Touring Europe on a Budget

by

Thomas Lewin

Grosvenor House
Publishing Limited

This book is published by
Grosvenor House Publishing Ltd
Link House
140 The Broadway, Tolworth, Surrey, KT6 7HT.
www.grosvenorhousepublishing.co.uk

A CIP record for this book
is available from the British Library

ISBN 978-1-83975-737-2

FOREWORD

TO MY WIFE BETTY JEAN LEWIN

It's funny what life throws at us. When I first met my wife Bet, neither one of us had two pennies to rub together, not a pot to pee in, like many people, of course. But when you come from the so-called slums it becomes magnified. No one could sink any lower. We decided to throw the dice and give things a go. No one ever knows how long or if a relationship will last. For the first five years I think both of us expected everything to fall about around our ears, but slowly and steadily, things started to turn around for us.

From buying our first house, with the everyday fear of losing it at any moment, we then bought a hotel, then another hotel. We had turned a corner and things started going right for us, our relationship was established. Strengthened, from hotels to shops to a country pub and caravan site. We did a great deal and covered a lot of ground. As things came together, we crossed off goals as we achieved them, to buy our kids their first car, then pay for their weddings. Eventually we started planning for our future retirement. To retire at fifty, then it became fifty-five, by the time we did it was sixty. We had a nice four-bedroomed house in a nice area when we bought our motorhome, unfortunately by then my wife had had a stroke.

Still we persevered and started to enjoy some quality time seeing places of interest around Europe and the world. We were just getting into our stride when quite unexpectedly she suffered a heart attack. Still we persevered. We were planning on touring Italy the following year. We had enjoyed a Caribbean cruise, short hotel breaks around England, life was good for us. Until she had her final relapse, we never did get to see Italy or Pompeii together. I was left to do it on my own as with many other places to visit. But as I go along, I look back and realise that without her I could never have done any of it.

Rest in peace Betty Jean Lewin, know that I always loved you. I just never realised how much. Until we meet again and can dance across the world, let this book, as with the others, be my tribute to you. You are with me at all times in life and on our travels, Que Sera Sera. To our children I hope you enjoy the memories.

TOURING EUROPE
ON A BUDGET

(And A Wing And A Prayer)

CHAPTER 1.

I have to confess, like most people, I like my holidays. But more, I like touring; I like seeing different places around the world, keeping my memories of them. Maybe it's the gipsy in me; my grandparents were barge people after all. But just as importantly, I don't like wasting money.

Most people I've spoken to, or know, will boast how much they will spend on their holiday, "Oh, I'll knock out a couple of grand on the missus and me." A couple of grand? A couple of f*****g grand? On two people in a fortnight? Two or three times a year? Then you will see them in Benidorm, or Marbella, up at nine, down to the beach, a left turn to their favourite café for breakfast, a nice fry up washed down with a nice cold pint of lager, then another, then another until they are both blathered or too p****d to walk. A couple of hours on the beach, or back to the hotel, a few hours having a kip, then back on the bladder. Not for me, thank you very much. I've done it, no more.

The first holiday that I remember was my parents taking me out into the country. Jackie Willis would come and pick us up in his great big van. Inside, there was a table and chairs. The van would be loaded up with food, and off we'd go. First, we would hit a field, and mom and dad would set out a picnic me and our kid would then chase the cows down the field until they got fed up. Then they would chase us back. Once the picnic was finished and the cows had worn us both out, we would set off to the nearby town where we were left to pass the time while they spent their time in the boozer. Not a lot, but happy memories. The only other way most of us kids got a holiday was the odd charabanc trip out with the local school, Charles Arthur street. We would spend all year paying in a little bit each week, for a day at the seaside or in the country, all of it magical for us kids compared to life in the slums of Birmingham. People would treasure for years; the little brass bells or porcelain ornaments they had brought in Blackpool or Weston-Super-Mare for a few coppers; no one had high expectations. As I got older and left school, holidays disappeared into the heather. None of us thought of holidays. In truth, I don't think many of us could afford holidays. It took up enough time and money just getting by daily.

My first job as an apprentice bricklayer paid three pounds a week. Three quid a week! A skilled bricky was paid ten quid a week. What kind of holiday can you get on that kind of money? No, most of our time was spent daily, just surviving. If anyone I knew went on holiday, they kept it quiet. Today, everyone and their uncle has at least one holiday a year. They let everyone know about it, bringing out the pictures to back it all up.

CHAPTER 2.

I never had my first proper holiday till after I got married. Even then, it was only after a couple of years struggling to get in front financially. Narrow as our field of vision was, it was always Wales. Not only was Wales close to Birmingham, but we also loved Wales. Well, I did, so I assumed Bet did as well. And the kids. The only problem with Wales is the rain, it's always p*****g down. We can set off on a nice sunny day in Birmingham, and as soon as we cross that border, I can guarantee the heavens will open up, and it will p**s down.

I left the house in the morning, telling Bet, "I should be getting paid this afternoon after finishing the job. Get everything ready. When I get back, we'll clear the gravel out the back of the transit van, put a blanket down for the kids to sit on, then we'll get off." We had bought a second-hand family tent, so we were all ready for it. It was a sunny Friday afternoon by the time we got to a field outside Barmouth. True to form, it was p*****g down with rain.

Putting a tent up while it's p*****g down ain't much fun, then finding out the tent is leaking like a sieve is even less funny. No wonder the previous tent owners wanted to sell it. As it was late afternoon, me and Bet had to sleep in the tent with our kids sleeping on the hard floor of the van. I don't think anyone was smiling with happiness the next morning. With two days to go, I shot down to Barmouth, where we found a six-berth caravan for ten quid, utter luxury.

A wonderful two days, despite the rain, even though we could barely afford that extra tenner. This went on for a few years till we made a nice pile of money from a land and property deal that we had made in Aldridge, as explained in my second book.

After three or four lovely holidays in beautiful, wet Wales, we felt we could afford a holiday abroad in the sun, the popular place of choice was Spain. We picked an all-exclusive hotel in Malgrat, so we didn't have to worry about food or feeding the kids. It was bliss. When we got out of that plane at 1am in the morning, we were hit by a blast of heat. At first, we thought it was the plane's engines because it was so hot, but no, as we walked away from the plane and check-out buildings, we could still feel the heat. Walking down to breakfast the next morning, we felt very posh and middle class. Yes, in just a very few short years, we had moved from the slums of Birmingham to a very nice, detached house in Sutton. We had arrived. We were not only posh; we were certainly middle class—some hope. You can certainly get carried away with your own b******t.

The fortnights holiday was magical. We got used to the kid's continuous whine, like the proverbial plane coming into land. "Mom, I'm bored." "Dad, I'm hungry. I'm cold." It was frigging non-stop. The holiday in Spain was bliss. We never heard a sound from the kids. Not a peep. We would get up in the morning, go across the railway tracks to the beach, then we would crash out on the sand. The kids played ball on the beach or sunbathed, then for lunch, we would walk back to the hotel before going back to the beach. All we had to buy was the odd ice cream. This was our way forward; Bet was as happy as Larry. I could see by her little face. The kids? Well, we wouldn't be going back to Wales for a good few years. Getting a boat up along the coast to Tossa, we decided to have mussels in sauce at a table on the beach from a silver platter. These were a million miles away from the mussels we were used to in Birmingham Bullring; this was star treatment, and I could see Bet felt like a film star. The holiday was very soon over, and it was back to England and home, but we had got the taste now; our only one slight smidgeon of discomfort was when we got to the airport. Looking out over the concourse to our plane, my heart sank with embarrassment at seeing a whole line of stuffed donkeys stretching the whole length of the plane ready for loading, for Christ's sake. When I brought one for our youngest Kristy, I thought we were giving her a special treat. Everybody with a child must have felt the same. That meant the whole plane. Bet as usual never said a word, for me I thought I ain't going to stand for that again.

We didn't miss out on our holidays abroad from then on, trying different places and different countries. We found we were happy with one holiday abroad a year as we went along, with little breaks around England when we found the time. I couldn't get my head around the difference in prices for different times of the year. You will pay one thousand pounds for a holiday in August that in May cost two hundred and fifty. It took me years to realise that the July-August period was the 'catch-all time' and the time to sting people for the highest price you can get. We found this out when we bought our first hotel in Devon. Whilst we would never consider ripping people off, certainly not our guests, I couldn't help but feel sorry for them when we were charging them good money to spend a week or a fortnight in our hotel. Many a time when it p****d down with rain. They were having to take their kids into the arcades, spending more money, whilst we were spending the same sort of money for six weeks in Morocco, in January or February with guaranteed sun. Ok, it was self-catering, but the food was very cheap anyway. Why do people put up with it? Maybe we were just lucky that we always worked for ourselves and the times suited us.

When I mentioned holidays, Bet would be on the phone or telly like a shot bringing up the bargain holidays in Spain, Morocco, or elsewhere. Some people might want a big flashy four-star hotel, but we would prefer to pay half the price for a two-star hotel. Our logic worked because we never spent our time in the hotel but around the pool. If not the pool, we were out around the town or pubs, the hotel was just for putting our heads down, seemed a no brainer to us.

Mind, we have come unstuck a couple of times. Once Bet booked a week's holiday for herself and a couple of the kids at a dirt-cheap bargain price with accommodation included. Well, the accommodation was a bleeding house of disrepute in Spain. The taxi driver had to put her right as she was heading to the place out of town. The kids had to wait on a bench while bet ran around like a blue-arsed fly, desperately trying to find some cheap accommodation with the little money they had. I ran around to the agents in Boldmere, screaming my head off about my wife and kids being conned. The owners were stunned into silence. It took me a good couple of hours for the penny to drop. They had to include the accommodation to get around the cheap flight deal- but why didn't they just tell us?

Better still, why didn't I have the brains to see it myself? We never stood for that again.

CHAPTER 3.

One of our favourite destinations was Morocco. Agadir in Morocco was quite deceptive, rebuilt following an earthquake in 1961. It's not far from giving the impression of being a bit like Spain, modern, clean, and civilised. It's only when you dig below the surface you start to see how backward it is, the third world. Our first experience was when Zaida, the maid, invited us to her home for dinner. Bet more or less kept her thoughts to herself, happy to go with the flow, but I thought it was absolutely fascinating to see how the real people lived. Zaida worked six days a week for a wage of £7 a week. Her husband was a chef at a nearby hotel on not much more. We just couldn't get our heads around how they could survive on that kind of money. Even back then, in 1983, Zaida had agreed to meet us outside the hotel after she had finished work at 6pm. Outside she had ordered a taxi to take us to her home. But before the taxi turned up, her husband arrived on his little scooter/moped before setting off to get the dinner started.

Once in the taxi, we set off to Zaida's home, which was some two/three miles outside the city of Agadir. After the first mile or so, the roads disappeared and turned to mud and dirt. We could only wonder how bad the suspension was on the cars as we drove over hills and little bumps in the road. All the nice buildings disappeared to be replaced with single story mud and concrete dwellings. I think the shops were simply concrete blocks with openings for serving customers. We could tell the butchers by the sides of meat hanging up in the opening of the windows, swarming with flies. Eventually, we came to a large opening, much like a football pitch, except there was no grass, just mud. This was surrounded on all sides by a horse trough and a tap. Well, we thought they were horse troughs till we clocked the women around them, filling their buckets with water from the taps, all dressed in black niqabs. They stopped and stared at us with fascinating interest. In the corner of the field was the mosque, giving out its call to prayer. Surrounding the barren field and the horse troughs were several rows of cowsheds. Well, I thought they were cowsheds, managing to silently mutter to Bet, "where the f*****g hell are we?"

"I dunno," she whispered back.

"Well, where do they f*****g live?"

"I dunno." Bet gave the same response again. After making sure that all the neighbours had seen us, Zaida led us down one of the cowshed rows. Our thoughts were a mix of anticipation and wonder.

Eventually, we arrived at a building where Zaida opened the door and led us into her home. Walking into a room some 12x12 ft, we realised this must be the kitchen. Bare and empty except for a sink and a small pantry door leading off to our right. Inside the second room, we were met by a table with concrete seating surrounding it, all with coverings. Bless her little heart Zaida had put little candles around, making it all look very romantic. Turning to thank her, saying there was no need to go to such trouble, she replied that they had to use candles as the electric didn't come on at 7pm until midnight. For Christ's sake. Everyone paid just one pound a month for the electric, which was strictly controlled by the king. For that, the people were truly grateful. Great ay. No wonder they work from 7am till 6pm six days a week. The mosque stood on every corner, calling them to prayer, a weekly wage just enough to enable them to live. And being a Muslim country, the only drinking was for the tourists, yep, that king has got his subjects well trained, come to think of it? Much as we were 150 years ago. The only difference was we were allowed to drink as much as we wanted. The idea was to keep us all zombified. Just different ways of keeping us down, I suppose.

With some difficulty, in the dining room, Zaida introduced us to her closest neighbour, who she had invited due to his understanding and ability to speak English. The only problem was, we caught on very quickly because he couldn't understand a word we were saying. His grasp of English was worse than Zaida's. The crafty little blighter had blagged his way in for a free meal. Sitting us down next to this guy, we were brought our starter/first course of popcorn. After a few handfuls, next came the main course, which was a very nice chicken tagine. All countries have the staple diet that sustains them. Back in the hard days, the Irish had the good old Irish stew, full of potatoes. The scots the same, as do we English. Why, we were brought up on our mom's famous stew and dumplings, with a turkey frame brought from Lewis's for a shilling. The Indians have their curry and rice. The further south you go, the hotter the curry becomes; each curry named after the region north to south. You have to ask yourself what they got away with when eating in the early 60s. Many Indian restaurants were closed down in England; in Birmingham, as many as a dozen or so dogs and cats were disappearing in droves.

The Chinese also had rice, and god knows what else. Dog is a delicacy in China, but anything will do. Dog, cat, rats, snakes, you name it, the Chinese will eat it. All with chopsticks, one grain at a time, so it lasts longer. You will not see many fat Indians or Chinese; both can s**t through the eye of a needle after a good meal. A habit several Brit's have picked up. It's not funny. Many a time, many a person has woken up with a very sore and burning arse.

With the Moroccans, it's the couscous. First, they will cook the couscous and pile it up on a tagine dish, like a pyramid. Then they will pour the chicken and sauce on top, or fish if it is a fish tagine. The way to eat your couscous meal is to roll a small bit of chicken from the top using your fingers of the right hand, or is it the left? As you roll, you bundle a small amount of couscous along with your piece of chicken and place it in your mouth to eat. The only problem is, our host, Zaida, keeps trundling little bits of chicken around the base of the tagine dish to us. As her honoured guest, her friend, the guy who can't speak a word of English, is passing it on. I can't work out what hand he is using, nor can I work out what hand they use to wipe their backsides. Is it the left or the right? Because they sure as hell don't use toilet paper. I decided the best course of action was to be cautious and pass it on. Bet caught on sharpish and decided to do the same. Little bundles of chicken going round in circles on the tagine dish. After the meal was finished, we were brought dessert consisting of an apple and an orange. We chose orange as we could peel the skin. At the first opportunity, Zaida's neighbour, having filled his little Hodge, made his excuses, and ducked out. Zaida went and booked the taxi.

The next thing is Bet wanted to use the toilet. Before she had got the second word out, I shut her up sharpish. Within minutes she was back on again, "I need to…"

"Shut up," I whispered. After three or four attempts, Zaida had caught on and guessed Bet wanted the toilet. Reappearing five minutes later, she came back moaning, "I wish I'd never asked."

"I did tell you," I said. The toilet was off of the kitchen. Bet had to take her draws off and hold her head on the wall to stop the door from swinging open. She then had to strategically place her feet and aim at a little hole in the ground, all the time watching little floaters from nearby dwellings passing by underneath. With the taxi's arrival, we thanked Zaida for her kindness, inviting us for a meal, giving her ten pounds for her children or herself. The next day, I noticed a rash on the back of my legs. I knew I had caught food poisoning.

The other nice thing about Morocco is the cost, food is dirt cheap, but the other big selling point is that it can cost you even less or nothing if handled properly. The reason for this is the tax. The King, in his wisdom and greed, had a 100% tax on everything imported. Mostly everything was imported. The locals could hardly afford anything. A £300 television cost £600. We caught on sharpish, as did one or two others before getting to the plane. We would trawl the charity shops looking for any electrical goods, in good or as new condition. So polaroid cameras that were obsolete in England or unwanted would be on sale for three quid instead of the usual 30 quid, or 60 quid in Morocco. We had no problem getting thirty quid. We would load our suitcases up with goodies, cameras etc., all would sell like hotcakes in Morocco. As the money came in, we would go down to the local souk and buy as many copper saucepans, jam pots and kettles as we could carry. In Morocco, they produced and made their pots as we did in England, over 100 years ago, so they were antiques for all intents and purposes.

The electrical goods we sold over there paid for much of the holiday. The antiques we sold over here. Well, the dealers thought they were antiques, paid for much of our spending money. We would buy a copper jam pot for £10 and sell it in England for £90. Morocco customs would give us big smiles. We spoke to one holidaymaker who spent three times a year holidaying in Morocco. One time I brought a full-length sheepskin coat for ten pounds. It was a bit tight, and I looked like a right pillock getting on the plane. Everyone staring at this idiot heading out into the sun, but within twenty-four hours, I had exchanged the coat for a very nice full leather trench coat. I still have it years later.

CHAPTER 4.

The only downside I found to any holidays abroad were and still are the Germans. It probably stems from the war and what they got up to, but they are so stereotypical, so f*****g arrogant. You would think they would have a bit more pride, a bit of self-respect. But no, they are all clones of each other. They will all get up at 5am, blag a sunbed, put their towel on it, then p**s off for most of the day, and none of them sees any wrong in it. No wonder they lost two wars.

I got into the habit sharpish of making friends with the swimming pool entertainer. First, I would let him know he was my friend and bung him a tenner, then said, "my friend?" in my best pidgin English. I cannot put up with these Germans fighting over sunbeds every morning. Well, I've never met any staff anywhere around the world who like the Germans, so they are quick to agree with me and find a solution. "Yes, find your sunbeds. I will see you when you leave at night, put your towels on the sunbeds." He would say. Well, we found a nice spot around the pool, and for the fortnight, our beds were there every day with our towels on.

We had picked the spot deliberately. It was on the side of the pool that the sun hit after eleven am. The Germans, in their greed, would dive to the opposite side of the pool, where the sun appeared in the morning, coming over to us in the afternoon. By the time they got back from the shops etc., the sun had disappeared. It took them a few days to clock on to this before they started to sneak there way over, surrounding us. I got p*****d off with this as well, so one day decided to play a little joke. Going over to Malik, the pool entertainer, I asked him if he would like to play a little joke? When I told him, he was well up for it, giving me an hour on my sunbed, he then came over and, looking serious, spoke to me in Arabic but pointing at the blonde German woman behind me. I answered him back in Arabic. Well, it sounded Arabic to me. First, he put up his one hand showing five fingers, "no, no," I refused. The argument kept on, then six fingers were held-up. I could see the blonde and her husband getting a bit concerned. When he got to eight and still looking serious, the blonde asked in her German accent, "vot does he want?"

I said, "don't panic, these Arabs love blonde Saxon women." When Malik's fingers reached ten, I could see their bottles were really going, so I raised my voice even louder, saying, "none, none." Eventually, he walked away. I turned to the Germans, warning them to be on their guard. There were no police here as such, and it was known for white, blonde European women to disappear. The Germans never came near us again, the blonde I never saw at all.

Everyone finds their own little way or niche to enjoy a holiday on the budget they have got. My only feeling is to do it with dignity or stay at home if you're going to be a cheapskate. We could see Jim, from a mining town in wales with his wife, had worked hard all their lives, he worked down the mines. After retirement, they both ran a small social club to supplement their meagre pensions. I dread to think what their pension was or whether they owned their own house or were in a council house. It didn't matter to us. As far as we were concerned, they were a nice decent couple. But they were obviously on the ball for a bargain. During the summer, they would grow vegetables in their garden. As soon as autumn came, they started looking for bargains. They had booked a six-week break in Morocco, when we first met them, for £320, including plane fare. They couldn't live in England for that. Living modestly, they ate well, even enjoying the odd couple of beers. Getting home after their holiday break, we got a card from them a month later. After going through the cheap holiday breaks, they found another six-week holiday in the same hotel for the same money. Well, fair play to them. Better to be in the sun saving money than in dreary wet Wales spending it.

The complete opposite of them was a couple from the midlands trying to leach onto us. I don't know how they survived, but their whole demeanour and attitude made our skin crawl. They couldn't understand why none of their neighbours spoke to them. Without realising they had already dropped it out to us, they were disgusted that some of their neighbours owned cars and didn't tax them. Not owning a car themselves, they had decided to squeal on them to the police. Very nice. One day, they walked back to the hotel as we walked down to the beach to a restaurant for a meal. Without hesitation, they did an about-turn and decided to join us. Sitting opposite us, me and Bet ordered our meal. Watching us, the wife kept on to her husband, "I'm feeling hungry, Ernie." Well, Ernie was giving her complete deaf. We could see what the scam was, low as they were; they were hoping we would offer to pay for their meal. We gave them deaf. Eventually, Ernie had to give in. "Well, you have one. I'm not hungry," with that, she ordered a cheap lasagne, which he then helped her to eat, albeit reluctantly; after all, he'd said he wasn't hungry.

After the meal, we got up to walk back to the hotel, the leaches following us. We had left a pound tip on the table, and after 50 yards or so, Ernie turned back, saying he had forgotten something, wondering what there was possible to forget. We turned back and waited, me nudging Bet to watch. True to form, he nicked our pound tip off of the table. Well, for f***s sake. Did his wife clock on, we wondered? What a contrast this was from the year before when we had mixed with, befriended, and enjoyed the company of such different people.

CHAPTER 5.

Mike and Mary were a lovely couple from Canada, where they had made their fortune from turkeys. "What do you do, Tommy?" he asked me one day.

"We own a hotel in Devon, Mike."

"Ah. So do I. I brought my son a 300-bedroom hotel in Toronto."

I had a job to stop myself from choking on my lager. "Mike, I think there is a bit of a difference. Ours is a small 17-bedroom family hotel."

It didn't faze mike. "It makes no difference, Tommy. Today, a 17-bedroom hotel, tomorrow, a 300-bedroom hotel."

Mike and his wife had left Yugoslavia during the uprisings. They had gotten to Canada without a pot to p**s in. What a lovely genuine couple. We became good friends. Sadly, we didn't realise they were on a six-month round tour of Europe. Mike was dying of cancer. This didn't stop us from visiting them later. After some initial urging, they joined our company consisting of a fair crowd of us, enjoying ourselves on a nightly basis: Dave, the English musician, and Fatima, the top belly dancer in North Africa amongst them. Fatima had a favourite little party trick that she used to great effect to welcome you or say hello. As Dave introduced us, she would lean over, grab your dick in a strong, powerful grip, and say, "Hello, I like you." It was really embarrassing, especially with my daughter Louise staring. I could never figure out what her motive or purpose was, but I would use it myself to great effect after an initial couple of times.

Brian was a little carrot head from derby, on holiday with his wife and two kids. Fatima came in to do her nightly show. As she passed us, she shouted hello, came over, gave me a kiss on the cheek, and said loudly, "I will join you after the show." The bar was packed. Brian was very impressed, his little chest swelling with pride, "do you know her?"

"Oh, yes. She is a close friend. Would you like me to introduce you after the show?" Nodding his head like a good-un, Brian clearly did. Shortly after, Fatima came on to do her routine. On the dance floor, Fatima looked fantastic doing her act. She oozed sex, but close up, she was frightening. She had thighs so big they could break your neck if she ever got them around you, and her mouth was as big as a horse. My missus knew she had no worries. After the show, Fatima came across, and I introduced her to Brian, who was sitting next to me. His wife was on the opposite side of the table, out of reach. "Fatima, this is my good friend Brian, and he likes you very much."

That was enough. She grabbed Brian's dick and started giving him a good squeeze. "ah, you like me, yes??"

Brian's face went bright red, but worse than that, he rose to the occasion. His missus clocked on sharpish, "Brian? BRIAN! STOP IT." Looking at Bet, she said, you've only got to touch him, and he's away. It was hilarious, but I don't think Brian got over it. Fatima thought it was very funny. Certainly, Morocco was a bundle of laughs and a plentiful supply of interesting and funny people.

Getting the plane from Birmingham airport, we couldn't help but overhear a loud, black country family. Big mouths, very black country, 'am yer' and 'bam yers'. So it came as a bit of a surprise to see them in the same hotel in Morocco. Only this time, they were totally and utterly different. This time they spoke more quietly; worse, they had lost their black country accent and were speaking quite posh. They were talking to another couple who were equally posh and talking about their restaurant back in England. I had to double-check with Bet, "Oh yes, it's the same ones alright," she confirmed.

"Really? But why change your accent? Why try to be something you're not?"

Sadly, we found this to be quite common on holidays abroad. Why I don't know. Were they going to keep this up for the next couple of weeks?

One day we walked into the bar to find both groups going at it, full blast with the manager. A part had packed up in the boiler, leaving no hot water. Now, we were in Morocco, it was hot. Even the cold water was warm. What were they screaming about? George, a guy in our company, saw fit to remonstrate with them, but they were determined to make a fuss. The manager turned to us, shrugging his shoulders whilst explaining that this was not like England. To get a spare part could take days, even weeks. I said, "look, take no notice. They are two penny halfpennies."

"Oh," he answered, "it is no problem, we will just offer them a bottle of wine in apology." As we looked across, we watched them congratulating each other whilst pouring a glass of wine, big smiles on their faces from the victory. Silly prats. Many a time I have made a prat of myself on holiday. It's even worse after I've had a drink. I've got up on stage and sung when I can't sing, and I've danced like a frigging lunatic on a cruise ship instead of acting with some dignity. Thankfully, most of the time, I've slunk away, knowing no one will see me again or know who I am.

CHAPTER 6.

For various reasons, Morocco started to pale into insignificance after a few short years. Why? I couldn't figure it out. The holidaymakers we were used to seeing were not coming back, especially in the winter, when we had got used to going away. Now it was filling up with people grabbing the cheap deals because it was cheaper to live on the dole or on disability benefits than at home. We used to see business people, builders, shopkeepers taking advantage of a cheap break, now it was full of people on the treacle. That in itself was no problem to us. The problem was they were so frigging miserable and petty with it. Yes, they were having a break, but they had no holiday, just surviving daily as they lived hand to mouth. The shopkeepers were feeling the pinch. "Why do we have no customers? No people on holiday?" one of the shopkeepers asked.

"Well, maybe it doesn't help that you're such a pain in the flipping arse," I said. With the blank look on his face, I followed up. "Look, when we come away, all Europeans like to look at things first, in the shops, in the souks. After a couple of times, it becomes a bloody nuisance with you pestering us to buy something before we've even got in the shop." The first few times, it's quite exciting. After a bit, it becomes a bloody headache. Worse is the bartering. Most of us know, having been warned, that the shop will ask 100 dirhams for a kaftan. As such, we then know we have to knock them down to 50 dirhams to get a decent bargain. That's fine, for a bit. But then you start to realise that the shopkeepers have also caught on to the tourist advice. What they do then is up the initial price to 150 dirhams, then 200 dirhams. It's non-stop. In the end, we stop going by the shops altogether.

Hopefully, seeing the light entering his brain, he might take it on board and then tell all his fellow shopkeepers. It was just as bad going around the souks. It was an utter pain, being harassed by some dodgy looking Arab who looked like he would stick a knife in you at the first opportunity. You would see they would blatantly get you to buy something from a stallholder at an inflated price, going back later for a backhander. For that, you had the privilege of being charged a tenner by the little bleeder. I have always felt quite confident in my ability to look after myself. But some of these characters made me nervous. God knows what a lot of the tourists felt like. It doesn't take a lot for a knife to slip into your back. Another problem was the increasing attacks and bombings by extremists. I almost felt sorry for many of the Moroccan people who, in the main, were modest, pleasant, god and king fearing, downtrodden people. It certainly makes you aware of what a free democracy we live in.

We all have our own ideas of what makes a holiday. I loved camping, sleeping under the stars, smelling the damp grass, wood smoke, the many smells from around the forest or meadows. Money doesn't come into camping. Plenty of people with enough money to have the best in the world can, and do, enjoy camping. The only problem I found was by the time, I could really afford to camp in a bit of comfort, with built-in groundsheets, decent beds to sleep on and sleeping bags and good cooking equipment, I had become p****d off with it. Sleeping on hard lumpy floors, making do with basic cook pots, and worse, a leaking bloody tent. Enough I say.

The last time we did a bit of camping was when we'd got a quiet period in the hotel and decided to take the two youngest kids Kristy and Rachael, over to Bodmin Moor. We had driven down onto the moor, then walked half a mile or so to a nice, isolated area, a nearby stream, forest, and even a small mountain walk. It was all exciting as we put the tent up, had a little reccy around to suss out the area, not another soul in sight. Getting our catapults out and bow and arrows, I was in my element till the whinging started.

"Dad, I need the toilet." The three of them would gang up on me, huddling into a little group, them against me, "For Christ's sake, just go over into the bushes." Then the face-pulling started, till I clocked on, they wanted to do a number two, not a number one. Handing them a shovel, I pointed to the trees, "there you are, kids, go over there. Get behind a few trees, dig a hole, and there you are." The face pulling kept on. It was much later when Bet told me the kids were on their periods, "oh, thanks for letting me know. What am I? A mind reader." So ok, we decamped and found an exciting little campsite just a couple of miles from a Jamaica Inn. That made the kids a lot happier. The campsite had an animal sanctuary, semi zoo adjoining it. We got on very well with the owners, who later offered us a partnership with the sale of the campsite and bar. It made for an enjoyable two or three days. Sadly, I think It became the last of our camping holidays. Certainly, our kids were not too keen on camping. In truth, I don't think Bet either.

CHAPTER 7.

Maybe it was the building works we had gotten into, and the landscaping. Certainly, the hotel business-focused our minds towards the prospect of having a large part of the year with no work. We are brainwashed into thinking that we have to work circa forty-eight weeks of the year because, well, everyone does. In the building trade, I found some builders who would build up a small batch of extension shells to work on inside during the winter months, from November till April. It was great for the builders to give them a dry working area, but its p*****d the customers off, having been promised the job finished for Christmas.

The landscaping was dictated by the weather, with no arguments. One year, having built a boundary wall making two plots, the weather changed mid-December. It still had heavy snow on the ground four months later, making it impossible to finish. You had to make your money while the weather was good, pulling your belt in for the winter months. The hotel again was a different game altogether. You had just a few short months to make your money for the rest of the year. This quite suited us and suited our mentality. We quite liked the idea of working hard for a portion of the year and enjoying a few months somewhere nice and warm in the winter. Back in the good old days, when most people holidayed at home and hoteliers made a killing, they could buy a little flat or villa in Spain at rock bottom prices. It was something we could only aspire to. First, we had to make more money.

In the meantime, it was making the most of what time we had got to enjoy the best that we could afford.

There is, I think, a distinct difference between working for yourself and working for someone else. Most people I've met who work for someone else don't seem to budget in the same way as the guy who works in the car factory, collects his wage each week or month, and divvy's the money up to spend accordingly. A certain amount for the wife, for the housekeeping, to pay the utility bills etc. Usually, the wife would take care of that side of it. In that respect, we were the same. Bet would handle all our bills. In my dad's day, the rest went into his pocket, the wage earners pocket.

Apart from holiday money, the rest was spent as the couple or family felt fit, many not saving or putting money aside for a rainy day, a real rainy day. To the self-employed, to us anyway, that rainy day was always just around the corner. Lurking quietly, ready to catch us out. Usually, it was in the guise of the banks who were always ready to jump on you without too much notice. Our very first experience of big s**t hitting the fan was in the hotel business, where we would first see a hotel go up for sale at 300-400 grand, only for the banks to start squeezing and dropping to say as little as 80 grand, with the hoteliers grabbing anything they could sell before running out and letting the banks snatch it.

It was a salutary warning to me and Bet to watch our pennies. As our mom would say, "watch those pennies, and the pounds will look after themselves." She was right, and we did. Besides, we never seemed to actually make much money. A living yes, a fortune no. Whether it be in the building trade, landscaping, or any other business, some people have a knack for making big money easily. We did not. In the hotel, we found that the only way to afford and pay for a holiday was to open for Christmas. Our takings for Christmas paid for our winter break. It wasn't until we put our hotel up for sale, we found the secret. Calling the local agent in, he said, "well, I've got another ten to value this morning." My bottle started to fall out. "oh s**t, don't tell me everybody's putting their hotels up for sale?"

"Oh, no," Bill reassured me. "They call me in every year to get a valuation; the value increases by around ten per cent. Then they go to the bank, borrow circa ten thousand pounds, and add a suite to a couple of the bedrooms. Keeping a couple of grand for a holiday in the Canaries."

I looked at Bet in total disbelief. "Well, for f***s sake." We had been questioning ourselves for years. Working our nuts off for the hotel. Chock-a-block during the main season, and still we had to work for Christmas to pay for a break. All the time wondering what we were doing wrong when other hoteliers were closing the first week in September before tootling off into the sun. Now we knew. Bernard owned a beautiful pub and hotel a few doors from us. We felt he had got a little gold mine, little realising the silly prat carried his scrapyard mentality into the business, ripping the customers off as mugs. Waving expansively one day, he boasted how the brewery had offered him a ten-grand loan at very low-interest rates. "Well, Tom, it's silly not to take it at 1%? So we'll have a bit of work done on the bar, then enjoy a nice holiday in Tenerife." Well, I believed him. Now we knew. We had thought the same when we saw people having extensions on their houses. We saved up and struggled. These borrowed the money on the strength of the valuations and properties rising. But what about when the rises stopped? Or house prices dropped? No, we decided to struggle through.

CHAPTER 8.

Instead of paying two or three grand or more for a holiday, Bet would always look for and find the bargains. Our saving grace was and has always been that we've never been dictated by dates. It's sad and disgraceful that no one has come up with a solution to that annual holiday break time; coal mines, car factories, school holidays, all timed to come to a stop during that short July to August period. Conveniently when all those prices seem to quadruple. Worse your packed in like frigging sardines with people you've never met and probably won't even like. Fortunately, we only came close to this a couple of times. Once, was our first holiday in Malgrat, Spain. The town was quiet, the hotel full, thankfully with quite civilised people: no Germans arguing over the sunbeds.

The next was Palma in Majorca. It was horrendous. Half the hotel was full of Germans, who nicked all the sunbeds. The other half was full of pig-ignorant French, who, when we passed comment, pointed out that it was because they all came from a certain region in the south of France. Worse was turkey. Maybe it's because it's that cheap it attracts a certain type of person. But who am I to talk? With the holiday dirt cheap and lager at 50 pence a pint, it's got to be popular.

Our only criteria when looking for a hotel break is somewhere clean, maybe with a bar and a swimming pool. A two-star is plenty good enough for us. Why bother with a five star and the extra cost it entails when we won't or don't need them? We get up in the morning, go down to breakfast, then a nice day around the pool. Only this time, the pool was chock-a-block. You couldn't move for bodies. We had to negotiate our way around the pool to find a quiet little spot in the corner. We soon spotted 'the daddy' because he had a big mouth. Some of the others spoke about him with tones of respect - he's a soldier! That's it then. The average age of the hotel occupants was about thirty, all with kids. The soldier was having a little bit of a competition with a scouser who was there with his girlfriend. The scouser was a nice enough guy, a bit thick but started a competition with the soldier. Each having different music on their radios that they played around the pool. Each would turn there's up to outdo the other.

Running over to us one day, the scouser shouted out, "ay Tommy, guess what? We've just been down into Marmaris and found a great English restaurant." Before he could get the words out, his missus jumped in, "yeah. A McDonalds." A McDonalds? For f***s sake. They were so excited we couldn't tell them that McDonalds was an American company that almost pulled out, as it was so difficult to get a foothold in the country. "Yes, we've had a great burger and fries."

It came to a head by the third day when the scouser and the soldier got into a fight trying to outdo each other around the pool. The cops were called. The scouser was threatening to take it further.

"I'm in a good mind to call my family Tommy. They would fly over straight away." He threatened."

The couple in the next room spoke in some awe about one of the pair. "Well, he is a soldier." This was enough for us. I went out and found the holiday rep, "sorry, love, I'm not prepared to put up with this. Hotel? It's like a frigging nut house."

"Do you have any complaints about the hotel?" was her reply.

"No, the hotel is great. Very nice. But I've never met so many fruitcakes in one setting." I explained.

She offered a solution by inviting us to use one or both sister hotels opposite. The problem was resolved. The two hotels opposite were great with a more mature clientele. Much better, we thought. Until my sense of humour got in the way. Well, you can't get it right all the time.

I had often had the odd joke with holidaymakers or even locals in tourist hotspots. The joke could be even better in strange out of the way countries, like Morocco or Turkey, where the holidaymakers were unsure of the inhabitants. In Morocco, the English just didn't know how to react to the Arabs, mostly Muslim. We had all heard the stories of the Arabs coming up in the night, grabbing the blonde English girls and ferreting them away on their camels. The thought alone was enough to make us shudder. I made sure to repeat it at every opportunity. Here in Turkey, I just never gave a thought to the deep-rooted fear we English had for the Turks and the stories passed down from WWII—Gallipoli, and how ruthless the Turks were.

Calling over to a restaurant one night, where a young couple were eating, I put on my best pidgin Turkish/English accent, looked at the woman, then at her husband and said, "I will buy your woman?" I felt his missus stiffen up, but he stiffened up, even more, trying to speak as quietly and firmly as possible, "go away," he replied.

"I will give you one million lire for your woman." He just didn't see the joke, and when I upped it to two million, I could see he was getting quite frightened. His girl was terrified.

I burst out laughing, "joke, a joke." I said before walking away. That should have been my lesson. But sometimes, when I've had a drink, even more after I've had a drink, I get carried away.

The hotel opposite had three pool entertainers who would practice mime singing and entertaining daily. There were two lads and a girl, all three of whom grew quite fond of me, often sitting with us, just having a chat. One night, having swallowed a few pints, I decided to have a bit of fun with the lads. In the next hotel was a group sitting around the pool, relaxing, having a drink also. I said to the two lads, "look, let's have some fun. See that group? We will go over. You will introduce me to them as a rich Turk who cannot speak English but wants to buy their women?" Well, the lads saw the joke straight away, so ironing out the details, we trundled over. Sitting myself down, I pointed to the guy opposite, a scouser, then his wife, then spoke in a gruff Turkish accent. Well, it sounded Turkish.

As agreed and true to form, the young Turk informed the guy opposite that I was a rich Turk and prepared to offer one million lire for his woman. Dead silence. I upped it to two million lire. About 200 quid. His wife got up and walked away. Being p****d, I missed the signals. The other two couples sat in silence. I thought, 'this ain't going down too well.' Surely, they recognise the two lads were the hotel entertainers. 'Oh, come on guys,' I thought, you could see straight away I was English? —well, that was it. The scouser jumped in the air doing his frigging nut. Unfortunately, he just didn't see or get the joke. He had sent his wife to the hotel room. The woman next to me tried to make small talk, her husband not saying a word. The other couple, equally as quiet, the husband, a jock, conceding it was funny, but I had dragged it out a bit too long. I thought, well, I was trying to see how long it would take for the penny to drop but thought it prudent to keep my gob shut. I thought it even more prudent to get the f**k away from them. I decided to be very careful when I tried that trick again. Some people just ain't got a sense of humour.

CHAPTER 9.

We don't get it right every time when it comes to grabbing a bargain. Sometimes it's swings and roundabouts. One year we fancied the idea of doing a Nile cruise. Bet had clocked a nice little cruise and stay in Luxor. Well, we had never been to Egypt, so as far as we were concerned, anything and all was part of the excitement. The choice came up of whether to choose a large Nile cruiser or a much smaller one, holding about 70 people, at about half the price. We couldn't figure out why. Speaking to our daughter Nicky, she advised that we go on the smaller cruiser anyway, citing the informality and friendlier atmosphere that we would find. She was speaking from experience, having had a similar cruise a couple of years earlier. She and Michael, her husband, had been on one of the biggest cruisers and found the atmosphere very formal and unfriendly. The very thought terrified Bet and me as we couldn't put up with that kind of falseness. The smaller ship suited us and became our ship of choice.

It was a wise decision and turned out to be the right one. The smaller boat was full of mainly younger people—young girls in groups who looked on me as old enough to be their fathers, much to my f*****g regret. No matter how hard I tried, I couldn't get them to look at me as younger. In short, there was a nice mix of couples of various ages, and it was friendly, informal, and relaxing. The food was a good standard and served by young, friendly staff eager to please. The first week consisted of cruising up and down the Nile, visiting places of interest. The Kings' tombs, Tutankhamen's burial chamber, the Aswan dam, each fascinating sites, including the needle that had us all utterly baffled. The tour guide took us the fair few yards from the ship to the needle, which remained unfinished, inside the base of the mountain. First, he asked us to guess why the needle was there, unfinished, so far from the river. Then to guess how the Egyptians would have got the needle to its destination. Well, none of us had a clue on any part of it. This happened over two thousand years ago with no lorries, no equipment, no real tools.

The needle itself was about 137 feet long and weighed about 1,200 tons. That in itself boggled my brain completely and left us both unable to comprehend it. I don't think we were the only ones. Climbing up to the lip of the crater of the mountain base, we were confronted by the sight of the needle below us in the base of the mountain. We could see the mountain had been cut down, bit by bit, ostensibly providing the building blocks for other projects or pyramids. Then, when the workers and engineers had got to the right width and depth of the mountain, they had started digging out the solid shape of the needle itself. At the one end, the base, at the other, it tapered to the top. Even the base, we noticed, was tapered from the base to the top. Getting that far was beyond our scope of knowledge or comprehension. The tour guide enjoyed seeing the ignorance and bafflement in our faces, savouring every long, drawn-out moment before enlightening us.

Over many years the Egyptians had cut down the mountain to reach the right height and depth, cutting out the needle itself. It was only when they got to the very base and as such the near end that they realised that there was a fracture within the needle itself. This, they were knowledgeable to know, made any further progress impossible. The Egyptians left the needle and walked away. Whilst this was sinking into our brains, he then asked how we thought they would have broken or released the base away from the floor and got it to its destination? Well again, feeble as any of the suggestions were, none of us could guess anywhere near what was correct. I kept my gob shut throughout.

He then explained how the workers would chisel holes every few inches along the base from end to end on both sides. They would then insert wet hemp into the holes, ramming it in as hard as possible. In the heat of the Egyptian days, the hemp would soon dry out, breaking the needle away from the floor as it did so. Truly amazing. Then, after cutting the surrounding rim away, rollers would be placed under the needle. The whole monument was rolled down to the river and on to a ship. From there, it would be taken to its final destination. Of course, at that time, the river ran much closer to the needle. Since then, the river Nile has been diverted via the Aswan dam.

After a very enjoyable week of sightseeing, we were taken to our hotel in Luxor. Another four people got off with us, heading to their hotel of choice, further along the Nile. Although we thought they were a bit standoffish, we agreed to meet up sometime the following week. We must have missed the offer, but they were offered an extra week for the bargain price of twenty quid. How did we miss that? The jammy buggers, we were jealous, well I was. Our hotel was in the centre of Luxor itself, which, in all truthfulness, was a bit of a scruffy s**t hole. The hotel was warm, comfortable, and friendly and was packed with a nice mixture of people of all ages. Being on the hotel's roof, the pool gave a nice atmosphere with views over the nearby houses, shops, and town.

After a few days and spending time touring the town, we decided to visit the two couples we had met on the cruise. It was purely, as a break, as we didn't think they were very friendly. Keeping themselves much to themselves. We got a horse-drawn carriage to their hotel and were met with a sight that blew our minds. Just a bit further along and on the banks of the Nile, the hotel was a sight to behold. It was massive. Owned by members of the royal family, it was a five-star hotel with four pools set out on the banks of the Nile. The shops inside were very select and expensive. There was a choice of four or five restaurants. Bet, and I were in awe and well impressed. We both felt we could have had a bit of that. Walking up to reception, we asked after our friends in the room numbers they gave us. After a quick check, it was confirmed they were not in their rooms, neither were they around the pools, which surprisingly, didn't have that many people around them.

Making our way back to our own hotel, we felt aware of the difference and saw the flaws in ours compared to theirs. Halfway back, we heard a shout behind us. It was the two couples, in a horse-drawn carriage, pulling up alongside us. As we had gone to meet them, they were on their way to meet us. Reaching our hotel and after getting the drinks in, we exclaimed how jealous we were after seeing their hotel. They were quick to jump in, "don't be jealous, Tom. This hotel more than makes up for it with its nice friendly atmosphere. Yes, our hotel might look nice, but the atmosphere is terrible. No one speaks to each other. Everyone is miserable and serious. We would much rather be in here." Well, I looked at Bet, blow me down with a bleeding feather. Not only did we think they were a bit hoity-toity, but we had clearly misread the hotel we had just visited. It went without saying that we had a very pleasant couple of days in our hotel. This goes to show you can never judge by appearance. We were to come across scenarios like this many times. Things are not always what you might think. People are not how they may appear. The two men were design engineers in well-paid jobs. We had felt on the first ship they were a bit reserved. But really, the people they were thrown in amongst in the top hotel, were reserved and they couldn't bear it. Ha-ha, funny, really.

I read an article once by Michael Winner, the film producer. This is a guy who inherited a lot of money, was helped immensely by his wealthy mother, private school educated, and used to the finer things in life. From what I can gather, he lost much of it through bad judgement or arrogance. His mother lost much of hers through her own stupidity. Thankfully, he was elevated to a position in society because of his work that allowed him to look down on others and speak disparagingly, as, and when he saw fit. If you expressed views that he didn't agree with, he would call you an arsehole. With his comments getting into print. Upon hearing that a famous footballer was holidaying at a famous resort in the Caribbean where Winner spent his holidays, he made it clear that he was disgusted that this working-class but wealthy footballer would be lowering the tone of his hotel. How unnecessary and how terribly snobbish.

The hotel in Luxor that our friends had booked into for a fortnight, they found to be awful with a terrible stiff atmosphere. So stiff, in fact, that they isolated themselves around the pool, kept themselves to themselves in the restaurant, and by all accounts avoided the bars like the plague. The more we travelled in life, the more experienced we became. The problem we found was that many of these people who booked into these hotels and on cruise ships were just ordinary, mainly working-class people. Thrust into that situation where they just didn't know what to say, how to express themselves, just didn't know how the etiquette worked. For me, in that situation, I just decided to say 'frigging hell' quieter but carried on eating a lamb chop or chicken wing with my fingers, just more delicately.

We found it the same on cruise ships, now and again. Once, Bet found a three-week cruise around the western med for three hundred quid. Three hundred quid! It was a steal. Get it booked. When my brother, Reg, heard, he wanted a bit of the action. We had to get the ship at Liverpool docks, the commercial section. That should have been our first warning. The ship was called the Apollo and looked magnificent. Reg was well impressed and couldn't get his breath. It looked huge. The first downer came when we saw the guests queuing up to book in. Along half the ships length, they queued, all in f*****g shell suits or tracksuits. Now, I'm far from snobbish but shell suits? To board a ship? Ok, things picked up on board when the shell suits disappeared to be replaced by more formal suits or smart casual wear. But then came the crunch that quite a few were happy to boast that they were on the dole. On the dole? Ok, be on the dole, fine, fair play to us all, but to boast about it? We palled up with a cockney wide boy and his bird and a scouser and his wife. Both very interesting, both funny and both good company. The cockney was the typical wide boy; every cockney thinks he's a del boy. "What do you do, Roy?"

"Nahhh Tom, I'm on the dole," he replied.

The scouse couple were a bit smarter and kept their mouth shut, but seeing as he was using a walking stick, I suspected he was on the treacle. Fair play to them. Meeting up at the bar after dinner, we all sat at a table, and I got my water bottle out, filled up with vodka. Going up to the bar, I got Bet her usual Martini and myself a pint of lager and a glass of orange. Clocking what I was up to, I invited the cockney and the scouser to enjoy a glass of my vodka. The scouser politely declined.

The cockney was more vocal, "no thanks, Tom. Thanks for the offer, but the bar prices are cheap enough."

Well, if that wasn't a chip, I don't know what is. The bar prices were the same as onshore pub prices, which I didn't consider cheap. This is how the ship made its money. Considering they were getting their booze duty free, I thought it was a bit of a liberty, charging us full whack. Bringing and drinking my own vodka was my little protest.

CHAPTER 10.

The ship sailed for four days to its first port in France. After a day out at the port, everyone sat at their usual tables in the bar. With everyone placing their bottle on the side, Bet and I silently observed the pint water bottles on the tables. If not water bottles, then coke bottles. The cockney and his missus had a coke bottle each, the scouser a pint bottle of water which they both shared. Neither one said a flipping word.

At the second port of call in Spain, the ship's crew were on to everyone. As we walked on board, they were jumping on everyone, kindly offering to put the drinks in storage for safety. Many got caught out and had their drinks taken away. Some were on the ball and managed to ferret their drink's away unseen. The bar takings took a dive. It was only when we reached one major port that we got the opportunity to compare our cruiser. In most ports, we were alone, but at one, returning to the ship, Bet, I, and the cockney couple were walking along the dock when we started passing this massive black cruise ship. It was magnificent, shining in the sun, like a mirror. Every deck filled with cabins overlooking the side. Some with guests waving to us. It was full of Americans. Our ship was a bit further on, workers running alongside it, painting above the waterline to hide whatever was underneath, rust, most likely. Some Americans were openly laughing. We thought they were just friendly, until we saw our ship in front of us. Both me and Bet dropped our heads a bit in embarrassment. The cockneys never said a word. We guessed they were aware of the difference as well. It was brought home even more to us a bit later on, as the big black gleaming monster pulled away, setting off in front of us with all the yanks on the side of the ship, waving. The ship giving two mighty blasts on its horn, everything about the ship was massive, even the flipping horn. Every one of us on board bowed our heads in shame. I quietly said to Bet, "I ain't coming on this frigging ship again." She never said a word. I think she agreed with me.

After the second week, the cockney came over to us after one shore trip, "Tom, we've noticed you never come on any of the day trips out?" Well, we'd never given it much thought, one way or another. Except to have realised that it seemed a bit silly paying 60 maybe 100 quid to go on a tour visiting someplace when we hadn't even seen the country, the city, or the port where we had docked. It was nothing to do with being shrewd, more to do with not wanting to waste money for the sake of it. We explained this to them and watched as the light entered their brains. They had spent an extra two grand on trips that they realised they didn't really want, having missed out on what we saw. Without further ado, they set off to the booking office to try to cancel any further trips. I don't think they were very successful.

The food onboard the Apollo was excellent, on a par with any cruise ship we had been on. The ship was very clean. The staff and passengers friendly with a nice atmosphere, but seeing passengers queuing up in shell suits and the ship being painted every time we docked was a tad embarrassing. Call us snobs, but we decided to be a bit more careful in future. It made us think when we stood listening one night to a guy on his third cruise on the ship and extolling its virtues. He had done his research on the ships history and proudly proclaimed it had been converted from a ferry boat into its present cruiser status with all its little quirks and eccentricities, I wasn't impressed.

CHAPTER 11.

One of our better bargains, and experiences, was on the cruise ship named Black Prince of the Fred Olson line. Still sticking to our mantra of finding a bargain, even after things were picking up for us financially, Bet had found another three-week cruise. This time around the eastern Mediterranean. The cruise cost us a grand each with an inside cabin on the middle deck. After booking, we were upgraded within a couple of weeks to an outside cabin with a porthole at no extra cost. We were well impressed. Checking the costs, we had saved over two grand. Normally we would never consider worrying or being prepared to pay more for an outside cabin, certainly not a porthole. Most times you're at sea, what are you going to look at? If you're not at sea, you're in port looking at a sea wall or blank view. So no, thank you, you get up in the morning, go up for breakfast, spend most of the day on deck or in the city you're visiting, then you're in the restaurant or bar—you're only in your cabin to sleep.

Finding our cabin, we were having a coffee when an elderly lady came over with her daughter. To say she was a little p****d off was an understatement. She had paid a few hundred quid extra for an outside cabin with a porthole but couldn't see anything at all. Bet, and I felt it prudent to keep our gobs shut. Having paid for the extras she wasn't happy with, she was even more p****d off to discover she was miles away from the lifts, having deliberately pointed out she was disabled and required to be close to them. For them, this was a bucket list trip. Being disabled and not in good health, the mother had asked her daughter to accompany her, even paying for her, as you do. We found a cruise is on the bucket list for many people, even more so for a few buggers with a terminal illness.

But then every ship had its fair share of little snobs. One day a couple came over, the wife gushing with enthusiasm over Bet's taste in dress. Introducing themselves, the wife spoke straight away in that put on posh little voice. "Oh, I do hope you don't mind my asking, but I couldn't help but notice that you seem to have the same taste in a dress like me, i.e. a Marks and Sparks dress, I think. Only I wondered what type of dress you might be wearing for the Captain's dinner?" Well, being her usually polite self, Bet invited her up to our cabin where she could see for herself. Popping round later on in the afternoon, Bet invited her in and pointed to the dress she would be wearing at the Captain's dinner. The woman walked off, swelling with happiness, now knowing what she would be wearing on the night and promising to meet us in the piano bar later on. After our evening dinner, we set off for a drink in the piano bar.

We had only been in less than half an hour before the couple came over, both looking expensive and pleased to see us. Hubby invited us both to have a drink; they had found kindred spirits. Sipping our drinks hubby asked, "in all seriousness, Tom, are you in the Fred Olson members club?"

Well, I looked blank, "what members club?"

"No? Well, Tom, you must become a member. I have been a member of the Fred Olson club now for three cruises. After your first cruise, as members, you get a silver tie pin." I was impressed. He then carried on. "After our third cruise, I am now a gold member." The pride on his face clearly visible as he pushed his chest out to show me his gold tie pin, "but the real benefit, Tom, is with the discounts you get? Now, as you know, this cruise would normally cost us over two thousand pounds each. With our twenty per cent discount, it only cost us eighteen hundred pounds each." I looked at him, not knowing what to say, completely lost for words. His face was ready to burst. I was frightened to look at Bet. I could see from a sideways glimpse she was looking down at the floor.

Before we could get our second wind, his wife jumped in, "I should be careful who you're telling that to Peter. I know there are some people on this ship who have only paid one thousand pounds and been given outside cabins with portholes. We're supposed to be loyal customers, yet we've been dumped in an inside cabin next to the engine room in the bowels of the ship." Oh, f**k. I felt Bet stiffen up. I just didn't know what to say. Feeling myself colouring up with embarrassment, now I couldn't look at either one of them. A deathly silence descended on the four of us. Following a short awkward silence, the couple spoke. Well, I don't know which one made their excuses first, but they said they would see us later before moving off.

Looking at Bet, I said, "fricking hell, what a dickhead. Did you say anything to his missus?" I never found out if Bet had said anything to her. I didn't imagine so. Bet just wasn't like that. Did the wife know it was us who had paid the thousand pounds, and if so, how? Or did she just take a calculated guess? We were fully aware that we had got a discounted last-minute reduction. That's the advantage of booking last minute and being flexible. But we also knew never to boast or even mention it. The elderly lady and her daughter earlier had expressed her anger at paying top price for a specific cabin with a porthole. We would never dream of mentioning what we had paid, no way. We didn't see the married couple for another two or three days. When we did, it was only the wife we bumped into, "oh hello, where's Peter?" I asked her.

"He's not very well. He's been ill in bed for three days. We think he's got a touch of food poisoning." Again we didn't know where to look. Jeez, it was so obvious and so embarrassing. He must have shot to bed straight after seeing us. The atmosphere was tangible, and after a short awkward silence, we said our goodbyes and off she walked. We never saw either one of them again. In truth, and in that situation, I didn't know what to think. Clearly, as new customers, Fred Olson had thrown us the sweeteners of the outside cabin with a porthole on the upper deck as an enticement to come back again. But what does that say to the married couple who had been bulls**t into a false sense of loyalty with gold tie pins? Then found themselves buried in the bowels of the ship next to the engine room? To be fair, I would be right p*****d off too. A couple of hundred quid is one thing, a grand extra, and an inferior cabin is quite another. It was unfair, and I felt sorry for them. We would have been quite happy with their cabin for the grand we had paid.

CHAPTER 12.

Sometimes it does pay to pay the full asking price. One year we had decided to spend Christmas at a hotel in Tunisia. Because of our numbers and being with the grandkids, we booked up well in advance to make sure everything went smoothly with adjoining cabins, decent entertainment, and food. It was only after we had paid for the specific hotel that we read up more about it and saw the words' golden oldies.' Whoa, f*****g golden oldies? We weren't golden oldies. We rang the agent up sharpish, who confirmed that yes, the hotel was specifically geared up for golden oldies. Panicking, I said, "we can't have that. We've got grandkids." He recommended and changed us to another nearby hotel that was more geared up for families without any further costs.

This turned out to be a major, major mistake. Getting to the hotel, we were not too impressed with what we were looking at—dozens of people milling around with unsmiling faces. Tired, we made our way up to our rooms and received our first shock. The rooms were filthy—blood spots on the mattresses, broken electric sockets, dodgy balcony railings. There was just no end to it. Straight away, I told the kids not to unpack. Going downstairs, we made our way to the tour rep and her table. There was a long queue, so I decided to check the pool and restaurant out. It was all equally unimpressive. Walking into the restaurant was like walking into a major food poisoning zone. Straight away, the grandkids wanted to eat. It took all my might to stop them from going to the buffet bars. No, no, no, we're getting out of here. I almost ran to the tour rep, still trying to pacify some of the guests, then I could see it. All the people were milling about in anger. The staff were sensing the anger and reciprocating in kind. To them, they were used to living in a s**t hole. As such, they couldn't understand the fuss. The tour rep was doing her best to fob people off, with some accepting their fate. That made me more determined to get out.

Fronting the rep, I demanded to be moved to another hotel with my family, including young grandkids.

"What's the problem?" she asked.

"The hotel is a s**t hole. Our rooms are disgraceful." I replied.

"Yes," she said, those rooms are about to undergo refurbishment. What about if we moved you to another part. Where the rooms have been refurbished?"

I could feel my eyes widen in horror, "you must be joking, aren't you? The whole hotel is a disgrace. It's disgusting. It's filthy."

She then asked what we had paid. When I told her we had paid the full price and originally for another hotel, she changed her tune sharpish, told us to get our cases and be at the main door within twenty minutes. We were there in five. As we walked away from her, we could see and hear her tone change when we heard the customer say they had paid the discounted price, "well, I'm sorry. You paid the discounted price. You have to accept what you are given." Their faces looked well sick as they walked away. Reaching the other hotel, which was the original golden oldies hotel we had first booked, we heaved a sigh of relief—what a bloody difference.

Within twenty-four hours, two of the grandkids had come down with some illness and had to go to the hospital for almost a week. We could never figure out whether they had caught something in the hotel's pool or some bug from the previous s**t hole. At any rate, we were fretting ourselves with worry about what kind of treatment they were getting. It was even worse when one of the doctors started asking Bet how to treat a breached baby. For Christ's sake. How backward were these people that they had to ask a holidaymaker what to do about an unborn breached baby? We began to wonder if the grandkids were going to leave the hospital. The hotel was great. The food was very good, but our Christmas was completely spoilt. Walking around the town and seeing the local's attitude towards us and the tourists in general, we decided there and then, never to return. We thought Morocco was bad enough, but that was an experience. Tunisia was a nightmare. On our return to England, we went straight to our solicitor and instructed her to sue the holiday company. We got our holiday costs back thinking we were lucky. In truth, we should have got double. Never again. I don't mind roughing it a bit if the holiday in itself is worthwhile, but Tunisia was, for us, the last resort.

CHAPTER 13.

We like to think we are sensible enough to realise that you don't always get what you pay for. Likewise, a bargain isn't always the bargain you might think it is. This applies to all areas or aspects of life. Whether it be food, clothes, or holidays, sometimes we've gone to a supermarket paid the asking price for a steak, or a pork chop, only to find the steak is tough as old boots and the pork chop, tasteless; with the number of injections and poison, put into it. Like most people, I think we have to learn as we go along in life. Our experience in the hotel in catering taught us to be more discerning when it came to food and what we were eating. The food in most restaurants, we find, is either frozen or pre-packed and tasteless. Making us prefer to cook our own food, even buying our own cod and cooking our own fresh cod and chips. Likewise, when it comes to clothes, and as things got better for us financially, I would push Bet to buy nicer, better quality clothes. For myself, I've never been really fussed.

I've brought a selection of cheap T-shirts with hesitancy thinking it's too good to be true. Only to find and be impressed with their good quality. I've paid high prices for jacket or trousers only to find it's of inferior quality. I've stopped in good quality four-star hotels and not been overwhelmed. Likewise, I've been into five-star hotels such as the ones in Luxor and been appalled by the atmosphere whilst being in awe of our surroundings. Life is a box of all sorts. It's a question of trying things out and finding the ones to your liking. Common sense tells us that we only get what we pay for. Sometimes, it's difficult to reason out what's the bargain and what's a really bad deal. When we got into the hotel business, I was shocked to discover who was really making money. Whilst we felt we charged a reasonable price and gave what we thought was good value for money, we were astonished to discover the difference between what some hotels were actually making and the prices the coach firms were charging.

This came home to us the first time we decided to put an advert in one of the papers advertising our hotel for the four-day Christmas break. Because we only had a 17-bedroom hotel, the coach company owner, John, suggested that we would have to share with a hotel of a similar size. This was no problem for us, and John charged us ten pounds to include the return coach to Birmingham with a full day out and a half day out for the local hunt. We thought it was a bargain and enabled us to reflect that in our prices. Seeing the opportunity for further business, I put to John the possibility of him supplying us with guests during the rest of the year. Straight away, John jumped in, "don't even bother Tom. You are far better off as you are. Do you know how much profit the Grosvenor gets off us?" Well, I had an idea of what they charged, but what the hotels actually got, I didn't have a clue. "Twenty pounds Tom. That's what they make." Well, knock me over with a f*****g feather; twenty quid? No, no, no, he was right. We were far better off as we were. One hotel was noted for its prices and its ability to shave its costings to the bone. They had the rooms to take a coach and were full for most of the year, even in low season. One day Bet, and I cost out what they spent on doing three meals a day. It was one pound per meal. We could make breakfast for one pound. But that was just for the one course, egg, bacon, beans, tomatoes. To do three courses seemed impossible to us, although admittedly it consisted of something like ham and salad for lunch. They were buying in bigger bulk than us. Still, one mistake, they were in the crapper. We realised that one of the biggest downfalls with many of the hotels was their inability to get their costs right.

CHAPTER 14.

A friend of ours in Sutton lived in a lovely, detached house opposite us. He and his wife had always lived on a tight budget which surprised us as he had been a design engineer for Jaguar. This is how we became friends. Bringing some plants over, Ted commented on my jag and that he had helped design it. I was impressed. He had admitted that he had served an extra five years to top-up his pension and because he loved his job so much. I realised that this seemed a bit of bulls**t that many people spew out. The simple fact is that most people get to sixty before seriously looking at their pension and what they will be getting.

In many cases, it turns out to be not a lot. Logic tells you to sell your house and downsize, but Ted didn't want to do that. He and his wife ran their life to the clock. Up at seven, breakfast at the table, then a few games of cards. In summer, they would be out in the garden. Both front and back were immaculate. I couldn't believe that they didn't find life boring. They were just passing the time. One day I said to Ted, "why don't you go on one of these long-term winter breaks?"

"What do you mean, Tom?"

He hadn't got a clue. I explained how the hotels cut their costs to the bone just to keep the hotel running and the staff employed. After a few more questions, I promised to get Ted a brochure. A couple of weeks had passed, and Ted told us that they were going to Malta, but only for a month. We were both dead chuffed for them. When they came back, we couldn't wait to see how they had got on. With an air of tiredness and resignation, Ted admitted that they had quite enjoyed it, but, you know, we've left it too late. The poor b******s. It never failed to amaze Bet and me. These people had worked all their lives, bloody hard, respectable. Ok, they had a nice house, in a nice area, yet they were living their lives in almost poverty. How much pension they were on, god knows? Their house was paid for, so Ted told me, but it just didn't add up.

Paying them both a visit after we had moved to another part of Sutton, Ted proudly showed me a side extension he had, had built. "Well, it only cost me twelve thousand pounds, Tom. It has even got insulation in the brickwork underground?" I looked at the plans Ted was proudly showing me. Twelve grand? With insulation below ground? I said, "Ted, why insulation below ground? This is a side extension with a plastic roof?" The poor f****r just couldn't see it. I could have knocked it up for him for about three grand; why hadn't he asked me? A few years earlier, he came over to my house panicking. A cowboy builder had knocked on his door, pointing out the ridge tiles were loose on his house. As they were in the area, they could do the job for three hundred quid. Like an idiot, he stood for and signed for it. Once on the roof, the cowboys found another three hundred quid's worth of work, a classic cowboy con. When Ted told me, I couldn't help but be angry, "why didn't you ask me, Ted? How come your house is the only one on the road that needs work? There was bugger all wrong with the roof." Nonetheless, going to court, the idiot of a judge found against him. He had to pay it off over twelve months.

Walking back into his house to join Bet for a cup of tea, we spoke for another short period before saying our goodbyes.

Getting into the car afterwards, I expressed my feeling of anger to Bet.

"You never saw what was on the table then?" She replied.

"No?"

It was an equity release form. An equity release form? For f***s sake. How stupid are they to go for equity release? I was shocked. Equity release is a noted rip off. You're lucky to end up with something from your house. Well, your kids will. I thought Ted had been stupid standing for the roofers. Now, to borrow money through equity release, then compound it by paying through the nose for a simple side covering was beyond me. This was an educated guy, with six kids, for Christ's sake.

A couple of years later, I decided to call around to see Ted and Margaret and show them my new motorhome. Knocking on the door, Ted invited me in. "I thought I'd pop around to show you our motorhome," I said. Ted looked outside and sneeringly said, "oh, that piece of scrap junk?" Well, I was staggered. I could not believe Ted could express or harbour such bitterness. For Christ's sake. I've seen this so many times. Here is a guy who's had a far better start in life than me. A respectable and professional job, a detached house brought in a period when many people could not afford a house after the war, yet here he was full of bitterness. Life was full of surprises. We were to see this time and again.

Never having been to Malta, we asked Ted how he found it, "Well, Tom, the only way I can best explain it is that you either hate it or love it." This seemed no answer at all to us. We just couldn't figure out how you could come up with such an answer. So when a five-week winter break came up a couple of years later, at what seemed a bargain price, we decided to give it a try. It was early March, so we tried to hedge all our bets. It had got an inside pool and sauna. If the weather was s**t, we could spend the days around the pool. If it was sunny, we could walk out and around the town or the island. We had booked full board, so if the food in the town was crap, at least we had three meals a day to choose from. Yes, all our bets were hedged. We had done our homework—big mistake.

CHAPTER 15.

Oh, there was a sauna. But we had to pay for it and give notice. Ok, fine, we could live with that. But then we found the pool was cold. To cut costs, the hoteliers had cut everything to the bone. They only switched the heating on for the locals at weekends, who paid to use the pool. By that time, there was that many it wasn't worth going in. The pool was empty all week. True to form, the weather was s**t. If we went out, it was cold, even if the sun was shining. Very few places were open, and the locals walked around with faces as long as the island—many confronting us at every corner, touting for timeshare. We were starting to wonder why anyone would want to spend more than a fortnight here. Nights were just as bad, if not worse, because it was so cold outside, we decided it was better to stay in and listen to the DJ at the bar. This was fine for the odd night, but the drinks were top whack. And everyone sat around with long faces. This was not much fun at all. Normally, you can at least find a couple of people looking to enjoy themselves.

Then it dawned on us. I had thought it was odd the way one group of people were behaving. They were making statements that seemed at odds with what I expected. I realised they were living in caravans. Frigging gipsy's, for Christ's sake. Not real gipsies. These were people who, for whatever reason, had brought and moved into mobile homes. Fair play to them. I've known a few who have done the same. Certain aspects of it can be quite appealing, but to me, you're there on licence.

No wonder they all seem so odd. How many were in the hotel? They don't carry signs on them, but one day after the second week, we were talking to another couple when I opened my gob and said, "I don't think I can take much more of this. It's one of the worst places I've ever been to." With that, I realised my stupidity. "Oh, I'm sorry. I shouldn't have said that." The guys jumped in, "no, no. It's fine, we agree with you. To be honest, we would be off like a shot, but we have nowhere to go to. We have to leave our mobile home for two months every winter." Well, now we understood. The whole hotel was full, mainly with caravan dwellers coming for the cheap break. They had to vacate their mobile homes as their campsite stipulated, they had to be empty for two months. No wonder they were such a miserable load of buggers. They were here under duress.

We hired a car for a week to break the monotony. The minor problem is you can drive around the whole island in two hours. Valletta? Interesting, once you've seen it. Visiting the Knights Templars was quite interesting. The next big focus was the home of Popeye, the sailor man. The filmmakers had built a town for Popeye and his friends on the far side of the island. In the main season, this might have been quite exciting to see and experience. But in the winter, it was not so much fun. Looking down at it from above, I just couldn't rustle up the enthusiasm to want to go down and see it. Bet didn't seem too keen either. It came to a head a couple of days later when we went down into the restaurant. The food was served buffet style where you got up and helped yourself. A plain-clothes security guard was on show watching like a hawk. Well, I confess I didn't give a thought to him being a security guard. I just assumed he was the floor manager overseeing everything was going to plan. This all changed when we finished our lunch one day, and I decided, I didn't feel like eating the apple I had picked up earlier.

Picking it up with the intention of eating it later, I went to walk out with Bet. In an instant, the security guard was on to me, "sorry, you cannot take that out of the dining room?"

I looked at him, stunned, "you what?"

"No, you must go back and eat it at the table or leave it."

I was that shocked I couldn't think what to say. How f*****g stupid are you? What kind of hotel are we in that we have to be treated or spoken to like this? I could have put it in my pocket, and he would never have noticed. What does that say about the guests, if they are looking out for you to nick a bit of food? That was it for me.

Now I was totally p*****d off. We went straight to the airport and got ourselves a flight back two days later. We didn't bother asking for any refund. Ted was right. You either love Malta or hate it. I've never wanted or felt the urge to visit Malta ever again. It is now a distant memory, along with a past nightmare. It was also the last time we looked at winter breaks as a bargain break. Maybe I was becoming fussy. Having run our own hotel and worked in the leisure industry, maybe we were becoming immune to it. Maybe it was the people around us who were forced to mix with.

We were far from snobs. Christ, we had both lived in and came from the slums of Birmingham. But somehow, the atmosphere was beginning to change. When we first started on our holiday breaks, most of the guests were determined to have a good time without even trying. We made friends easily with people who had just come to enjoy themselves and make the most of the fortnight's holiday, from Spain to Morocco. It couldn't be the hotels. In some cases, we were going back to the same hotels. No, it was the people who were beginning to change. Maybe it was the economy, the insecurity of the workplace. I couldn't put my finger on it. We never looked too deeply into the national economy or anything like that when we brought a business. When interest rates went up to eighteen per cent, the only ones who suffered were the ones with heavy borrowing. But in the hotel, people still wanted to come away for a break. Now, we were hearing stories of people who would boast about having so many holidays a year. How much they spent, the places, they were visiting worldwide. "Oh, we went to the Philippines' this year," or "we've been to the Great Wall of China," they would say. Well, all I can say is they must have been leaving all the miserable f*****s behind because that's what we saw on a more regular basis.

CHAPTER 16.

Bet, and I were still trying to find what was right for us. Some holiday breaks were great, some not so great, some a bit mundane. When we sold the hotel, we decided to push the boat out a bit and give the two youngest kids the holiday of a lifetime to Florida. Louise didn't want to come, so it was just Kristy and Rachael. Rachael was about ten and Kristy eight. It was a great holiday for all of us. The kids couldn't catch their breath. Everything was as true as we expected, and everything in America was bigger than anything we had experienced. A friend who owned a travel agency in Devon got us a bargain break for one month. The downside to this was that we had to divert to New York first, then to our apartments in Florida, which we only found out after a few days was a timeshare complex, hence the low price. We wondered whether our friend was really our friend. At any rate, it was great. The apartment was first-class and calling into New York first allowed us to get a look at the big apple. We were grateful for the experience because it saved us a fortune on making the same mistake again.

Our apartment was on Treasure Island, about ten miles from Disney World, which suited us a treat. The second day we picked up our hire car and having got over our jet lag, drew up an itinerary of places to see. This was a deliberate policy because a friend back in Devon told us a few of the places to visit, even giving us brochures and posters to many places. Busch Gardens, Alligator World, Disney World, etc., the list went on and on. Even then, we vastly underestimated the size of Florida and what it consisted of. In reality, Florida is one big playground. We were stuck in the world of England and the leisure and tourist venues around the country; Dudley Zoo, Twycross Zoo, Buckingham Palace. Plus the various country estates and homes. Florida, we found very quickly, was a different ball game altogether. First, Florida is not far from being the same size as England. Looking at the map, we just thought of it as a little tail on the bottom cheek of America. First mistake. Then, we realised that Florida is one great big playground, a leisure venue just a few miles apart in any direction.

Taking the kids for a drive the first night, they couldn't catch their breath, glaring neon signs everywhere. The main high street was like Las Vegas. Even though I had sensibly realised that the best thing to do was build an itinerary by the first week, I discovered even that was a mistake. Building the kids up, I explained that we would go to Busch Gardens the next day to give us a taste of what it would be like at Disney World. We had brought a three-day ticket to Disney World and had realised that it would be better spreading it over three weeks. Getting to Busch Gardens the next day, I realised I had yet made another mistake. I had assumed Busch Gardens would be like Twycross or Dudley Zoo. Smallish, navigable in a couple of hours. It was massive. That big that there were three forms of transport to get you about: from an overhead rail, a bus or horse-drawn coach. The brewery who owned Budweiser, Busch, had sought planning permission for a plant in Florida. It was granted as long as they built a leisure venue around it. They did, hence Busch Gardens. The actual brewery plant was hidden away in the centre of it; unless you knew, no one would have a clue. Any visitors were invited to a free tour of the brewery and a few samples. We just never had the time to do it. Touring the park itself took the whole of the day; gardens? —a bit of an understatement, I thought.

After a long, tiring, but thoroughly enjoyable day, we decided to call into the supermarket to get a couple of steaks for dinner. Another eye-opener. Along one side of the supermarket were trays upon trays of fish and prawns. There were about eight counters with the prawns, trays alone, with prawns of various sizes from small things that in England we call king prawns to gigantic things, the like of which I had never seen. The steak counter consisted of steaks varying in size from what we call a medium steak to steaks that big I didn't think a cow was big enough. Everything was big, again the kids couldn't get their heads around it. I also realised that the dollar equated to the spending power of the pound. So while the dollar was about 1.75 to the pound, we effectively got everything at half price. Which meant, as an extra bonus, we could live very cheaply.

The weeks soon passed, and we realised even with the time we had got, it was not enough. Some people we spoke to had booked a three or five-day break to Disney World alone. Crikey, what could you possibly see in just a few days? We only touched on a few major attractions around Orlando and Disney World itself. With a three-day ticket to Disney World, which included the Epcot centre, and having learned my lesson from Busch Gardens, I rethought our planning schedule. Setting out early for Disney World on the third day of our holiday and in our hire car, we got ourselves onto the highway following the signposts to Disney World. All of us were constantly open-mouthed and in awe at everything we were looking at and experiencing. Whoever said that everything was bigger in America was right. The steaks, the prawns, the lobsters were twice as big as in England. The roads were like our frigging motorways. That joke about the American from Texas, coming to London and listening to the tour guide boasting about the size of the river, replying in that loud Texan drawl, "why, when we take a piss in Texas, we make bigger rivers that that." Well, I don't think it was a joke.

One minute we were on a three-lane highway, following the signs to Disney World, the next, we had filtered into a five-lane highway. Then a ten-lane highway before it dawned on me that we had actually left the highway and were now on what must have been the Disney World filter lanes. From there into Disney World itself and one of the car parks. At the edge of the car park were small trains taking us to the booking offices where we brought our tickets. The tour guide informed us through a loudspeaker to please remember our car park's name for when we returned, looking over we could see ours was Goofy. Within ten minutes, I had forgotten it, so did everyone else. All the car parks were named after the Disney characters. Well, all I can say is there are a lot of chuffing Disney characters. Getting back in the night, it took us hours to find our hire car.

Leaving the ticket office, we were guided down to the lake. We were confronted by ferries leaving and returning with passengers to Disney World itself. We still couldn't get our breaths. Flipping hell, even the ferries were as big as the seafaring ferries we have in England to take us to France. Oh, ok, maybe I'm exaggerating a bit, but they looked big enough. Getting off the ferry, we had to reconsider our position yet again. How big was this Disney World? For starters, there were about four means of transport to get about. There was an overhead train, a horse and carriage, a bus, and the train. I thought it wisest to get the train, following the outer circle of Disney World while stopping off at every venue along the way. From Frontier Land to Adventure Land to Micky Mouse Land. In all, six different lands. Getting on the train, we were assailed with a non-stop assault on our senses from every angle. Passing Frontier Land, we did our first jump off at Micky Mouse World. At every corner were life-size characters from Disney World. The kids were in heaven.

I made a mistake, again, of working out that due to the vastness of Disney World, we would spread the three days over the three weeks. Leaving the Epcot centre to the last evening of our last day at Disney World. After all, it was not all that big—big mistake. We only realised how big it was when we got the overhead train into the Epcot centre, at around six o'clock after an exhausting day. We ended up running around the Epcot centre like idiots. Only leaving at closing time. Getting back to our apartment, we had just enough energy to grill and eat a steak before flopping into bed. We never moved the next day except to get to the beach and crash out, all of us, even the kids.

The complex manager had asked if we were here for Mickey's birthday, as usual in that drawn-out American twang. We looked at him blankly, "Mickey, who?"

"Why, Mickey, of course."

Then it dawned on us. He meant Mickey Mouse. For f***s sake. We are talking about a cartoon character here, and here's this guy talking like he was a real person, and he was serious.

"Why. Its Mickey's 60th birthday." He grinned.

For Gawd's sake. He had offered us a family ticket to Busch Gardens. All we had to do was attend a presentation on the complex we were in. Obviously, they were out to sell their timeshares. While we'd never be stupid enough to buy a timeshare, we thought it worthwhile to get a family ticket to Busch Gardens.

Well, I did. Bet as usual never said a word—another big mistake. We'd clocked on that the price for our bargain holiday was the chance of the complex trying to impress us into buying a timeshare. What we were not prepared for was the hard, mind-numbingly two-hour hard sell by the manager. Followed by a video of the complex. The guy knew we were not in the least bit interested but persisted in torturing us anyway for taking the Busch Gardens tickets. I was sorely tempted to shout, "here, take the f*****g money, enough."

Two doors away from us were an American family consisting of Bob and his wife, Trudy Pickles, and their daughter, Cindy. Bob and Trudy had bought a week's timeshare and travelled down in their car from Pennsylvania, North America. Bob owned a very large Cadillac and would drive the circa 2000 miles from their home, non-stop. Each taking it in turns to do the driving. With petrol at some 40 odd pence per gallon, it was cheaper than them getting a plane. Bob and Trudy owned a ranch in Pennsylvania. Well, it was actually a bungalow, but they call bungalows a ranch in America. At any rate, we became good friends and continued our friendship ever after.

They kindly showed us some of Florida's sights that we would never have considered visiting without them showing us, including a visit to the Kennedy Space Centre outside Miami. That in itself was yet another eye-opener. Heading there, we passed over the main highway bridge that ran alongside the existing bridge that had been damaged by shipping. Instead of repairing or dismantling the bridge, the Americans simply built another bridge alongside. Bob was quite proud to point that out, making it clear how wealthy America was.

Soon, our months holiday in America had come to an end. Shaking hands with the Pickles family, we swapped addresses, vowing to keep in touch from then on. We realised we hadn't seen anything like what Florida had to offer. Even a real Indian reservation further south in Florida, we had to miss out on, such as our time limitations.

The flight to America was horrendous. Just over eight hours, first heading to New York, the plane was shaking like a rusty f*****g can. At first, I accepted that as normal; all planes shake when taking off, right? So the lights were on to keep our seatbelts on and no smoking. For the first hour, I was fine. Then it crept into the next hour, at which stage the pilots voice came over the loudspeaker apologising for the heavy turbulence due to us heading into a heavy westerly wind. That was fine, but we were sitting over the wing, and my mistake was looking out over that wing. Well, that wing was shaking like nobody's business. For the first hour, I was fine with it. Going into the second hour was ok.

Then the shaking started to get to me. The wing was flapping with what seemed a ten-foot spread. Now, I don't think I'm stupid or of a nervous disposition, but I was starting to wonder how much bending and shaking a wing could take? How much can a plane take? We are talking cigar can here. I'd got my overcoat on and was starting to sweat, and it wasn't the heat. After four hours, I had to get up. The plane was bouncing all over the place, and so was I. At one stage, I hit the ceiling, falling into a woman's lap; she snottily reminded me that I should be sitting in my seat. I snottily pointed out that she might have the contents of my stomach in her lap if she wasn't careful. That shut her up. I made my way to the back of the plane, where I smoked three fags on the trot.

The plane never stopped shaking for the whole 8 hours, thirty-five minutes and sixteen seconds of the flight. Ok, it wasn't so bad getting back, but I vowed I would never get on a plane to America again unless we were going for at least a six-month break. Bob would keep inviting us to visit him in America. Each time I made excuses. Whilst he and his family made many visits to us in England, we never did visit them in America. Our kids did, but not us. Getting back home, we all simply collapsed for the first two or three days. None of us could even consider a holiday, anywhere, at all, for the next year, so we stayed where we were after our experience in Florida.

CHAPTER 17.

We had been in Devon for ten years when it started to occur to us that Devon was not somewhere, we wanted to spend the rest of our lives. This was no disrespect to the Devonshire people. We had bought two hotels, a guest house, and various other properties, including a fish and chip shop, and letting properties that gave us a nice income. No, it was more that we still never felt, even after ten years, that it was going to be our home. The fact is we were Brummies', and whichever way we looked at it, we felt we would always be outsiders. This was brought home to us at a friend's New Year's Eve party that we had been invited to. Fred and his brothers had lived in the town since they were kids at school. They were now all successful. Fred inheriting the building company from his dad. They had moved from Wolverhampton some fifty-odd years ago. Yet after all those years, it seemed he hadn't got a friend in the world. The atmosphere was stiff and unfriendly, strained. No one seemed to know each other, and Fred and his wife didn't mix or say much. We had been invited along with our friends Malcolm and Janet, who owned the local bingo company. We had been to a few parties like this over the years. People go about their lives not bothering much with friends until a specific occasion then seems to scrape the barrel to find a few people for the party. Each not knowing anyone else there. Such was the case here.

Sitting on the sofa next to us were a couple of elderly guys. Clearly, Devon born and bred and reminiscing that the town had changed so much over the years that there were now very few of them around.

"Ay, ay." replied his pal in the strong Devonshire accent, counting off who they knew.

"There's Peter down St Brannocks Road. He was born here. Then Billy over the hill," and on they went. All the time eating the free food and slurping the free drinks. I nudged Bet to listen. "Would you f*****g believe this? they're scoffing all the free food and drinks whilst slagging of their host as a non-Devonian."

So much for Auld Lang Syne, linking arms at midnight and wishing each other a Happy New Year. We had been there for about an hour, and it was still only 9:30pm. It was unbearable.

Sidling over to Malcolm and Janet, I said, "I can't f*****g put up with much more of this. My head is ringing with the pain."

Malcolm, who had been keeping a blank neutral face, admitted he was finding it equally painful. "But we can't go yet. It would be offensive and insulting to Fred. We've just got to stick it out till a decent time after midnight." I knew he was right; of course, painful as it was, I knew we had to stick it out. After a few minutes after midnight, we strained to put a smile on our faces while saying goodnight, a Happy New Year to all and thanking them for inviting us. Outside I turned to Malcolm and said, "f**k me that was terrible. Never again, never again." We had gone brain dead listening to that clock, tick-tock, tick-tock. Building its way up to midnight.

Maybe Birmingham wasn't the greatest place in the world, but it was home. The people, proper Brummies', were genuine and friendly to outsiders and strangers. This petty mentality was just too much for me. It wasn't just Devon. We'd seen it in Wales, in Hereford when we'd brought a country pub and caravan site in Five Acres. There the pig-ignorant local yokels made it clear to my daughter Kristy that unless she could talk about tractors and cows, she 'wouldn't be no good behind the bar.' A local girl of the same age told her she could live in Hereford for fifty years, and she would never be accepted in the community. After another bit of the same treatment, she said, "sorry, dad, you did not bring us up to put up with this crap." She was right, and I couldn't really object when she walked away after a few more weeks. We had learned our lesson from Devon. Instead of sticking it out, if it didn't work out after a few weeks, see it for what it was and get out sharpish. With that in mind, I went over the accounts, put a bit of work in and put it up for sale. We sold it straight away to a brewery letting company.

When we rang the agent up, he burst out laughing when I told him our reasons for leaving. "What's so funny?" I asked.

"You're the only one who's been honest, Tom. Most people come up with all kind of excuses. A stroke, a heart attack, anything but the truth." He explained.

He was dead right, any country pub up for sale would have the same excuses. Reason for selling, wife, had a heart attack. In our case, the agent turned up on the very day our pub was busy, and the campsite was chock-a-block.

He was in awe and felt we had a gold mine. "I know, I know," I agreed. A week later, the pub boss turned up on the agent's recommendation, had a quick look around, went back and put an offer in. Not only did we get out by the skin of our teeth, but we also made a nice few grand profit. Two years later, the smoking ban came in. A few short years after that, I saw the pub back up for sale at almost half the price. Every time I think about it, I give a little shudder and thank my lucky stars for getting out when we did. So, no, we had decided to sell up in Devon after ten years and get out, and that was harder than we thought. Or I thought. First, we had to sell the property portfolio that we had built up.

Selling one house is hard enough; selling a business or business property is ten times worse. It took us over ten years to sell up. As we sold, we transferred our finances into property in Birmingham; having moved and bought a grocery shop in a small village outside Birmingham, we then moved and brought a nice house in Four Oaks, Sutton Coldfield, our main priority being to get the kids stabilised and in a decent area.

It was over two years before we could find the time, inclination, or the money to have a nice holiday. By this time, we had become a bit disenchanted with some of the holidays we had. Everyone has their own opinion of what they feel constitutes a holiday. A working guy used to book into our hotel with his mates whilst working in the area. One night he was having a bit of a moan about how he would love to stop at our humble two-star hotel with his wife. He loved the friendly atmosphere and intimacy, but his wife was very demanding and insisted on a minimum four or five-star hotel, I could see by his face that it p****d him off. No doubt, he was on good wages as an engineer, but he was just an ordinary working guy. Not only did it cost him a fortune, but he also had to dress accordingly and found the atmosphere very stiff and formal. I felt sorry for the guy, but it was not new to me.

Time and time again, I had come across couples where the wife, in most cases, demanded a top-quality hotel from her husband who wasn't on great money. A friend, Brian, came to visit us, who dejectedly told us he was on the floor. With his business doing quite well, they would have regular top-ups on their mortgage. Everything was going hunky-dory till the interest rates started creeping up, the bills started mounting, and the s**t started to hit the fan. Now they were lucky to escape with just a few grand that enabled them to move into rented accommodation.

At the same time, he was imparting this to us, his wife was boasting how she was insistent on demanding a balcony suite when they went on a cruise and for a hotel to be provided whilst they had a kitchen extension, all on the top-up mortgages, of course. Bet, and I could only stare while trying to keep a poker face. Typically, Brian and I are no longer friends.

CHAPTER 18.

FINDING OUR MOTORHOME.

To me, I just couldn't get my head around how people's minds work. I've seen it many, many times. We expect it in poor working-class areas, but I've seen similar stuff in and around Sutton from people who appear to live in very wealthy houses and appear very well off. In truth, people tend to hock themselves up to the eyeballs. I've done it myself on houses. But as I go along in life, I never fail to be staggered how people then hock themselves up even more, on fancy cars, either on hire purchase or lease. Our friends Janet and Keith would have top-up mortgages then ramp their credit cards up. Go to the best store in Birmingham to order the best fitted carpets, all on the mace. No, thank you, the thought terrifies me. I don't mind being the flash harry, but not on thin frigging air.

So no, call me over-cautious, but when we go on holiday, the last thing we're interested in is a nice flash expensive hotel. If you've got the money fine. If not, cut your cloth accordingly. The cruises were great. We thoroughly enjoyed our cruises. Enjoyed the thought of living and eating very nicely of the best of food. We also liked the cross mix of people from ordinary people like ourselves, to the snobby set, to the millionaires. It was also interesting watching how each comported themselves. Mike and Mary from Canada were millionaires but came from very humble beginnings in Yugoslavia. They saw no need to put on a show or try to impress others. They were happy in a basic 2-3-star hotel. All these people taught us is how we wanted to live and lead our lives. A cruise was great for us now and again. Some people actually live for and on cruises. Others have a cruise more than once or twice a year. No, a cruise to us was to be treated as a treat, a little luxury. Plus, our money was always tied up in property. I don't think a lot of people understand money. We assume very rich people carry or have millions in the bank, not so. Many people see money in the bank as dead money. My dad and his peers carried there wad around in their pocket, pulling a roll out in the pub; everyone would assume they were loaded, they were, but that's all they had.

Equally, we were starting to get a bit fed up with the hotel holidays. How many times can you do the same thing year after year? Blimey, the same hotel. We had met people who went to the same hotel year after year. Up in the morning, down by the pool, in for a dip, out for a rest, a pint of lager in your hand. Into the bar at night, maybe a few excursions. Why, we even met people in some places like Morocco who never left the hotel, so frightened were they, then they would boast about how they went to Morocco.

Camping? No. The memory, the nostalgia of it was beautiful, but the reality of waking up on a cold and damp floor, a stiff back with arthritis creeping in, digging a hole to have a crap, made it a no, no, for us now. We had done the cruises; how many cruises can you have? Mountaineering? Cobblers to that for a lark. Hiking holidays, great if that's your thing. From experience, our worst nightmare would be to stay in a five-star hotel where everyone walked around like they were in a hospital ward. But then, one day, the future opened up before us. We had decided to have a day at the caravanning exhibition at the Birmingham NEC. Apart from a lovely day out, it opened our eyes up to the potential opportunities. There were all kinds of holiday ideas to satisfy every taste, tents that sat on top of cars or on the back of vans, brilliant but not for us. The boats, from little dinghies to million-pound yachts, were great, but we had tried that. But no one would get in the yacht or dinghy with me, so no, that was a no, no. Then we walked into the motorhome section.

Seeing the motorhomes on display started to get us excited by the minute. We had never looked that way, never met anyone that had owned one, so we didn't have a clue what we were looking at except for the fact that they looked absolutely fantastic and beautiful. The insides on some of them were utterly jaw-dropping, cookers, fridges that were better than we had in our home, a separate bedroom with a double bed, a separate shower and toilet, but it was mind-boggling in its diversity. You could have as many as ten variations in one model alone, one with rear bunk beds, or single, double bed, another with end kitchen. Some with overhead beds, others with storage over the cab, yet others with drop down over cab beds. Then there were different makes and models. There is the coach built, or alcove, low profile or integrated. Then there were the conversions. As we started to look around, the more we looked around, the more terrified we became. It was f*****g mind-boggling.

Walking into and around the Benimar, we fell in love with it. It was beautiful inside and even came with air conditioning, very wow factor. Well, it was to us and could hold up the promise of what lay in store for us. It was on sale for thirty-one grand, which seemed reasonable to me. However, it was still a lot of money, so being cautious, we decided to carry on having a mooch around. In the next section were the Hymers. The one we were looking around was very austere and bland. We felt it was ugly. No style to it, no beauty, no character. And it was priced at fifty-four grand. Fifty-four bleeding grand. Over twenty grand more than the Benimar. I'm trying all ways to see the difference in the price, surely it couldn't be the fact the furniture was rearranged differently. In the end, the salesman strutted in, alone, and fearing making a prat of myself, I asked him why there was such a price difference between the Hymer and the Benimar? Looking at me sneeringly and with a typical air of arrogance, he flung his arms wide and said, "well, it's the quality, of course!"

Looking suitably blank, I asked him for an example of the difference in quality. Again giving that air of superiority of knowledge, he pointed to the seats, "why, just look at the quality and difference between the seat covers?"

By now, not only am I feeling totally ignorant, but I'm also feeling bleeding angry. Now, I'm looking at him like he's an idiot. As calmly as I could, I said, "well, surely seat covers don't justify a twenty-odd grand difference?"

This time he went into a bit more detail, "well, you see, the walls on these Hymer motorhomes are 40mm thick and very well insulated." Then, to push his point home, he said, "you could travel up to the north pole in this and not have to put the heating on!" I stared at him in astonishment and a wave of growing anger.

"Is that it? I could drive to the North Pole." The guy is treating me like an idiot, and I'm thinking, how bloody stupid are you? As calmly as I could, I said, "I ain't looking to buy a motorhome to drive to the f*****g North Pole. With that, we walked out, Bet keeping her little cheeks tightly together.

Walking out, I said to Bet, this is ridiculous. I'm completely lost. We had learned nothing, and the salesmen were completely useless and seemed to know bugger all, either that or I was as thick as two planks and couldn't see what was in front of my eyes. The only thing I had learned was on seeing a motorhome with a rear garage, it answered the one big question and worry I had. A motorhome, like a tortoise, is your home when you go away. Every time you want to go to the shops or the beach you would have to pack everything up and put it away. The garage was the godsend. We had never heard or seen anything like this before until we hit the NEC.

After a long and tiring day, we set off back home, none the wiser except for the fact that we knew the way forward, we knew what we wanted, and we knew our future lay in having a motorhome. From then on, I had got the bee in my bonnet. It was just about finding the right one to suit us. That took us another two years of searching and viewing. It was worse than buying a house. With a house, you look at the front, the area, and if its three or four bedrooms, dead simple-- a motorhome? It's a bloody nightmare. Asking one owner, he pointed out how it's all about compromise. He'd got a scooter ramp on the back of his van; some people have a trailer. "It's all about compromise," he repeated. He was helpful, but I was still no further forward. Going along, we tried another tack; let's try and imagine every scenario, and jot down what we wanted and expected. First, we wanted a fixed bed, so we could just flop into it after a day of driving. Also, if we're driving abroad and Bet was tired, she could sleep during the journey. We also wanted a separate toilet and shower. Next, two separate sofas so we could sit or lie down after a long day on the beach and have a nap without having to get into bed.

Along the way, we slowly started to sort the wheat from the chaff. We started to see the difference with the Benimar, a Spanish built motorhome by a company set up specifically to jump on the motorhome market's growing popularity. In short, they were rubbish, and we came across many complaints. The Hymer? My first thoughts were correct, and my feeling was and still is that they are overrated.

We looked at small motorhomes, medium motorhomes, and big motorhomes. Eventually, our eyes were opened to the Autotrail range. Again we were dazzled by the sheer array of different models. There were what seemed like dozens of them. The Tracker, the Navajo, Comanche, Apache, Tribute, Cheyenne, it just went on and on, all evoking the excitement of adventure and travel. Then the variety of layouts. Autotrail was a British company based in the north of England. It also seemed to have a good reputation. It also had that vital 40mm insulation which meant if we did by any chance want to go to the north pole, we could do so. We then nailed it down to two models, the big Comanche, and the Cheyenne. The Comanche was about six foot bigger than the Cheyenne, but inside we couldn't justify the difference. The lounge had an extra two foot; we didn't need it. The bedroom another two-foot, we didn't need that. Looking at the Cheyenne, we found the bed was above the garage. Realistically we considered we never went to bed to enjoy the landscape, we went to sleep, so the lack of windows was more than made up by the extra room in the garage below. The lounge was exactly right for us with the two full-length sofas that could turn into a double bed, a pull-out double bed above the cab, all ideal if we had the kids along, or, maybe, even if the kids were lucky enough to borrow it. As an extra bonus again, we found the SE model, with a television built into the rear-view camera in the front, an outside tap with a shower connection, great for those sandy days on the beach, and barbeque connections. It was great. It was everything we could hope for. After looking at everything, having a test drive, getting some generous discounts, that was it; we brought it and were on our way.

CHAPTER 19.

FREEDOM BECKONS AND
ON THE ROAD, WE GO.

Our motorhome was delivered to our house a few days after purchase. This followed a full vehicle and habitation check. Bet was handed a very nice bunch of flowers that pleased her immensely. A photo was taken, giving us the memory forever. But this was only the first bit. Next, we had to survey the workings inside the motorhome itself. There was the Sargent power converter in the overhead locker. This provided power to the whole unit. It also converted 12 volts to 240dc.

Then there was the Sargent power unit display. Very simply, it displayed the condition of the main battery as well as the leisure battery and the freshwater capacity as well as the wastewater capacity. Then there was a timer to enable us to have the lights come on at a specific time when we were out. It was great. But I just never got around to using it or figuring it out. For that, I needed a degree, which I was lacking. It took us about a week just to figure out the basic workings. Then stock the motorhome with what we felt was needed for a holiday abroad or in the country, clothing, shoes, cutlery, towels, soap toothbrushes etc. all this in itself not a five-minute job. We were to find it takes many, many months to get to a satisfactory position, then you still ain't got it right.

But eventually, we reached the stage where we felt we could build up the courage to set off on our first venture. We had joined the camping and caravanning club and the camping club. Both of these are supposed to be charitable organisations. This bemused me as I found in many cases, they were dearer than anyone else, charging a couple for putting a tent up some twenty-odd quid for the night, to lie on a patch of grass and use the toilets and shower. Nice money if you can get it. We were charged twenty-five quid a night to park up and plug into the electric. Sitting on our little sofas, I turned to Bet and asked what we were paying for? We have our own shower, our own toilet, ok, the facilities are there, but we didn't need them. We were paying twenty-five quid for a bit of turf and a couple of quids worth of electric; it started to rankle with me.

There are two trains of thought with motorhomers. There are those who would never go anywhere except on a site. Then there are the free campers or wild campers as its commonly known. Out of these, some will do nothing except wild camp, refusing to go on any site by any means. Others will go on a site out of desperation after every few days simply to empty their cassettes and use the showers. This I could see the sense of as it puddled my brain, wondering where some of these people empty their cassettes after just a few days. It doesn't take long to fill a little chamber up after all.

At any rate, the idea of paying 175 quid a week just to sit in a s****y field wasn't in my vocabulary. Worse, some of these places had no decent bar, café, or restaurant. If it did, we found people generally a bit anti-social, keeping to themselves as a couple or a group. If you went over to say hello, you would either get looked at a bit sniffily or get the cold shoulder. Motorhomers generally liked to keep to themselves, and caravanners we found liked to be in their own little groups called rallies.

Generally, caravanners don't talk to motorhomers. Why I could never figure out. Do caravanners resent or look down their nose at motorhomers because we cheapskate by wild camping? Do motorhomers look down on caravanners because they feel a bit superior? Again I never knew. I had heard instances of people having brought a very expensive motorhome, looking down their nose at someone in an older motorhome. At any rate, the whole thing sounded utterly bleeding stupid. I assumed caravan sites would be a nice opportunity to meet nice friendly, likeminded people, share experiences and have a nice meet up in the bar or local boozer on our little travels. Not so. Maybe I've got a stamp on my head saying p**s off. Maybe I just look miserable. But looking around, we felt that most campers of either side kept to themselves.

One site we pulled on; we had inadvertently pulled up next to a rally group. This was fine with us, but they kept to themselves, fine, we're not snobs. But if they prefer to keep to their own little pack, that's their choice. Well, we hadn't been there a day when the rally leader came over and asked if we could judge their potato competition. A potato competition? For Christ's sake. Feeling we had no choice but to agree, we were asked to give them twenty minutes before going over. I could feel the stunned look on my face as I said to Bet, "a f*****g potato competition? How the f**k do you judge a potato competition?" Bet just looked her usual blank self. Saying nowt. After twenty minutes, we walked slowly across. Looking around, I wondered why they had picked on us? There were other caravanners around? Why us, just because we were the nearest?

Trying to keep a straight and serious face, we set about looking at the potatoes. All had little faces of one kind or another on them. Some had hats on. Some had beards, looking around at the group, about ten of them, all sitting in a circle, anticipation and excitement filling their little faces. I couldn't look at Bet. Not having a clue, I tried my hardest to pick a winner, with a runner-up coming second. Eventually, after trying to keep a serious demeanour, fitting for such an occasion, we picked out the winner and the second runner-up. Looking across, we could tell the winners by the look of smugness on their faces, the losers by their dropped mouths. Heading back to our van, I said to Bet, "would you want to do that?" These people were over fifty, sixty, for f***s sake. They were pensioners. Doing potato heads that we used to do as ten-year-olds in junior school. Bet shook her head with some vigour, "no, I wouldn't."

Maybe that's why caravanners kept to themselves. At any rate, I'm no snob, but this is something I couldn't get my head around or with people I could never socialise with. Maybe I've been self-employed for too long. I mean, I left school with barely any education, but this? Playing potato heads. No, thank you. We started to see, very quickly, that the little negatives were adding up. We had a very nice comfortable motorhome completely self-contained with all the facilities we needed for wild camping. All we had to do was get out on the road and start exploring.

"Western-Super-Mare is a nice place. Let's go down there?" So off we set. The only problem that we quickly found out was that Western, like a lot of seaside resorts, just doesn't want or welcome campers. Unless you pay for out of the way sites, of course. No, Western-Super-Mare is very money, income orientated. Even the disabled spots are limited to one hour instead of the usual three hours. This is where the camping clubs, very cleverly, come into their own. If you own a small site, a pub with land or smallholding, you can be granted a CL status giving you permission to let up to five campers on to your land. This would be included in the caravan club's booklet. In theory, it sounds great, and it is for the camper.

We found a little site, a couple of miles up from Western called Kewstoke. It was only six quid a night, in a crappy little field, which was a lot better than twenty-five quid a night in a slightly better field. But it was out in the sticks, miles from anywhere, and a short walk from a desolate beach. After one day, we were pulling our hair out and having to travel the couple of miles back to Western for the day. This was not much fun. We started to notice that quite a few campers would get round the restrictions by hiding away in the back streets, like sneaky gipsies. The thinking was that if you keep all the blinds up, the lights off and the doors locked, no one will know or be able to prove you were sleeping or living in it. This is something that didn't appeal to me or Bet at all. After a few trips to Western, we decided it wasn't the place for us. To paraphrase the actor, W. C. Fields, 'if you don't want us, we don't want yow.' We cut Western-Super-Mare out of our favourite places to visit.

Calling into Brixton one time, we found it impossible to find anywhere to park. Out of desperation, we found an empty industrial estate just outside the resort. Settling down to sleep, we woke up to find ourselves surrounded by cars, vans, lorries, and workers. We were mortified and drawing the blinds back, we got out as quickly as possible. Further along and just outside Paignton, we noticed three camper vans on the leisure car park. One of the campers was the same model as ours, the Cheyenne. Pulling up alongside, the Cheyenne owner pointed out that the leisure centre provided free toilets and showers, and we could park for the simple cost of the parking fee; this was fine by us. And we decided to have a few days there.

The second day, in the late afternoon, I noticed a camper pull up in front and to the side of us; this was a big camper like a bus. As I set off over to the leisure centre, I couldn't help but notice the ramp under the van lifting it up and levelling itself off. Coming back, the sides were now out, giving more room inside. Impressed, I went over to the guy and complimented him on his motorhome, "oh yes," he said, "that's the self-leveller, and putting the sides out gives us the room inside." But then he went on to tell me of the difficulty he had experienced, going to France. He explained that the journey was a bit of a nuisance, being as big as he was. Once on-site, great, but coming back, it was even worse. Ringing up every campsite in the area, he found no one would accept him. He was simply too big. I must confess it was something I hadn't thought about, neither it seemed, had he.

In desperation, he rang the local council, which directed him to this car park, and to simply pay the parking charge. Asking me, which was my motorhome, I pointed to the Cheyenne. Giving a sigh, he said, "you know, I looked at one of those and considered buying one. I wish I had." Now there's me thinking what a lovely outfit he had got, and he's standing there regretting buying his. It must have been well more than one hundred grand. It made me sit back and take stock. Going across to Bet, I told her the chat I had just had. Looking across, I think we both felt the same. We had brought the right size motorhome for us. Yes, it was a bit tight when we had got the kids and grandkids, but for only short periods. Although it was a six berth, we realised that it was only suitable for the two of us for comfort and space.

CHAPTER 20.

VENTURING FURTHER AFIELD.

Our plan was quite simple and straight forward, that was to spend our winters abroad in the sun and our summers enjoying the beauty, character, and diversity of touring England and what it had to offer. This was mistake number one. Everywhere we were hitting may as well have put up big signs saying camper vans ain't welcome. Weston-Super-Mare was a choice example. As soon as you pulled up, the wardens were around like a shot. Cornwall and much of the south coast was much the same. You could almost feel the 'not welcome' signs. Inland wasn't much better. I pulled up at a pub car park at Holt Fleet near Stourport. I called into the pub and asked the young manageress if we could park overnight as we expected to come in and have a few drinks and a meal. Without hesitation, she said "yes, no problem." With that, we drove over to some out of the way spot in the corner. Within half an hour, she was over like a shot, panic-stricken knocking on our door, "no, no, no, I'm sorry, you can't park here, the landlord won't allow it." Jeez, I couldn't believe it. What have my fellow campers done to deserve this, I wondered. You would think these places would be chuffed to have anyone calling in. The place was dead.

I was frustrated as I walked around, trying to find somewhere to park up when I came across the warden on the mooch. Pulling him, I asked, "what the hell is going on here with the barricades?" After quite some time, and I could see with some reluctance, he told me, two years earlier, a bunch of gipsies had pulled on to the car park and refused to leave. It cost the council thousands in court orders to get them off and clear the crap up they had left. So was this the answer then all over the country? Well, if so, why couldn't these councils bloody do something about it?

One of the main points of buying our motorhome was to enjoy the freedom that comes with it. To tour the country, to tour Europe at will, and at a time that suited us. To pull up on or near the beach at Western-Super-Mare or Barmouth, tour Scotland pulling into quiet bays and coves. Much to our concern, well, my concern at least, I was finding this less and less so as we explored and set out around England. Slowly, and it was slow, we would find little places that we could park up for one or even a few days at a time, if not made totally welcome, a blind eye was turned so long as we paid the local parking charges. But real freedom would come from abroad. Now that, we were to find was more to our liking.

CHAPTER 21.

After a year or so of tootling around England, trying to find out decent places to park up without being kicked out before we had even started or got our heads down, not to mention in between paying through the nose on caravan sites that offered nothing except a bit of ground, electricity, and sometimes grubby showers, we made our first venture abroad.

We had decided to drive through France from Calais straight into Spain. Spain was the go-to place. The sun always shone, the people were friendly, the beaches pristine, sandy, and beautiful. It was sangria and castanets all the way. France seemed unfriendly and inhospitable. This was a big mistake. But I have to say for a few years, most of our touring was made up of big mistakes. Down to me, every time, of course.

Our motorhome was fully equipped, serviced to the hilt, packed with back-up food, swimming trunks, shorts for the day and the hot sun, smart slacks, and a jacket for those cooler nights, when we would be eating out under the setting sun, and books and puzzles to keep us occupied on the quiet nights in our van. We had considered taking our evening dress and dinner jacket but decided to drop that idea, just as well.

We had decided that the best plan of action was to get to Calais on the 12 or 1am ferry from Dover, thereby driving overnight through France and away from the port of Calais and all the misfits, immigrants and other dodgy chancers lurking around. This was where our little motorhome came into its own. Pulling up at Dover at least two or three hours before our ferry booking, we simply booked in and drove to the allocated bays. Pulling up, we switched the power on, put the kettle on the hob, got the cups out and proceeded to make a nice hot cup of coffee. Settling down on our full-length sofas; feet up, coffee in hand, we looked across at our fellow travellers, mostly in cars, cramped up four to a car. Boots chock-a-block with luggage. Faces weary and tired. Not only did we feel very smug and comfortable, but we also felt a great sense of gratitude that we were heading abroad in total comfort. It was something we were to find time and time again. We could turn up, and it would be p*****g down with rain. Watching people walking around in the rain, desperate for a break from their cars or motorbikes, made us grateful for our motorhome.

By now, the sat-nav had come into its own. Thank the lord for the sat-nav. Bet, bless her heart, just couldn't read a map. It led to countless arguments over years driving around England. A simple trip to Wales would lead to heated arguments, with me having to stop every few miles to see if we were on the right road. I would see her little brow furrow up as she tried to work out the little lines and squiggles. But now, with the sat-nav, all our prays were answered. Now, Bet could just sit in the seat and enjoy the views. If she wanted, she could just get into the fixed bed at the rear and have a sleep as we tootled along. We were both in our oil tot.

We would head straight for the restaurant and have a snack or a meal before the two-hour ferry trip. This was to become part of our rituals and would put us in the holiday touring mood. Before docking, we would be called down to our motorhome along with all the other travellers in their lorries, vans, cars, and motorbikes. Sometimes I would not catch my breath at the wonder of how many bloody lorries and arctics could be piled onto these ferries. Watching them drive off the ferry seemed never-ending.

Between each body, whether ferry company or government departments, they had got everything worked out for perfectly well-oiled running. With the doors opening, we would be called off, line by line, five or six lines in a row in single file. Smoothly driving off into the customs stop and checkpoint, then away, sat-nav fired up and finding a route. We were only stopping in France for a break or a kip. Instead of setting the sat-nav for any stop-off points, we would just put in, say, Alicante or Benidorm, picking it up each time we stopped and started. From customs, that was it. We were off with the wind. We were aware of some of the stories about the traps set for motorhomers, in particular, being waved down was an obvious trap. There were the spikes to give you a puncture. A little party would follow you along the road, and when you stopped, pull in and mug you. Obviously, motorhomers were noted to be carrying all their personal possessions, cash, credit cards etc. We were, after all, in our own homes, safe and secure. So we thought. I was determined to take every precaution.

We would drive at least 150—200 miles before pulling in for a break or a sleep at the motorway services, of which there were plenty. We were to find that there were Aires aplenty throughout France. We seemed to be seeing them or passing them every few miles, some in small villages or towns. The ones we were passing were absolutely great for toilet facilities, water, and to empty our cassettes, but also seemed dangerous as well. Pulling into one such Aire, we pulled into a suitable spot just away from the main toilet block. Before settling down, I walked over to have a piddle while Bet put the kettle on. By the time I had finished and walked out, the few cars that had been around and a couple of motorhomes had disappeared, my bottle went sharpish. We were a sitting target.

Clearly, these Aires were very isolated and meant purely for a break, not for overnight stops. We decided that the service stations were the safest places. Almost everyone had restaurants and facilities, even Wi-Fi. Unlike in England, the attitude was totally different. In England, there are two- or three-hour-time limits. Here the welcome sign is up. There were sections for cars, motorbikes and even sections for motorhomes and caravans. All free, no charges, and no little puffed up jobsworths coming around demanding money. The more times we pulled into these places, the more relaxed we felt. It was heaven.

Instead of going to the parking lot's far side, which could be some distance from the main service area and restaurant, we would find somewhere nearby. This served two purposes, it was close to the restaurants for walking and most times within Wi-Fi range, it was also safe. Again, no one ever came out to chastise us or move us on. We found that, unlike the English, the French and Spanish had a life. Their mentality was very different.

France is bigger than Spain, and both are more than twice the size of England. France has 60 million people. Spain has circa 40 million, whilst England has 70 million, plus. That's without the ones we don't know about. The facts speak for themselves. We in England are overcrowded with not much quality of life. It only stands out a mile when you tootle around both countries. Many English, who live in France, will tell you it's like England in the 50s, which sums it up.

Sometimes we would be driving during the day, which gave us the chance to see a bit of French life, or so we thought. But this was a big mistake on our part. Stupidly, I made snap decisions on just a few of the places we visited or passed through. For instance, many of the little villages seemed bland and barren, quiet, with no one about. At night it seemed even worse. It seemed to me that after 7pm, everything closed down, the shutters went up, and everyone seemed to disappear. Where did they go? Whole families disappearing behind closed doors hunkering down and watching the telly? Like us? Of course. We did exactly the same, but seeing as we had almost double the population, we saw more people. We didn't shutter our windows.

CHAPTER 22.

It was in my makeup to make the mistakes I did. We all start the same way on many published and internet camping sites. Asking the same questions, looking for the right answers, what we carry, what we need, and what about insurance. With all these questions, we have to find out much comes in learning as we go along. I was to find, very slowly, that my mistake was to rush about so much I was just chasing my own tail. Missing out on so much in towns and villages, we were too busy flying through to get to Spain and the sun.

Getting to Spain, we found it was everything we had expected - sunny and hot. That to us was everything that Spain was about. I had set the sat-nav to Alicante. From there, I guessed we could tootle along to any of the coastal towns and holiday resorts. To reach them, we travelled across a varied Spanish landscape. From mountain views to lush valleys to acres upon acres of crops growing from vines to tomatoes to olives, all throwing up amazing and tantalising smells that would hit the nostrils every few hundred yards. This, coupled with the heat that bore down on us, left us exhilarated and with a never-ending feeling of anticipation of what was to come next. Cutting into the left, we had decided to coast hop for the last few miles down to Alicante, Benicassim, Gandia, then into Denia, spending a couple of days in each. Each having its own character and personality whilst still being intrinsically Spanish.

For some reason seeing any fellow Brits was a bit of a rarity. Mostly, we came across the French or a few Germans, dotted about in little clusters, many on the beachfront or within walking distance. Taking our cue from them, we would pull up, leaving plenty of space between us. We were to find very quickly that there is a difference between camping and parking up when wild camping. When you are wild camping, you are simply parking up at the discretion of the local council and police. This means no awnings, tables, or chairs out. That is camping. If you want to camp, go to a campsite. We were quite happy with this especially being just a short walk to the beach carrying our towels and deckchairs. We were quite in our oil tot.

A fellow camper once said to me, when choosing a motorhome, you will always have to compromise whether to have a trailer on the back carrying a motorbike or scooter, bunk beds, fixed beds and so on. He was right. We had chosen the fixed raised bed with the garage underneath, ideal for us. The bed was separate, and whilst we had to climb a couple of steps, it gave us a massive amount of space in the garage. This left our living space completely uncluttered and spacious.

From Denia, we headed into Benidorm, which we found to be very different. Benidorm was bustling. Firstly, there were no Aires or places to park up anywhere near the beachfront or within a mile of it. The Spanish were well on the ball to the importance of money and how to make it. If you were in a motorhome, you were diverted to the designated campsites. For the first night, we parked up on what seemed like a bomb peck a mile or so back from the seafront. Although there was another couple of vans parked up, we didn't know if they were parked up empty or whether someone was living in them. We guessed it was the latter when we saw a glimmer of light creeping out of the one. This made us feel even more like gipsies.

I found out more and more of the camper's attitudes to camping. Some would hide away in the back streets to avoid paying camping fees. This not only seemed wrong to me, but it also seemed a bit cheapskate. For Christ's sake if you're not welcome, go somewhere else, don't be like a gypo. To be fair, the state pension for some of these people is in the region of circa £170 a week. Some of the campsites were charging that for the week. After spending one night, we decided to book into a campsite a short walk from the beach. We had joined a camping club called ACSI, which guaranteed all sites from between £11-£15 a night out of season. Showing my card and seeing the ACSI sign, I asked, "ACSI?"

"Si, si, signor." As he said this with a smirk on his face, I offered to pay in advance, and he was having none of it, "no, no, it is £35 per night." He knew he had got me by the short and curlies, it was either pay his fee or go somewhere else, and we wanted to enjoy what Benidorm had to offer. We booked in for a couple of nights at least, deciding to give it a go. Finding our site, we pitched up and hooked into the electric. From there, we made our way to the central café and bar to see if we could get a snack or a breakfast.

It was clear from the people around us that many were long termers. They sat in groups and spoke like they owned the place, loud and confident. They reminded me of the people in the back streets of Birmingham, where I grew up. No, thank you, I couldn't see myself wanting to be their best friends or get into their little cliques, the thought horrified me, and I could see Bet weren't too keen either.

Locking up, we set off for a little mooch around the town. It was great, and everything was geared up for you to spend your money. The booze was dirt cheap, and it made no difference what time you went out; you would see people drinking. Traditional breakfast? And a pint of lager, please. Beef dinner?

And a couple of pints of lager, please, it seemed the whole town was full of Brits banging back lager. I had to wonder how much or how many ended up in the local hospital with pickled livers.

Many of them took to hiring little mobility scooters to help them get around and to the next boozer as quickly as possible. It seemed every other Brit was tootling along on a shop rider, and every other shop was selling trinkets or 'kiss me quick' hats. Then you had restaurants and pubs. I don't think anywhere else on earth held so many. It didn't take us too long to figure out this didn't suit us. Worse, we were wondering what we were paying for. £35 a night works out at £245 per week. That's two hundred and forty-five pounds a week; just to park up, use meagre electricity and empty our cassette. I don't consider myself a cheapskate, but I just couldn't justify this cost when we didn't need it. Benidorm seemed great for a fortnight, but for too much longer, no, I don't think my liver would have stood for it. On the third day, we decided to set off along the coast, past Alicante and onto El Campello.

On our way to El Campello, we decided to call into Torrevieja. Torrevieja was famous for its salt lakes, and I reckon its cheap properties. We had holidayed there a few times and just couldn't weigh it up. We rented a small villa on a complex about four miles out of town towards the salt lakes the first time we went. The complex was one of a few dotted about in little isolated groups. Why the government or developers allowed or stood for this, I don't know. Cost and convenience, I suppose, but it allowed them to sell the properties cheap, and I mean cheap, and it showed.

Our little villa was fine, and it was clear the owners had put their private possessions into the separate top bedroom. We weren't complaining. We weren't complaining it was only £100 for the week, but first things first, we noticed the pool was empty. Later on in the evening, we called into the one and only bar to find two sulky looking individuals propping up the bar and nursing half of lager. Saying hello, I asked if I could buy the guys a pint. They weren't slow in saying yes. Opening the conversation, I mentioned how quiet the place was. Like a shot, the older guy was quick to spew out that "well, it's alright for people like your landlady. She brought the place but never visits. She just rents it out." Interested in finding out about the place, we considered buying something, as prices were cheap. I offered them another drink, the visible shock on their faces showed this wasn't an everyday occurrence. I then commented on how the pool was empty and wondered why? Quick as a flash, the older guy got it in, "It's only people like you who use it, us who live here have to pay the service charges and never use it." Blimey, I couldn't get my breath; what a miserable old bleeder. And I'd just bought him a pint. The guy next to us told us he was a retired bricklayer from Germany. Upon retirement, he'd sold up, brought this little villa to retire to and that I think explained things.

A lot of these places had been built and sold off very cheaply. The people who brought them in the main were ordinary working guys who sold up to move here. The only problem I found was they didn't do their homework properly. The average pension was never the best. If the pound dropped, so did their pension. If one partner kicked the bucket, they were well and truly in the doo, doo. No wonder the old b*****d had got a face like Livery Street. But didn't he realise he was paying a maintenance charge?

We found this time and time again around Spain. One year a friend loaned us there two-bedroomed apartment, again in Torrevieja. Offering to pay, they insisted they didn't want any payment. Just give it a good clean. When we got there, we could see why. There was an inch of sand all over. The place hadn't been used for months. Using the pool, we learned very quickly that no one could make any sounds between 12pm and 4pm. This was siesta time, and as most residents were Spanish, the rules were very strict. That was another community we weren't interested in. Another thing we found about Torrevieja was that there was a large Russian community not too far away, resulting in a lot of robberies. It was a shame because the port and harbour area were beautiful, clean, tidy, and buzzing. Maybe it was us, maybe we expected too much, but at any rate, it put us off buying. The more we saw, the less we wanted to buy.

Because of its reputation, we decided to seek out and stop at a campsite on the edge of town. A story that was gathering in strength was the gassings we heard about. We had heard that people were going around inserting a pipe into the vents, gassing the people asleep inside, then breaking in and robbing them. This was a frightening thought, but when I mentioned it to the English campsite owner, he dismissed it out of hand, "I don't think it's happening he said. I think it's for insurance claims?" Hmmm, that's a thought. But then we heard Germans in Torrevieja were leaving in droves because of the robbing. Whether gas was involved, we never knew. But a guy calling himself a doctor wrote an article in a camping magazine who said it would be impossible, on the basis that the crooks wouldn't be able to carry a canister big enough. At any rate, one night and two days were enough in Torrevieja for us, late afternoon, we tootled off to El Campello.

CHAPTER 23.

El Campello was a complete contrast to Torrevieja and Benidorm. El Campello was more sedate, quieter, and posh. Driving up and around the town, which was now becoming our modus operandi, we came upon a car park right on the seafront at the edge of town where we saw a few motorhomes pitched up. This would do us, and we settled down for a week or so of sun, sea, and relaxation. El Campello was lovely. It had a nice town centre, a very pleasant beachfront, a nice line of shops and restaurants, and a more sedate attitude with a nice mix of English and Spanish. When we mentioned Torrevieja to a couple of English people there, noses turned up in horror and disdain. Oh no. Oh no, thank you very much.

When you're camping in a motorhome you can spend as little or as much as you want. Food was not on our list of priorities, and Bet and I ate to live, not lived to eat. In El Campello, the parking was free, our only cost was the diesel for getting there. We would stock up before we even set off abroad, cornflakes, tinned tomatoes, tinned soups, and sardines from Aldi. Some of Aldi's food is crap but a lot is also very good. Considering most supermarkets buy from the same suppliers- this shouldn't be too surprising—one box of cornflakes for 70 pence, which lasted a week. But the food wasn't expensive anyway in Spain. Two kilos of fresh mussels were two euros. Two kilos of mussels with a bit of bread as a main meal for us, we could afford to eat out at our leisure, but it just wasn't in our nature. It's great to find a nice friendly little restaurant with a nice ambience, a nice view overlooking the sea, sit back, eat a nice meal or a snack, a few drinks and then a nice steady/unsteady walk back to the motorhome. One day it hit me how little we were actually spending, so I said to Bet, "you know what? I'm going to keep a tally of what we are spending."

Having our normal breakfast, we set off around the town, stopping off for our usual coffee and pot of tea for Bet. After a bit of people watching and soaking up the ambience, we'd be off again, having spent just over two euros. Lunchtime, pulling into another café by the seafront, we had a burger with fries and a bit of salad, followed by a coffee and a Fanta. Further on another coffee, another bit of people watching. At the end of the afternoon, I said to bet, you know, that's a normal day for us, yet we've only spent ten euros. On average, even having the odd meal out, we were only spending around 100 quid a week. We were doing exactly what we wanted to do. In Spain's warm climate, I daresay a couple could easily live on about fifty quid a week, maybe less.

One morning I was walking around and checking the local garage for a tap and a water supply. To the side of the garage was a side road adjoining the local rambler. The ramblers are the gullies dotted all around Spain, bringing water down from the mountains when there is heavy rain or flooding. Seeing some motorhomes, I decided to have a slow walk across to see if there were any Brits amongst them. There were at least a dozen motorhomes of various ages and conditions; some really old looking knackers. All appeared to have Spanish number plates. Walking back alongside the rambler, I noticed a brand-new motorhome in front of me with a KA car on a trailer behind it. It was only as I got up closer, I noticed it had an English plate: a man and a woman sitting to the side overlooking hedgerow and the rambler in front. Saying hello, I asked what they were doing here, in what I thought was not a very good position, instead of the far more attractive base by the sea where we were sited. The man told me that they were all indeed on the front up until last month, when the gendarme, anticipating a major flood which would have hit the car park, advised them all to park where they were now. Having settled in, they had now got themselves comfortable and felt disinclined to move.

I couldn't get my head around the pair of them. They were both sitting there, ten am in the morning, and he was dressed in smart casual. His missus had got an evening dress on, face fully made up, hair perfectly groomed. They could have been dining on a cruise ship, both steadily waving their hands back and forth with a couple of fans. When I asked where they dumped their cassettes, the man very casually looked around. He gave a wave of his hand towards the rambler and nonchalantly said, "well, I suppose most of the others would dump them in the rambler." Then pointing to the hedgerow a couple of feet away from them, he motioned towards some blue tissue paper clinging to the gorse bushes. Casual as you like, he said, "it looks like someone's tipped right there." Well, I couldn't get my frigging breath. No wonder they were swatting away with the fans. It wasn't the heat they were wafting away. It was the flies.

I had a job keeping a straight face. I was astounded. Their motorhome must have cost at least sixty grand, and the KA on the back was brand new. Yet, here they were, squatting like gipsies on the side of a rambler, on a dirt road, overlooking gorse bushes littered with cassette waste, probably theirs, and fanning the flies away, without a care in the f*****g world. Ha-ha, it takes all sorts. They just seemed to sit there, day after day, getting the KA out on market days to get some supplies in. Getting back to Bet and explaining to her, she seemed totally unfazed. We were witnessing many strange or odd people and motorhomes along on our travels, all interesting, all fascinating.

Pulling into a campsite one night on our way through France, the owners explained that they were closed for the winter, but for security allowed us to stay on the grounds for five euros, without electricity. Settling down, putting a pie in the oven, we prepared for an easy, relaxed night. Eating our meal, we heard this loud chug, chug, chug. Looking out the window, we saw an old three-tonne work van chugging along the drive. They pulled up, and a lady called over asking if the campsite was open. I told her it wasn't, but to see the owners, who, I'm sure, like us, would allow them to stay. A few minutes later, the chug, chug, chug started again as they pulled in behind us. This I had to have a nose at, so slipping out of the door, on the pretence of checking our motorhome, I had a good look at what there set up was. Instead of a motorhome, they had simply got a three-tonne van. Put a double bed in, a portable cooker and a table and chairs. I couldn't help but be impressed. Our motorhome had cost us forty-odd grand, and this couple were travelling the same roads and seeing the same sights we were seeing. Bloody fair play to them. It was probably their work van back home, so serving two purposes.

We were to see this time and time again, one night on one campsite, a little five-hundred weight white van pulled in next to us. A young couple got out, casual dress, went over to the toilets, freshened up, came back to the van, tootled about for a bit, then set off over to the bar, presumably for a meal and a few drinks. Getting back about eleven pm, we heard them get in the van and watched as the van started rocking. Obviously, they were having a good time, and I couldn't help feeling a bit jealous. Getting up in the morning, they came out of the van, over to the toilets and showers, then returning to the van in a dressing gown and head towel. I was dead impressed. Turning to Bet, I couldn't help but comment, this couple were touring Spain for ten euros, having a fun time, at very little cost. We found the restaurants on these campsites were very reasonable with their prices. Obviously, they knew they had to be competitive to get tourers in, so they cut their prices right back. On average, you could get a decent meal for about a fiver. It was cheaper to eat out. So for about twenty quid, excluding drinks, the young Spanish couple had got somewhere to wash, shower, and eat in a warm, safe environment.

On another campsite right on the beach further south, we found a young German opposite us. He was in what looked like the ambulance in the film Ice Cold in Alex with John Mills. On the roof, he carried a canoe. On the back double doors, he carried a small four by four. He had a BBQ set up and a table and chairs. He was obviously well camped in. He was a nice lad of about thirty and was quite open in telling us that he lived in the north of Germany. Divorced from his wife, he was left with five grand. Looking at the s****y weather with heavy snow, he spent the money on the van, fitted it out and drove south and into Spain. He had been on this campsite for over eighteen months and had a job in the nearby town. Obviously, he had got the rent a lot cheaper than we were paying for the night. This was supplemented by any leaving campers who left him with surplus food or drinks they had. He was living quite comfortably.

CHAPTER 24.

There is a rich tapestry of life and people wherever you go in life. In the main, we live a nine to five existence and assume everyone else lives like us. In reality, many people live really interesting and varied lives in all parts of the world. Once in Majorca, we walked along the harbour front in Palma when I clocked this old knacker of a boat tied up. On the deck were dozens of plastic bottles tied together through the handles by rope. Behind them, hopping about the deck, was a fit wiry old boy sporting a grotty T-shirt. Seeing the ensign on the back, I shouted hello and asked if he was English. Confirming he was, he came off the boat and gave us his story.

He lived by and worked in the docks in Liverpool. When his retirement came up, his wife asked him what he would like to do. He said you know what, love, I'd like to buy a boat and sail around the Mediterranean."

"Well," she said, "if that's what you want to do, I'll do it with you."

So off he goes and buys this boat. Seeing my face, he said, "don't be deceived by her. She's rock-solid, and the engine is spot on, why we've been all around the med and even over to Morocco." I was well impressed. I had this image in my mind of a guy in a low-level job living in a cheap terraced house. Selling up, he had told his kids to help themselves to whatever they wanted and dumped the rest in a skip. Keeping just a few personal items on the boat and set off. He'd never been in a boat before, buying an AA road atlas they set off navigating the coast till they got to Dover. They spent the winter learning about the boat and the basics of navigation. From there, they set off across the channel then followed the canals down to the med. "After all, we're retired, were in no rush." He told me. I was flabbergasted and couldn't get my breath. I was so full of admiration for this couple. He was quick to point out that there was no snobbery looking at the other boats and yachts. The owner of the million-pound yacht further along often invited him to any parties that were going. Gave him little jobs around the boat, and any surplus paint was his. That answered why the boat was painted in different colours then.

The shop across the way acted as the post office and mailbox for all the post. He was only here for the winter and normally spent the summer around the opposite end of the island, where he could berth up free. Here it cost him six euros a week, and for that, he had the electric and as much water as he wanted, hence all the containers. I had got a thirty-two-foot sailing yacht and had considered berthing it up somewhere in Spain and using it as a holiday home. Turning to Bet, I couldn't help saying, "When is enough, enough? We've got a nice hotel, rental properties. And here's this guy having the time of his life with his wife and living on what must be the basic state pension." I knew I was hitting a brick wall. Bet had seen the thirty-foot waves in a force-ten gale outside our hotel. There was no way she was ever going to set off on a boat like mine. It didn't stop me from admiring the guy or his wife.

CHAPTER 25.

People of all ages set off and hike across the world. Once I had a dream of hiking around India, my daughter Rachael was well up for it. Riding elephants, seeing nature and wild animals in the raw natural environment. Unfortunately, by the time I was in a financial position to do that, Rachael had left home, and I didn't fancy the idea. The motorhome was, to me, a great compromise. It gave us complete freedom to go where we wanted when we wanted. Most people who think of, or intend to buy a motorhome, have the same questions; what's it like? What motorhome is most suitable? Which layout is best for them? Well, in all cases, we have to compromise. The next big question, is where are the best places to go? What are the best sites? Caravan club, camping and caravanning club, motorhome club? There are clubs to suit every type of camper. Once the confidence is built up, many of us start looking abroad with a small helping of trepidation and fear.

When it came to travelling and driving abroad, I was filled with excitement and a reasonable dose of fear. I had seen the roads around Paris from sitting behind the coach driver. It seemed every car had dents, and they all seemed to drive like lunatics. Without a doubt, keeping away from any major city would be my number one priority. Then there are different types of people who buy a motorhome and their reasoning. We are all individuals, and as such, typically, this shows in our choices of what suits us. There are numerous online Facebook sites set up for motor homes. Everyone is very helpful, but advice can only go so far. At the end of the day, it all boils down to finding out for yourself.

We were finding more and more that the continent suited us better for touring. One way or another, we had spent much of our life exploring and touring England. But there are only so many times you can go over to Wales, pitch up your tent only to spend a week in the p*****g down rain. Coupled with the no welcome signs, we were slowly coming to the conclusion that England was for short pleasant, enjoyable breaks. For longer breaks, we wanted the sun. For most of my life, I had gone along with the con that England was beautiful. We were so lucky to live in England with all the beauty it entailed: breath-taking mountains and lush valleys. Quaint little towns and villages, for that alone we were the best country in the world. If that's the case, why does every other country say the same about their own countries? France? Germany? America? When you're skint, you have no choice. When you can afford to get abroad, your eyes open up to the beauty in those countries. Our first couple of forays were straight down into Spain, into the sun, and we weren't disappointed. Sometimes we went onto sites, sometimes we wild camped. When we wild camped, we found no problem finding somewhere to park up, most times close to the beach. The only downfall with wild camping is the longer-term facilities, toilet, shower, water etc. Water wasn't too hard to find, facilities for emptying the cassette were harder. In major towns, we would use the restaurant toilets.

Once in Benalmadena, Louise and the grandkids had flown over to spend a week with us. Another great bonus of a motorhome. The kids could fly over on a return flight for a nice cheap holiday. The public toilets were disgusting. Speaking to the kids, I said, "look. Wherever you are, don't use those filthy places. You don't know what you're going to catch, just look for a nice 4-5-star hotel, walk in like you own it, head for the toilets and use them."

Once my kids had the experience of expensive marble-clad walls and floors, pristine toilets cleaned every ten minutes, and oodles of toilet paper that was it, it was never mentioned again. The same applied to the swimming pools. Soon we were sitting around the hotel swimming pools like we owned them. Walking in just like everyone else in our trunks and a towel bag, incognito. We were in our oil tot. Now it was just a case of polishing all the little edges. As novice beginners, we were still trying to find our way. Why do people go on sites? Are we missing something? Why do people go wild camping, parking up anywhere? Are they skint? Cheapskates just looking for a cheap night? Well, the truth is, it's all down to the individual. Some people prefer the comfort and security of a campsite. We've done it ourselves a few times. In Italy, I spent a month on one five-star site with three swimming pools and great facilities, for less than one hundred quid a week. One friend and neighbour in Sutton was not short of a few quid and lived in a very nice, detached house, yet it was anathema to him to spend money on a campsite. He was vehement on the odd occasion, asking complete strangers if he could park on their drive. Amazing. He considered it his right to park up free, anywhere.

With a lady partner, I found that a site was essential for at least one or two nights in the week. Not only to have a decent shower but to top up the batteries, fill up with water and empty the cassette. But campsites are in many ways restrictive. You're stuck on a pitch and constrained in what you can do. Its freedom, but you ain't free.

One time in Italy, I pitched upon a very large car park on the beach road within walking distance of all shops, restaurants, and beach. A bigger bonus was as I sat in the motorhome one night enjoying the ambience of the early evening, I felt rather than saw a little dog walk past my open cab door. It then walked past again, gave a little grunt, and looked up at me through the door. I was thrown back in surprise to realise it wasn't a dog at all but a baby boar. It was cute, friendly, and inquisitive. As it walked off wagging its little tail, I poked my head out of the door to see mommy boar, daddy boar, then another. Soon there was a whole group of them mooching about. I clocked along the low car park wall, a group of locals with their families, feeding the wild boar. Clearly, this was a regular event. It was brilliant. The wild boar were used to it, knew where their bread was buttered and behaved themselves. It made for a wonderful evening and something you would never see on a campsite.

Incidents like this or other different situations cropped up regularly. If it weren't seals or dolphins, it would be people travelling around in motorhomes or yachts, all adding to the rich tapestry of life. In the Derbyshire peak district on a small CL site, a Rolls Royce pulled up towing a caravan. Out stepped a guy in a smart but slightly dishevelled Crombie overcoat and a titfer. Casually, he unhooked the caravan and brought out a miniature trap/cart. I was intrigued, to say the least, and sat gawping at him whilst trying to act disinterested. Having set the trap up, he then went back to the roller, opened the back door, and brought out a f*****g great St Bernard dog. Slowly he backed the dog up and into the cart and placed the harness around him. By now, I had clocked the guy was eccentric, to say the least. He was in a little world of his own, totally detached from everyone else. Once set up, he

slowly started walking the dog, which was as big as a little pony, around the site. Slowly and surely, little crowds started gathering around him like the pied piper. Before long, he would invite one or two of the young children into the cart and give them a lift around the site, it was hilarious and a sight to behold. At first, I was a bit cautious, wondering if the guy was a pervert, but he wasn't. It was clearly his little bit of joy and pleasure. It was obviously a regular occurrence. Once he was out of sight, I sidled over to his roller to have a nose. He had removed all the back seat and backing, putting a large bed for his little pet in its place. The dog was treated like a king.

I tried to picture the guy in his home environment and wondered how he lived. He was an eccentric millionaire, perhaps living in a mansion, his sole pleasure getting out and about with his dog/pony. Maybe a gipsy living alone in a luxury caravan somewhere. Reliving his past life in a different era when he travelled the country in his horse-drawn gipsy caravan. Maybe a combination of the two, either way, he seemed to give out the vibe that he wasn't up to getting all pally with anyone's kids or their parents. He was certainly eccentric.

We often came across folk in motorhomes with an unusual little pet. Not the normal pet dog, no, maybe an owl. One guy pulled up to a beachfront site in Italy. Parking up, he first brought out a little branch, placed it on his luggage rack on the back of his motorhome, then brought out a massive, fully grown owl, placing it on the branch. He came around the other campers, knocking on our doors and asking if we wanted to take a picture? Before long, the German a little way across from me, brought out his small push along with Wurlitzer and started playing tunes. Then the Chinese couple popped out to tell us they had travelled from China to get here. Before long, a party atmosphere was going full out, cameras clicking all over the place, everyone chatting or laughing, the ice broken. I couldn't figure out if that was the owl owner's plan or just to get a bit of attention; either way, it was a great moment.

CHAPTER 26.

FURTHER AFIELD, PASTURES NEW.

We were now getting into our stride for travelling abroad, finding every trip a delight and exciting experience. We would try different ways of reaching Spain or the south of France. From Calais, it was some 750 miles to the Spanish border. It would cost £200 in diesel to get there. On the plus side, the roads in France were a delight to drive on. Getting used to the right-hand side of the roads was simple. My sat-nav gave out a warning every time I set out, even from motorway services. This is mainly due to the balanced level of population. France is over twice the size of England with a third less of the population. Away from the major cities, there was very little traffic on the roads, even at peak times.

In England, our government, in its wisdom, has decided to welcome millions of immigrants into the country. Great, not only do they take what's left of our jobs and houses, but they also add to the traffic density. All in the name, I suspect, of cheap labour and more money adding to the economy. Great for our standing on the world stage, not so much fun for those on the ground trying to get home after a day's work. For myself, being self-employed, I was, most times, lucky to escape the rush hour nightmare. But we get used to it. We accept it. It becomes the norm. It's only when you drive around Europe that you realise how we are being brainwashed. To reach Spain, which was our main goal, it could also take us two or three days of steady driving. Adding to the £200 fuel costs was the wear and tear on our motorhome, plus the added risk of any potential accident just getting to Spain, on top of the food costs. Not a lot, I know, but it all added up.

We found it easier, cheaper, and quicker to drive down to Portsmouth and get the ferry to Santander or Bilbao for a one-way 300 quid ticket. Good value, we felt. We would set off in the afternoon, reaching Portsmouth well in time for the 10pm ferry. Pulling into the port, we would be directed to the correct lane, park up, put the kettle on and our feet up on the sofas. By 8am the next day, we were in nice warm sunny Spain, leaving the rain and cold behind. I was to find this was a big mistake indeed, yes, we were saving money by cutting out France to get to the sun. But we were also cutting out one of the most beautiful countries in the world with such a lot to offer. Besides pleasant driving, there were plentiful national parks, amazing medieval villages, and towns like Carcassonne. Then there were the chateaus and the Loire Valley. Ahh, well, we were slow learners. Well, I was. Bet was just enjoying the tours. There was plenty of time to catch up. There were a lot of countries to see.

This time around, we decided to get the ferry from Portsmouth in mid-April and have a steady drive coast hopping down to the Benidorm, Alicante area. Stopping off at Benicassim, Tarragona, Cambrils, Gandia, and Denia. All beautiful towns offering something different and interesting. All with somewhere friendly and convenient to park up for a night or two. The only thing that surprised me was the lack of English during our travels. Motorhomes were becoming more and more popular, more people were buying them, but where were the Brits? We were meeting plenty of Germans, even more French, but very few Brits. Were they all sticking to England?

Was it too expensive for them to travel abroad? Were they all hiding away on sites? It cost us £300 for the ferry. £150 in diesel to cover the 550 miles to Benidorm Alicante, so all in all, a £900 round trip. Bear in mind the lower cost of living in Spain, food, heating etc., we found this a bargain. For a couple of days, it would be expensive. For a month, it becomes cheaper. Quite simply, the longer you spend, the cheaper it becomes. For two months at say £100 a week, is around £800, £1700 in total, excluding wear and tear.

I'm sure a lot of people can live a lot cheaper than that. We found it more convenient a lot of the time to eat out. We would also spend some of the time on campsites, but we used our ACSI camping card, which was one of the best discount cards around. Spending around a month in Spain and Benidorm, we started to make our way down to Tarifa in southern Spain, then getting the ferry over to Ceuta, a Spanish enclave in northern Morocco. We had been to Morocco many, many times over the years. Each time protected by the blanket of security offered by the tour companies and hotels, we stopped in. Now, on our own, independently, in our own motorhome, we were setting out on a totally different adventure.

I had read an article in one of the camping magazines about a group of motorhomers who had set off in convoy, from northern Morocco down to near enough the Sahara and back again. Following a circuitous route. We had decided to follow that route more or less. It sounded exciting. It was, and more. Along the way, we came across lots of French and German campers. The French because Morocco used to be a French colony. Most of Morocco spoke French. The Germans simply followed the sundown from cold, wet Germany. Like swallows, they would set off in early September, hoping, like us down to southern Spain, then getting the ferry in October to Morocco where they would spend the winter in the sun. Very nice too.

CHAPTER 27.

CEUTA AND MOROCCO.

The ferry from Tarifa to Ceuta took just over an hour, Tarifa giving us a taste of what was to come. As soon as we had pulled into the port, we were surrounded by Arabs at the grab. Leeches swarming all over you, trying to get you to buy your ferry ticket from their agents dotted around the port. Having been to Morocco so often, we should be used to it, but we never were. It's debilitating, it wears you down, it's incessant. Getting our ticket, we were glad to get on the ferry.

It's in the psyche of some of the Arabs to harass and pester the tourist. To them, every white European is rich and, as such ripe for the picking. You can't walk more than ten yards in the local souks or towns without being jumped on by the local shopkeeper or tradesmen. On our very first visit to Morocco, the tour guide advised us to always haggle the price down. If they ask for 100 dirhams – about ten pounds—haggle it down to fifty or sixty. In theory, this is fine. The only problem was the Arabs very quickly caught on to it and upped the asking price to 200 dirhams.

On one of our final holidays to Agadir, one of the shopkeepers asked us why so few Europeans, tourists, were visiting them. Looking at the pleading desperation in his face, I wasn't sure how to tell him that I thought it was due to all the killings and bombings going on in the world by the

Muslim extremists. Morocco had a strong Muslim population. Instead, I pointed to another white European outside a shop on the opposite side of the square being pestered by the shopkeeper. Keeping my frustration under control, partly, I said in exasperation, "look, look." I felt like saying f*****g look. "maybe it's because we are all getting fed up with being harassed. I come past your shop, I stop, wanting to have a look, in peace. But I can't. Every shop I stop to have a look, I am pestered to buy something. In the end, I just walk past." I didn't like to hurt the guy's feelings, but cobblers to it, I thought maybe he might pass it on to the other shopkeepers. Let it filter around. Now, here we were, entering into the lion's den again.

Ceuta is a small enclave on the northern tip of Morocco of some 18 square miles. When the Spanish recognised the independence of Morocco in 1956, they nicked Ceuta. They kept it under Spanish rule, considering it part of the Spanish state. Morocco disputed this, but the Spanish were adamant it was part of Andalusia. It was also directly opposite Gibraltar. Another little enclave, this time nicked by the British and claimed as ours. Poetic justice maybe, either way, the Spanish have got a bit of front demanding we give them back Gibraltar whilst they tell the Moroccans to p**s off.

I couldn't get my head around Ceuta. It didn't seem to serve any point at all. What did the inhabitants do? Where did they work? Not in Morocco for sure, its only purpose was its disputed ownership by Morocco. We could drive from one side of the colony in fifteen minutes to the seafront in ten. Having a walk around the shops, we could see everything was duty-free. We bought a couple of duty-free watches at a bargain price only to find one didn't work once we got out of the place. Finding a place to pitch up for the night, we awoke refreshed, ready to set off into Morocco the next morning.

We reached the border in about fifteen minutes, but we were pulled in by a couple of Arabs just beforehand. I thought they were part of the border force. They were asking me if I had filled in the required entry forms. Puzzled, I told him I hadn't. In truth, I hadn't got a clue, and they gave me a form to fill out. I noticed other cars just whizzing past and to the border; presumably, they had all the forms filled out.

Wrong again. The fact is it was a con just to extort the money from us. They succeeded. I was used to how they acted in Morocco but couldn't believe they could get away with this kind of shakedown so blatantly on Spanish soil so close to the Moroccan border. We were less than fifty yards away. At the border, we had to go through the same process all over again, pointing out how we were shaken down just a few yards back and pointing to the group. I looked at the border officer and asked why nothing was being done about it? Nothing. I just got a blank, faraway look and a shrug of the shoulder. This again was part of the Moroccan psyche, ask a difficult question, and the eyes go blank, a shrug of the shoulders, and that's it, we were to see it time and time again.

Getting through the somewhat chaotic border, we were glad to set off. We were now in a different world, the third world. Within minutes of leaving, we were out in the country. There wasn't any traffic in sight, yet we were pulled over by the traffic cops. Pulling a jar of sweets that I kept by me for just such purposes, I gave them the biggest smile that I could muster and threw the jar at them, inviting them to take a sweet. As hoped for, this threw them completely. They couldn't even ask me for a bung because of my kindness. Half-heartedly pointing out that I was speeding and seeing my surprised expression, they let me carry on. Leaving the border, I'd never seen any speeding notices or knew what the speed limit was. We were out in the middle of nowhere without a soul in sight. We had decided to head for Chefchaouen, a city in northwest

Morocco and in the Rif Mountains, known for its striking, blue-washed buildings. We found a campsite just a few minutes outside of the town where we were quoted seven euros a night including electricity, which we thought was a good price.

There were no pitches as such; we were just directed to space and told to park up. After we pulled in a few minutes a one tonne transport van pulled in next to us with the occupation signed up on the side, D.E Transport. Out stepped a middle-aged couple who started bringing out the tables and chairs, then a little cooker that they set up on the table. They were a very nice couple who spoke good English. Like us they intended to tour Morocco. We had been watching them with interest as they unpacked, confirming again how you didn't necessarily need anything expensive to get out and see different countries. These guys were using what I presumed was their works van. And why not. In the magazine article detailing their motorhome tour of Morocco, the author mentioned how happy they were to have their own shower and cooking facilities; we soon saw why.

Getting out to have a little nose at our surroundings, I walked over to the restaurant's main hub, shop, and toilets. Bet wisely decided to stop in the van. The restaurant was closed. Walking over to the toilets, I popped my head in to see what the facilities were like. Christ almighty, I knew that many European countries went for the French toilet system, which basically was just a hole in the ground, like a shower tray, but this was filthy. It was disgusting. Whoever had built the place needed locking up. It just looked like the owners had thrown the job at the local jobbing staff, supplied the materials and told them to get on with it. The blockwork was all over the place, the tiling a joke. If you built it for a dog, you would want something better. I certainly wasn't going to go in there for a shower or a tomtit. No way. Bet didn't even want to look. My next port of call was the shop where Bet had asked me to get a loaf. Walking into the little shop, I was hit with an unpleasant smell that assailed my nostrils. Looking around, I couldn't see anything that we would want except the bread. Thankfully, we had well stocked up with the basics that would see us through times like this.

A young lad about 20 years old sat on the floor behind the counter, looking like he was bored out of his brains. Asking him for a French stick, he got up and walked into the back storeroom. It was then I noticed he had sandals on. That was the smell that surrounded the room like a fog. It was his sweaty feet. I could feel my nose turning up in disgust. Everyone walked around in sandals, obviously to cut out the constant washing. But surely the bosses must walk in and notice? Didn't they care or not?

As he walked back out with the French stick, I tried to formulate a way to refuse it. I couldn't. He had taken me by surprise. Holding the stick gingerly, I headed back to the motorhome. Inside I just said to Bet, "the dirty bxxxxds." Explaining how the shop stunk of dirty feet. Heading straight over to the sink, I cut six inches off the end of the stick and threw it out for the birds. They wouldn't notice the smell. Ok, I know it's cheap, and I didn't expect the Ritz, but there was no need for this. In front of us was a tatty little well, filled with filthy water and a fountain that didn't work. The whole site was an eyesore. We were in low season, yet I counted forty vans spread about the site.

At seven euros a night, that adds up to nigh on £300 a night, £2000 a month. The average wage was twenty quid a week. Surely, they could afford to pay a skilled workman and a labourer to work around the site permanently. Building a new toilet block, making the site more attractive. Making a nice feature pool. But this seemed to be par for the course in Morocco. Everyone was on the grab, and no one seemed able to see the benefits of spreading it around. Employing two men would give work to the local community. This, in turn, would benefit them by spending their money in the community. I mentioned this to a pal back home, and he told me this was quite common in many backward countries like India and Pakistan. Those who were raking it in kept it tight to themselves, oh well.

Refreshed after a night's sleep, we set off the next morning for a drive down to the main city of Chefchaouen. There had been some rain during the night, and pulling up in the town centre, we noticed puddles dotted all over the dirt road. Within minutes we were approached to the side of the van by a little urchin of about ten. Usual pose, hands out, head leaning to one side and a pleading look in his eye. Some don't speak at all, leaving the eyes to do the talking. Others will slowly mutter, "please, dirham." Within minutes a guy of about forty came striding across and shouted at the little brat to bugger off.

You might make the mistake of thinking this guy is kindly doing me a favour. He's not. He's simply getting rid of the brat so he can jump into his place. Trying our best to just ignore him so we can enjoy a quiet, pleasant walk around the town, I can see he's determined. Once they get a grip on you, they don't let go. Walking just a few yards, he pointed to the mosque in front of us. With deep reverence and bowing his head in awe, he proudly told me that this was the main mosque in the town, hundreds of years old. Proudly and with due deference, he informed me that the King had donated one million dirhams to refurbish the mosque. Keeping my face straight, I looked at him, "you are very proud of your King, aren't you? Nodding his head vigorously, he said, "yes, yes."

A million dirhams is less than one hundred thousand pounds, and here was this guy dripping in gratitude. I could not believe it. I had been shown one of the king's palaces just outside Agadir. One of many around the country. It was very nice, indeed, very ostentatious. And here was this guy drooling in gratitude, all misty-eyed. The roads were filthy, mud-caked with puddles all over. The town was in dire need of a few quid spending on it. But here he was, dead grateful to his King.

Walking on up into the shopping centre we did our best to ignore him, but no, he wouldn't let go. Stopping to gaze into a carpet shop, he jumped on us again. We had looked into the shop, hoping he would walk on. Still, no, he simply saw this as another opportunity. Grabbing my arm, he led us across to the carpet shop opposite. "Please, this is my cousin," he said, leading us into his shop. Trying to be polite, we had a quick look around. Pointing to one woollen Berber carpet, I asked how much it was. It was a nice carpet with a nice pattern. We had the room on the motorhome to hide it without getting ripped off by customs. But that was it. As soon as he opened his mouth, the deal was lost. How much do a few pounds in weight of wool cost? Whether by hand or machine, how long does it take to make a carpet roughly six foot by four foot? You can buy a week's food for a few pounds. The average wage is peanuts, yet here he is asking me for some seven hundred euros. Yes, euros, not dirhams, politely telling him, "no, thanks" we walked out, our guide still determined to latch onto us. Eventually, we got rid of him. I told him we didn't wish to buy anything at this stage with a kind smile; simply, we were just looking around. Not seeing a dirham coming his way, he walked off, shoulders drooped, thank f**k for that. With some relief, we carried on with our little tour.

Sadly, I have to say neither one of us was too impressed with Chefchaouen. It was filthy and smelly. Maybe we had come on the wrong day. It had been raining, nowhere is nice after a downpour of rain, but things didn't improve on our way over to the market. Ok, we expect the market to smell.

It's a fish market, but it was the dirt that gets into your pores as well as the smell. It pervades the whole atmosphere. We didn't fancy buying anything even though the prices were displayed and on show—something very rare in Morocco.

After a short walk around the town, we headed back to the campsite after getting a feel for the place. Stopping off on the way to enjoy a coffee and a snack on the balcony of a four-star hotel and restaurant overlooking and giving us a nice view of the town. This was more like it. We could enjoy the view, enjoy the ambience, without the stink getting into our noses. Refreshed, we headed back to the campsite.

Making our way along, we were alerted to the slow chug, chug, chug of a single-decker bus struggling to fire-up on a piece of wasteland. A long-haired woman with three kids was standing around outside the bus. Stopping to watch, the driver gave up and went to have a look at the engine. Going over, I shouted hello and asked if they were ok. "Yeah, man, we're fine. It's just a bit slow, that's all," Hippies! They had converted the bus and used it to travel. Trying again, the engine gave another chug, chug, chug, before slowly starting up and roaring into life.

"Thanks, man, see ya. We're off up into the hills." He looked like he was away with the fairies. His missus, I couldn't quite make up my mind about. They were obviously here for the cheap hashish, marijuana. I could picture them sitting in their coach at night, smoking themselves brain dead. Happy as little pigs in s**t.

CHAPTER 28.

We weren't overly impressed with Chefchaouen, so we decided to move on after a couple of days. The Danes in the van next to us had decided to do the same thing, getting up early and disappearing before us. Great as our TomTom sat-nav was, it was simply no good in Morocco. Guessing there would not be many roads and not having much confidence in a road map, even if we could find one, we decided to simplify things by just going by the compass.

Getting out of Chefchaouen, we simply took the first road out to the left and south. Well, we weren't dictated to by anyone or anything, were we. Our idea was to head south-west and down to the Sahara. Then do a right turn to the Atlantic and the coast before heading north and back to Ceuta. We were not dictated to by destination or time. Driving out through the Rif Mountains, we headed up into the Atlas Mountains. First, the lower than upper Atlas to reach the famous blue lake. The contrasts here up in the north were quite staggering. The valleys around the Rif Mountains were lush with greenery, yet not a goat or sheep around. I couldn't get my head around it.

Lambs' meat or goat's meat in Morocco is quite scarce and very expensive. Even allowing for us being ripped off, it was more expensive than England. You would see goat herders walking along, all day, herding their little flock of twenty or so goats from scarce grubby little patches of grass to grass along the sides of the road, week in week out. Yet here, up in the valley's there are thousands of acres of grass and food and not a goat in sight. I'm missing something, but what am I missing. Maybe it's the fear of bandits. Maybe any enterprising farmer or goat herder simply can't do what he wants. Maybe everything belongs to the King. I had worked in farming as a kid. The sheep are just sent out to live off the land, just brought in for dipping and shearing—a truly organic animal. Bred at a very low cost, why can't the Arab's do the same? We were to see examples of this all over Morocco.

We would stop off in fascinating little towns and villages along our route, each in contrast to the other. Some were busy industrial workplaces. Lorries and tractors belching out smoke. Kicking up dust from the dirt roads. No such thing as tarmac or concrete over here; it was just muck or dust. It was almost like the old wild west of America. Stopping off for refreshments, we would see shops or a little café serving drinks and food. But these little cafes were a million miles from what we were used to seeing at home or around Europe.

Crossing over the road, we called into an open plan café bar. There were plastic covers on the tables and tagine dishes on a side bench set over little burners to keep them warm. Bet chose a chicken tagine which was brought over with a few chunks of bread. I gave it a miss preferring a bottle of coke.

Tucking into her tagine, I don't think Bet gave a thought to the butchers behind her. Well, I don't know if it was the butchers or simply meat being served in the café. Sides of beef, mutton, and chickens, hanging from hooks over the front counter, open to all the smoke and dust from the road, swarming with flies. It was almost medieval. Food was served like this in medieval Rome, Pompeii, before the volcanic eruption. But Bet didn't see or wasn't bothered; she was enjoying her tagine. Finishing our meal, we set off. Paying the higher price than we expected, being the rich, white Europeans.

Off on the road again, we headed off to Timoudi and Sidi Daoud and the famous blue lake. The blue lake was surrounded by a host of tourist shops selling the usual stuff—copper and brass ornaments and kaftans. We pulled into the campsite that was part of the venue and headed off to the famous blue lake. Reaching a small pool outside of the motley group of shops and cafes, we stopped for a coke and to get our bearings. Bet, and I were of the same mind without even mentioning it. Don't eat anything cold. Don't drink anything unless it comes in a bottle with a cap on it.

As the waiter came over with our drinks, I asked where the blue lake was. It's a good job. I kept a straight face, jumping back a couple of inches and showing the surprise on his face. He pointed to the lake in front of us, "there, sir, that is the blue lake."

"Of course, of course," I replied with a smile. I hoped he thought we were kidding. After he walked away, I looked at

Bet. "Famous lake? It's a little f*****g pool." Due to the natural elements in the water, it turned it or made it appear blue. Some lakes are blue, some lakes were grey, some green. Different places around the world had different lakes of different colours. Maybe we were not looking at the right lake?

After a night and a good look around the complex, we headed further south to the ghost town of D'alouli, or Al-houli. The French set up this town in the 1930s as a mining town employing up to some 60,000 workers. It was abandoned in circa 1961 leaving just one Berber family living there, I was keen to see it. I don't think Bet was.

It was some thirty miles outside of Midelt, a major town. Getting directions, we headed out along a made-up road. After a few miles, we left the road behind and carried on along a dirt track. I think Bet was getting a bit worried. Coming to a rickety wooden bridge over a small stream, I got out to check it for strength. Figuring other motorhomes had made the trip, I risked it and slowly made our way across with some nervousness. Made it. We headed further ahead into the ghost town. The stream had now opened out to a river that we followed until we came to the town. Pulling up, we were surrounded by high buildings on both sides, some five-six or seven storeys high built into the mountainside.

It was eerily silent. All I could see were little washing lines outside of some of the units or houses above us. I could feel rather than see the eyes staring down at us.

I made the mistake of whispering to Bet, "the hills have eyes." Which was a reference to an American film about a family heading through the mid-west in a camper van, attacked by a bunch of retards. This was a big mistake. Bet was already hesitant about many aspects of Morocco. This place was making her very nervous. As we were sitting there. A taxi pulled up alongside us, "are you looking for the ghost town?" the taxi driver said. Puzzled, I replied, "yes."

"This is not the ghost town. Follow me."

Bet's bottle was going even more. The taxi driver led us on for another couple of miles, following the course of the river until it opened out into a plateau, forming a massive 'U' shape surrounding what used to be the original ghost town, housing sixty thousand people. It was now abandoned.

To me, it was awe-inspiring. It was like a scene right out of the wild west of America. Looking around, we were surrounded by little clay huts scattered around—some derelict and falling down. To the side a well supplying water for the village. Outside one house was a weary-looking Berber, sat on the floor, looking at us with tired interest.

We had brought a load of cheap pens, writing books, and second-hand dolls from charity shops to give out as gifts. They came in quite handy wherever we went. Telling Bet to give a few gifts to the many inquisitive urchins, who quickly gathered around while I was invited to have a mint tea with the Berber, sitting outside his house. I was amazed. There was no way Bet was going to move from her seat in the motorhome, so she threw gifts out of the window to get rid of the gang. Heading in, the guy brought the little battered kettle off the gas boiler to make me a cup of mint tea. Hesitant as I was, I had to admit the tea was quite tasty.

Sitting opposite me and not saying a word was the Berber. Obviously, none of them could speak English. All he could do was smile. Looking around, I could see we were surrounded by four walls in what looked like a two-bedroom dwelling. His bedroom must have been next door. We were in the lounge come kitchen, come shop. On the bare floor lay a carpet. On the one wall, another carpet hung, and in the corner of another wall lay a small crudely made bench table. This held various minerals that the Berber made to sell. That was how they made their living. Next to the meagre minerals was the little burner with the battered kettle on top. That was it. His whole life and possessions were in that room.

It was a scene straight out of Jerusalem and the days of Jesus Christ. It was staggering. As we had brought a few gifts, I didn't feel inclined to buy some minerals that we didn't want or need, so thanking him, I headed out and back over to the motorhome. The kids had mostly disappeared; Bet had thrown everything in the van at them to get rid of them. I was in awe of the place and wanted to spend the night. I envisioned pulling up over by the side of the river, getting some wood and having a little fire, maybe a barbeque. Just like Davey Crocket or John Wayne in the wild frontier. I was in my element. Bet was having none of it.

"You must be bloody joking. I am not spending the night here, they could come out, chop us up, and no one would know we had been here."

I looked at her in disbelief. Surely, she was winding me up. Any protestations from me fell on deaf ears. These were peaceful Berber people. A lot more than the initial families that left there in 1961, but it was quite safe. Still, that was it.

Saying goodbye, we got into the motorhome. Along the dirt and dusty road, over the rickety bridge and headed back to the city of Midelt and civilisation, of sorts. I didn't realise how glad Bet was to get out.

CHAPTER 29.

Travelling through Mid Morocco, we were now on our way to the Ksar of Ait-Ben-Haddou. A medieval city that had played host to a whole list of films including Sodom and Gomorrah, Jesus of Nazareth, and Marco Polo, to name just a few. It was a small fascinating town set on the Ounila Riverbanks, just a few miles from Ouarzazate. It was founded along the old caravan route between the Sahara and Marrakesh, nestled under the Atlas Mountains. Our plan was to follow that route down to the Sahara.

The medieval city was surrounded by four-star hotels and small shops selling the usual trinkets and kaftans. For sure, Morocco was very limited in its ability to cater to visiting tourists. The souvenir gifts looked cheap, tatty, and dusty; the shops were dark—none inviting. Arabs sat outside on their backsides, looking like they had just left the medieval city with a death sentence put on their heads. Nothing was inviting to want us to visit their shops. A smile was hard to come by. Maybe it was us, maybe we expected too much, it was low season, and there weren't many people about. Walking into a couple of the hotels, we found them a bit dark and quiet, seemingly waiting for the tourists to arrive. Fresh blood to liven the place up and bring in some money.

The only way to reach the place was by coach from Ouarzazate or the nearest coach station seven miles away, car, or like us by motorhome. Maybe that was part of the answer to the reaction we were getting. Seeing us in our motorhome, the locals would know we weren't going to be spending any money on accommodation, and maybe, not on food either. Making our way down the steady incline to the riverbank, we could see there were only two ways to get across: to wade across the river by steppingstones or by camel. By the bank were three camels standing next to their owner, who looked as long in the mouth as his camels. I decided to walk across. Bet preferred to stay by the shops whilst I had a look around before heading back.

The town itself of Ben-Haddou was quite fascinating and not too difficult to transport yourself back in time to two thousand years ago and the life of living in that period. I didn't visit the whole town as I didn't want to leave Bet for too long at the mercy of any passing Arab. But it was enough to get a feel for the place and the films that were made there. I found it just as fascinating to imagine being a fly on the wall in the hotels, as major film stars relaxed after a day's filming, discussing the day's events.

We had a good day around the town, stopping overnight before setting off the next day to Ouarzazate. Every country, every city, has its own unique individuality and charm, or no charm, if you like. But much of Morocco constantly surprised and intrigued me. Marrakesh itself was very much unchanged over hundreds of years. It was easy to transport yourself back to its early days. Agadir, on the other hand, was very modern. It was rebuilt following an earthquake in 1961. It was clean, smart, with nice two- or four-star hotels. You could almost imagine yourself to be in Spain, almost. But that was the mirage. Step four miles outside of the city, and it was like stepping back five hundred years.

Apart from the hotels, maybe a few jewellery shops and a major supermarket outside Agadir, it struck me that there didn't seem a lot of initiative around Morocco. Morocco people seemed to not think out of the box. Outside of the major cities, the people seemed subdued, obedient. Even the police who were quick to jump on the locals who even seemed ready to approach us stepped back when we actually spoke to them.

At the bottom of the incline leading to the river and Ben-Haddou, was a small café I'm sure would have done very well. Just an open style café, smart, tiled, with nice seating serving mint teas, European teas, coffee, sandwiches etc. Maybe the big hotels served them, but here you have ideal weather for outside dining, and no one takes advantage of it.

In Agadir, I had queried with a restaurant owner because none of the restaurants seemed to serve English breakfast. Ok, ok, I know I risk being lectured on being a typical anglophile trying to change the culture and habits of the indigenous people, but these people are desperately trying to bring in western people into the country. English, German, American. I don't think it's a lot to ask. The restaurant owner asked me how they would cook such a meal. Their idea of an English breakfast was some chunks of ham, two eggs and a chunk of bread.

Taking me into his kitchen, I showed him how to mash tomatoes, fry them in a pan. Serve with two eggs, some beans and mushrooms, all ingredients available in the town. I said, "your restaurant will be heaving once you put a big sign outside saying English breakfast." I don't think he could see it. The Spanish did, now you can get an English breakfast all over the major resorts. There were cafes, of sorts, around Morocco. In Ouarzazate itself, we went into one of the cafes set out in a semi-European way. Mind, it was there to serve the Moroccans themselves more than Europeans. Two young Arab lads sitting on the next table put their bottle of shared coke down to give a gob on the floor, not deliberately to insult us, I'm sure, it was just a natural thing for them to do.

In one sense, we could see the progress being made. Calling into one small town, we parked up to meander around. Again, no hard road, no tarmac, no concrete. Just a dusty dry road running through it. The lack of free health facilities struck me when I saw a young lad of about ten in a makeshift pram/wheelchair. Walking through one alley, I felt, rather than saw, something hobble past me covered in some kind of jalabiya. I just caught a quick look at the face of an old man with a grey beard. It frightened the bejabbers out of me. What was it? Was he walking on his hands or his feet? I couldn't make my mind up, I tried to keep up with him, but he was off like a shot. By the time I had taken a picture, he was a good distance down the road, contorted and twisted over, going at a good pace. I couldn't help but give a shudder. How do people live like that?

On the local market stalls selling fresh food and vegetables, we bought some carrots and potatoes. These were truly organic, given their shape was naturally twisted all over the place. I had purchased some lamb chops earlier from the local butchers, an open concrete square with the usual sides of meat hanging from the walls with flies whizzing all over the place. I felt more comfortable when he brought the chops from out of the back. This didn't live up to expectations. The next day, when I went to retrieve the chops from the fridge to make dinner, they were swarming with flies. We were getting more and more queasy. The constant dirt and dust were getting in our nostrils and pores. Now we were hesitant about even buying our own food and cooking it ourselves. I was getting frightened that we might pick something up.

Along the routes of our journey, we would pull in anywhere it felt safe. Parking areas within towns or villages, always within sight of living accommodation and people. I just didn't feel confident enough to sleep parked up out in the wild. Once or twice someone would approach us and very kindly invite us to stop by their house or dwelling, electricity included. A few times we stopped at Kasbahs we came across or forts and fortresses dotted all over Morocco. There were walls fifteen feet high or more, heading into one swimming pool and a nice restaurant. We ordered a meal giving us food for thought on the need for such security. Was all this a throwback from two thousand years ago, or was it still essential today? We didn't like to dwell on it too much. If it had been more in season, some of these Kasbahs would have been ideal in themselves to stop. The prices were reasonable both for camping and eating. They were like little cities, but we wanted to see more of Morocco, so we headed, right down deep south to the Sahara.

CHAPTER 30.

Reaching another little town, we set out to have a walk around. Another setback outside the main tourist traps was the lack of alcohol. It was a Muslim country. Muslims were strictly forbidden even to purchase alcohol, never mind drink it. In such areas, the only real place to get a drink was the hotels or campsites, maybe. Fortunately, just in the area and on the edge of town was a nice-looking little campsite with shops and restaurants just a short walk away. Better still, it had a swimming pool. Even better, apart from two French motorhomers, the place was empty. I looked at Bet, giving her a big smile, "we've cracked it here, Shug. we've almost got the pool to ourselves?" We could have a couple of months here chilling out good and proper. I think she was in agreement.

Calling into reception, I was directed to a pitch; I think it was a case of pull in where you want. The fee was six euros for the night, inclusive of electricity. Food being so cheap we were living on less than one hundred euros a week, the weather was great, what could go wrong. Having been travelling for most of the day, we decided to bunker down and eat in the campsite restaurant that night. Again, we weren't over the moon. Sitting down, we got that certain smell again, sweaty feet. It seemed to be everywhere except maybe the bigger hotels. It got into the nostrils and made the food go down in lumps.

Maybe I'm too fussy, maybe we're both too fussy, but we grew up in the days when Indian and Chinese restaurants were being closed down by the dozen in Birmingham for serving up cats and dogs. Ok, it was back in the day, but what's to stop these places from not being back in the day? And we weren't seeing many cats and dogs about. We decided to do any future cooking or eating in or around our camper with our own food. Calling around to the shops, we did a bit of shopping to supplement what we had in the motorhome. Another advantage to us was the lack of having any washing. We spent our days in our shorts, only putting a T-shirt on when we walked out among the crowds or in the town. Here at the campsite, we were in our shorts.

Mooching around the shops and bars, stopping off for a leisurely drink, a young lad excitedly asked if we had seen the lion? Lion? What lion? Pointing to the mountains in front of us, he again said, "the lion—it is famous in all of Morocco!" Well, I wondered if he was taking the mick. Looking at Bet, I could see she was equally as blank and saying nothing. To save further embarrassment, I had no choice but to say, "oh yes, yes." His little face beamed with pride, but where was the lion? Were they that desperate in this neck of the woods to get tourists? They would come up with anything; it's like finding a dog or Jesus in the clouds. We both kept looking up for the lion over the next couple of days. Still not seeing it. In the end, we threw the towel in. We had got into the camp on a Wednesday, the next day, the French left, not saying a word. We weren't bothered. We had the pool to ourselves, the height of luxury.

Come Saturday, things changed. A local man came into the camp with his two sons, each wearing the traditional kaftan with a towel, each under their arms. Taking their clothes off to reveal their swimming trunks, they then went over to the toilets. To the side of the swimming pool were two toilet cubicles. Again, very basic, no locks on the rickety doors and a shower tray on the floor, a tap to the side and a small water bottle. Just the view of it was enough to turn the stomach, so we pointedly ignored it. Clearly, the owners, to supplement their income, allowed the local population to use the pool for a small fee. We were fine with this. After all, we couldn't expect the whole pool to ourselves. But it was Bet again who brought my attention to the next phase. Both the Arab and his two sons had gone into the toilets one by one, coming out all three had jumped into the pool, facing us. Obviously, and completely oblivious to us, they started washing their arses. It was Bet who first brought my attention to it. "Look, the dirty b******s. They're washing their arses in the swimming pool." Was she making this up? Slowly I walked over to the toilets. In both, they were splattered with s**t. My stomach did a roll. Bet was right; they hadn't come in for a swim; they had come in for a s**t and a wash. The pool was the ideal venue. We delayed going into the pool, preferring to sit on the deck chairs to the side. Maybe after a bit, the pool might cleanse itself, with the crap spreading out and dissipating into the heather.

After a bit of splashing about and a respectable time, the three got out of the pool, gave themselves a quick rub down then put their kaftans back on before heading out. I felt inclined to go over and remonstrate with the owners. But what purpose was that going to serve? Surely, they must know what's going on? They have to clean the bogs; maybe this is what all the locals do. "Ok brothers, it's Sunday, wash day. Let's head off down to the pool for our weekly wash before lunch." It hardly bared thinking about, maybe it was us, maybe we were too fussy. Neither one of us fancied getting into the pool after that. The shine had gone off it. By Sunday, we had decided to make a move, so much for our two-month sojourn.

CHAPTER 31.

From the western Sahara, we headed west and up to Sidi Ifni, stopping off to take pictures or sample the local culture along the way. No one bothered us except to stare in awe at us as we travelled along. Passing camels as they walked wild and in groups or stopping to watch the goats that climbed the Argan trees. In the process, the goats eat the fruit from the trees then release nuts through their waste that produces the famous Argan oil. We knew from experience that Argan oil had brilliant healing powers. Many years earlier, our maid Zaida had spent the night crushing the Argan nuts to produce two litres of oil for her arthritis. It was brilliant and worked.

The only problem was we were sometimes frightened to stop. If we stopped to watch the goats climbing the trees, we would notice the local farmer or herdsman some distance away, far enough away to not bother us. Big mistake. These Arabs were nothing if not resourceful. The farmer might have been some distance, but his son would creep out of nowhere to stick his hand out, begging for a few dirhams; what for? For taking pictures, of course. Driving across the mountains, I stopped in the middle of nowhere to pick a tortoise up that was meandering across the road. I had hardly got out the door before some young Arab shot out from behind a boulder, asking for dirhams, for allowing us to keep the tortoise. We gave him a pair of trainers and the tortoise back. How long had he been sitting there? Do they sit like that all over Morocco, waiting, like spiders, ready to pounce?

We would see litre bottles of water. To test our theory, we stopped by a plastic bottle. Sure enough, within seconds, an Arab shot out from behind some bushes. The bottle placed there for the weary dehydrated traveller. Then we saw the litre jars of what looked like an orange liquid; was it honey? Stopping to have a look, I picked the jar up. Before I had even got the lid off, a young Arab shot over from out of nowhere. I wasn't interested in the slightest, not knowing what hygiene methods were used in gathering the honey, but out of politeness, I asked how much? I had stopped after all. Quick as a flash, he replied, "ten euros."

"Ten euros? We don't even pay ten euros in England." I replied. He was adamant it was a bargain price. Handing him the jar back, I got back in my motorhome and put my foot down.

Reaching Sidi Ifni, we found we were at a little sedate holiday resort. A few shops, restaurants, and a nice pedestrian walkway along the seafront. It was very pleasant. Looking around for somewhere to pitch up, we noticed a whole line of motorhomes on a raised bank overlooking the sea. Driving up, we noticed it was almost full of French and Germans, spending the winter in the sun. Some had electricity hook-ups. When we enquired, we found the hotels behind us allowed us to camp up for a fee of two euros a night. You could have electricity for an extra two euros, provided via a long cable from the hotel. This seemed good value to us, twenty-eight euros a week for a park up and electricity, what more could you ask for?

The only English guy was next to us in a small 5wct van. He was sitting inside the side door, cooking some shrimps on a little colour gas burner, a little mattress tucked away to the side. He was about fifty-five and invited us to have some of his shrimps. He explained that the local's called around regularly selling fish, seafood, and bread to the campers for pennies—no wonder the German and French headed here for the winter.

We were 2500 miles from our home in Birmingham. For the French and Germans, even less. It would cost us 500 pounds to get here. With the cost of living, food etc., you could live a relaxed, easy life in the sun here for seventy-five pounds a week. If you consider the average English state pension is around £180 a week, you're quid's in. If you're in a council property, the rent is paid for you. We met a guy in Spain who locked his flat up every year, spending the winter in Spain in his caravan. He was on full disability, and no one knew if he was in or not. Fair play to him. The French and Germans had an even better pension. I did feel sorry for the guy in the van next to me. What was his story? A young couple coming away for a weekend in a small van was one thing. An old boy living for months at a time was another. I was starting to feel a bit guilty in our comparative luxury motorhome.

After a few days, we were starting to get a bit bored. There are only so many days you can sit about twiddling your thumbs. It wasn't hot enough to swim in the sea or to sunbathe. So we set off, making our way to Agadir, stopping off at different towns and seaside resorts as we tootled along. Most of the time, we found the people pleasant and friendly. The poverty and hardship were clear to see, but the people were used to it; they accepted it as normal. It was part of life. In the main, they just looked at us with mild curiosity. It was only when they got close to us; they would see an opportunity to put their hands out to beg or try to find some way to part us from a few dirhams.

If we felt comfortable, we would call into some petrol stations and ask to spend the night. If we didn't, and we saw one, we would call into a local campsite. Mostly quite cheap. In all our travels around Morocco, we only ever once saw another English motorhome. That was an Autotrail like ours. Settling onto our pitch, I popped over to say hello, only to find no one there. Again, plenty of French and Germans. Just no English. We found this quite strange. There are hundreds of motorhome owners in England. Most I suspect stuck to holidays in England, quite a few travelled across to France or Spain. Again, we saw not a great number in those places, yet Morocco has a lot to offer. And it's quite cheap.

CHAPTER 32.

Getting to Agadir, we felt on familiar ground. We had holidayed in Agadir many times. We had friends in Agadir like Zaida, our hotel maid, or Mohammed, the swimming pool attendant. Plus, there were lots of hotels with swimming pools. We first called into the local campsite set down towards the seafront. This was an improvement from the campsite in Chefchaouen, in northern Morocco, but only slightly. The camp exuded an air of dirt and dust, there was a swimming pool, but it was closed. I didn't see much point in stopping. After a few days, we decided to drive further up into the town close to the hotel we had stopped at before, the Igoudor. Our first couple of holidays at the Igoudor had been pleasant and enjoyable. We made many friends, including Mike and Mary from Canada. Both had escaped from Yugoslavia during the 50s uprising and made their fortune from turkey farming through hard work and perseverance.

Sadly, the hotel had gone down the pan with no improvement plan or refurbishments made since we had first stopped there. Mohammad was still tending to the pool, but there were very few around it. With no parking outside, we pulled into a lay-by next to another hotel a short distance away, next to another camper with its German owner. Within minutes a security guard came over and demanded two euros a day for us to park there. We considered this a fair price. We would have the security umbrella of the hotel and the possibility of using the hotel facilities. Sadly, the hotel was much like the

Igoudor, with very few guests. It's not much fun sitting around an empty pool.

We were becoming starved of English-speaking company. Heading down towards the seafront, we walked into a very big, four-star hotel. My mistake was asking the security staff if we could use the hotel facilities.

"Yes, sir, please, of course." Lovely, in we walked, making our way down towards the pool. The hotel was rammed with holidaymakers, mostly if not all, English. Plonking ourselves down by an English couple, we started asking about the hotel and entertainment etc. When they asked when we had arrived, we told them we had been touring all around Morocco for two months. This quite shook them up. They had been in the hotel for nigh on a week and hadn't been anywhere.

"No, we go down to the harbour, have a walk along the seafront, look in the shops, then come back to the hotel." He said this as a simple matter of fact. I never failed to be amazed at how many tourists came away somewhere like Morocco yet never left the hotel. What was their purpose in coming away? I could understand them not going out at night to isolated areas, but here we were in the main tourist spot. We had always found it perfectly safe. Do people wrack up trips around the world simply to boast that they had been there? What is the point of having dozens of holiday breaks around the world when they never see the place? Maybe they were simply fed up with being harassed by shopkeepers and locals. But they had never been out to experience that.

Having settled in a bit and having got our bearings, we made our way down to the pool. Finding a couple of sunbeds, we put our towels down before deciding to have a snack at the poolside restaurant. This in itself was a wonderful change to what we had been used to. The settings were clean and welcoming. The food set out was also immaculate. Chips clean and well cooked. Bet had a ham salad, I had ham chips and eggs. We were in our little oil tot. We would be having more of this. So we thought. Finishing our meal, we ambled over to our sunbeds, let the meal settle down for a bit, get the sun on us, then a few dips in the pool. What more could we ask for? We hadn't sat down more than ten minutes before security was in our face. "Excuse me, sir, you are more than welcome to come into the hotel and enjoy a meal, but you cannot use the pool."

I was gobsmacked. "why didn't you say that before we had spent good money on meals." I replied, offended. There was no point in arguing. That was their policy, and that was that. Indignant, we got up and walked out. Lesson learned, and we wouldn't make that mistake again. Never ask the hotel for permission to use the pool. Just walk in like you own it like you are a guest, plonk yourself down and use it. Sometimes in life, it just doesn't pay, to be honest.

Whilst we had a couple of hotels with pools that we could use, this was a nice, classy hotel with some life. It was all we needed to make ourselves at home, a nice pool, clean food with nice facilities. We spent almost a couple of weeks in Agadir before heading north and back home. Our first stop, Marrakesh, was one hundred miles away. The cities were all well signposted, seeing there were not that many roads it worked in our favour. Whilst there were plenty of roads, of course, between major cities there was only one main route, great.

Driving around looking for somewhere to park up, a scooter rider pulled up alongside us. "Are you looking for a campsite?"

We weren't, but if he knew one, why not. Off he set, us following behind. Sure enough, within a short time, he guided us into a campsite. Seeing us in, we paid up for the night and headed for our pitch, the scooter rider behind us. I should have guessed; he was after his fee. What is it with these people? Everyone is on the f*****g scrounge. I had assumed he was touting for the campsite. Wrong, he was touting for me. "What do you want?"

"Fifteen euros for showing you to the camp."

"Fifteen euros, are you having a joke? Are you taking the p**s?" Why do businesses like these campsites allow this kind of thing to happen? It is widespread all over the place. The arguing was getting me down. He was not going to leave till he had some money. In the end, we settled on five euros, effectively five quid for bringing me half a mile to the campsite, it was almost funny.

It also took much of the shine of our touring. I enjoyed Morocco; it was an interesting place to visit. There was a lot to see, but the constant begging, scrounging, and harassment gets to you after a bit. If a cop is about, he will jump on whoever is about to approach you before he gets a chance. But there were very few cops. If you're in one town, the locals will get used to your face. After telling them to p**s of four or five times, they will eventually leave you alone. We were hitting a town every other day; it seemed non-stop.

It was still low season, so Marrakesh was very quiet, almost desolate, and not very appealing. It's amazing how much of a difference the tourists can make to a place. The tourists bring out the locals. When the tourists disappear, the locals hibernate. This wasn't new to us. We had owned hotels in Devon. When the season ended, the town almost died. I had worked at seaside resorts as a young man, and the contrast was quite startling. It suited some people to travel in the low season. Indeed, it suited us around England, so long as it wasn't too low season. Otherwise, it was as dead as a doornail. In Morocco, it was totally dead, quiet, and not at all welcoming. Worst of all, we couldn't figure out if or where any hotels were open to take advantage of.

CHAPTER 33.

Bet, and I had never been on a Caribbean cruise. In early March, we never gave a thought to whether it was low season or not. We were on a cruise, surrounded by people. Pulling into each port in the Caribbean, St Kitts, St Lucia, Dominica Grenada etc., we never gave much thought to the market stalls, taxi drivers and others awaiting our arrival. Preferring to find our own way around rather than go on guided tours. This was fine until we found that the taxi drivers followed the same routine. They each had their little favourites who they would take us to, a little bar out in the sticks, a mini market stuck up in the mountains. Clearly, the taxi driver was supplementing his fee by taking us to his friend, cousin, or uncles store. Most of the stalls sold cheap, tacky tat, or oils, soaps, or powders—none of which we wanted.

After we hit the third or fourth island, we started to notice the long faces. The taxi driver had taken us to the islands famous sulphur eruptions, pulling us to the side of the road halfway up a mountain. We then had to walk by foot uphill along a track until we reached the sulphur emissions. I wasn't too impressed; I don't think Bet was either. Walking back, he introduced us to a little bar set up along the track where we were offered a pleasant cocktail, for the sum of some ten euros equivalent. The bar was beautifully made out of the local bamboo and fern for the roof. It was cheap but authentic. The young girl serving us the cocktails had a face as long as Livery Street. Her jaw couldn't drop any lower, her eyes dull and lifeless, the taxi driver didn't look any happier.

"Where is everyone?" I asked him. There were some three thousand passengers on our cruise ship, were we the only ones to visit the bar. They both looked dejected, not having an answer, then he dropped the little nugget out. Although he was the taxi driver, it wasn't his car. He was just brought in when the tourist ships came in. It was the same with the market stalls. Knowing the ship was coming in, everyone would come out bustling, setting up stalls around the island. Driving down in their tour buses and open-top people carrier's. As soon as the cruise ships departed, everyone packed up and went home. It was frightening, to think so many people relied so desperately on the tourists was sad.

These islands were part of the windward islands owned by the British, yet the poverty was clear to see. Even taking a casual walk around the towns on each island, you could feel the hardship and poverty. It was only in the main tourist parts of the island you could see the difference. I bet they were dead grateful to be part of the British islands. Owned by the British. It was much the same in Morocco. Drive five miles outside Agadir, and it was almost like stepping back 2000 years. It almost takes your breath away. For many years Spain was supposed to be reliant on the tourist industry, but away from the main tourist spots, you can see the country is thriving in all areas.

CHAPTER 34.

HEADING HOME.

We were now feeling travel weary. We had been driving for some two months from Chefchaouen down into the Sahara. We had seen and experienced some amazing sights, from Ben-Haddou to the Ghost town outside Midelt. But the poverty, the dirt and the dust were starting to tell on us. We were now almost glad to be heading home and back to civilisation.

From Marrakesh, we made our way back to Chefchaouen. It took us a couple of days, pulling into pretty little villages along the way, the locals either cheering out to us or gawping in amazement. The only people driving along these routes would be the odd, rare motorhomer, French, or German. We were way off the tourist route. If we saw some unusual sight, we would pull up and take a picture.

Communal wells were quite common in Morocco. At these, we would stop and take pictures. Most of the ladies would stand up from their scrubbing and wave madly at us. Passing one lady drawing water from the well, we pulled up, and I took some crayons and a drawing book over to her, indicating that I would like to take her photo. Gesturing her approval, I took her picture. She was standing on top of the well's wall, which was about two feet from the ground, a canopy covering the well and a pulley to draw the water up. It was quite an eye-opener to realise this was still quite common in this day and age. To a westerner, the main tourist areas like Agadir and Marrakesh showed a completely different picture. This lady pointed to her house some fifty or seventy yards up the hill. Every day she would have to walk down that hill for water or with clothes to wash, spend a few hours washing, then the slow, gruelling walk back again. Having accepted our gift of a drawing book and felt pens, she wanted to return the gesture. Diving under her gown, she reached somewhere in her nether regions before pulling out half of a crusty loaf. Gesturing to me to come over, she handed the crust over to me. I was f*****g horrified and had great difficulty keeping a straight face. Where had she brought it from? Where had it been?

The poor girl was doing me a kindness, I realised that. I had no option but to accept it with good grace. As soon as we were half a mile out of town, I opened the window and threw it out. Before heading to Chefchaouen, we realised that we couldn't leave Morocco before seeing the ancient city of Fez. The oldest city in Morocco, Fez, was a medieval walled city with 10,000 streets and hundreds of shops. There were tradespeople of every kind throughout the city.

Pulling into Fez, we were confronted by the walled city of Fez itself. Fez was a city within a city. The medina streets were long and narrow, no cars, no motorcycles, anything that had to come in was brought in by donkey. Gas bottles, food, and goods, all came in on the back of a donkey. Getting in was the easy bit. Walking around it was an amazing experience. The air filled with a variety of smells, including the famous tannery, which can be smelt all over the city. The tannery in Fez is one of the oldest in Morocco, if not the oldest. They still treat their leather as they did since at least the 16th century. The smell is disgusting and overpowering and can be seen from balconies overlooking the tannery.

Watching the people working made you realise what hard work was involved in making leathers. Then coloured and sent to the different workshops around the medina to be made into various items and garments. We were told that originally urine was used to treat the leathers. To my mind, they were still using it because that's what it smelt like.

Within a short time, we were lost. The streets seemed to go in one big circle around the medina. Seeking out one exit, we got outside only to find we hadn't a clue where we were. We had no choice but to go back inside walk around until we got to the next entrance. We didn't even know where we had parked the motorhome to ask anyone for guidance. I was starting to panic. Trying to keep calm and show a calm front, I had a nightmare vision of walking around into the night, lost forever. People lived, worked, and spent their lives in this busy medina. I felt we were going to be one of them.

After three attempts, we finally found our way out, with some immense relief. Fez and the Medina was a fascinating city. It deserved more time to be spent exploring it, but for us, it felt so claustrophobic we were glad to get out, to fresh air. The most memorable part of Fez that sticks in my mind. The antiquity. The feeling of being stuck in a time warp. Of being transported back in time over 2000 years, to narrow cobbled streets barely wide enough for two or three people to pass side by side, hundreds of them. A donkey being lead carrying two gas bottles barely leaving room for another to pass by. The vibrancy of the place, it was all bustle, noise, and movement. In the ghost town outside Midelt, I felt we were back in the time of Jesus of Nazareth. No electricity, no gas, no toilet facilities, no running water, only water from a communal well. Here in Fez, it felt like we had just walked out of the ghost town to spend a few dirhams in the local medina. The one seamlessly blending into the other. So natural, was it. I never even noticed the electricity or even if there was common electricity, so convincing was it. As we walked out, small crowds followed us about. Yet it was a mecca for tourists with coach parks aplenty.

Finding our motorhome, we headed out of town. Up to Chefchaouen, 130 miles further north. Making it after a steady three-hour drive. When we reached Chefchaouen, we decided to pull into the very same, the only campsite that we had left only a few weeks earlier.

Pulling into the campsite in Chefchaouen, who did we pull up alongside but the Danish couple in their works delivery van, who we had parted from a few weeks earlier. We each gave the other big smiles like we had undergone a major life-changing situation and come through it the other end. Well, we felt we had. They had left the site early in the morning on the day of their departure. Going over their tour, it was clear we had more or less followed the same route. Where we had been, they had been. For overnight parking, they simply pulled into fields or quiet spots for the night. We guessed that by choice or otherwise, they had kept to a very strict budget. They gave us the impression that they didn't drink. They didn't seem to socialise or mention using any restaurants, hotels, or bars. They merely toured and enjoyed the sites they were visiting, and why not. This was the beauty of travelling with your own means of transport. You just don't need a great deal of money. They mentioned that it would have cost them £500-£600 in diesel by the time they returned home to eat? If you're careful, you can literally live on a few dirhams a day, it is so cheap.

CHAPTER 35.

In one small town, we were approached by a young English guy who lived there who had moved to live in Morocco because it was so cheap. He had an incurable disability and felt it better to live there than back home. I daresay the cheap, wacky baccy might have had a bit to do with it, but either way, it was cheap to live there. I could imagine this Danish couple wouldn't have spent much more than ten euros a day if that. There was no snobbery. They were just a couple enjoying a break and fair play to them in all. I imagine they wouldn't have spent much more than £1,000 for a four to six-week break. That's around £150 per week, per couple, all in. We were spending not much more, yet we ate out a lot, we had plenty to drink. We do like our little comforts. Having a couple of days to chill and wind down, we then headed off to Ceuta, the Spanish enclave in north Morocco, 116 miles away. It was a pleasant, steady drive, along rugged, dusty roads, and perilous mountain roads where we encountered mad Morocco lorry drivers whizzing along at breakneck speed. My only thought was to keep well out their way.

Reaching Ceuta, we made sure to avoid all and any touts leading into customs. Upon reaching customs, we duly filled out the forms handed out to us. Handing them back, the customs pulled a right long face because my writing was ineligible. Well, very sorry but I'm very tired. Getting on the ferry, we were quite pleased to be heading home, back to civilisation, a nice meal in Spain in civilised surroundings. The facilities on board the ship were not very nice at all. We didn't even have a drink. Even on the ship, we were still in Morocco.

Driving out of the port on Spanish soil, we pulled into the first suitable restaurant we came across. Ahhh, a lovely clean, nicely cooked egg omelette and chips, heaven. It was great to be back, well, almost. From Algeciras, we set off north-west heading for Benalmadena, Sotogrande San Diego, then up to Estepona. The driving was a delight. The roads were great and well set out. I thought the Spanish were milking Brussels for all they could get, banging in roads all over the place. The only problem was we would be driving along, sweet as Larry, watching my little car on my TomTom, but the red road would be a couple of miles to the right or the left. At first, it was a bit disconcerting because I couldn't see another road, maybe a dirt track, but by persevering, we soon came back together.

Until we hit the major cities, the roads were almost desolate, no big traffic hold-ups, no jams, no slow crawling cars, just sweet, pleasant, steady driving. This was like driving in England in the fifty's, but with better roads. It's only as you trot along in France, Spain, or even much of Europe, you see the contrasts. Driving in England is, much of the time, a nightmare. Thankfully being self-employed, I was mostly able to avoid morning and evening rush hour. But I'd put a bet that anyone who has to drive through Spaghetti Junction at rush hour doesn't get out of it without a severe dose of migraine.

Simply put, England is utterly overcrowded, and the government just don't give a toss for the people. There are some 70 million people in England, that's without counting all the illegals. In Spain, there are some 45 million, yet it is over twice the size. France has almost a third fewer people than us yet is almost twice the size. Property is cheaper, and more of it, people have a better quality of life. In England, the government simply sees more bodies, more money to act the big s**t on the world stage. Everyone in a motorhome starts in the same way, an eager beaver wagging our tails, desperate to learn and get out on the road. Finding our way slowly, we found more and more our way around, and where it was acceptable to park up without causing a nuisance, being discreet and not offending the locals or even the holidaymakers. If we saw one or two motorhomes, we might pull in, keeping a discreet distance from them. If we saw too many, we would drive on until we came to somewhere more suitable. Once, seeing three German motorhomes in a parking area behind some restaurants, we pulled in for the night and got our head down. The next morning, the gendarme turned up and politely asked us to move. I suspected that maybe the restaurants had seen the growing number of motorhomes, and thinking of their customers, had panicked. It was understandable. I bet the Germans were giving us some stick.

Many years ago in Morocco, we saw hundreds of motorhomes literally on the beachfront in Agadir during our first holiday there. It was a sight to behold and one of the incentives for us to buy a motorhome. A few years later, the beaches were empty. Asking our friend Mohammed he told us that the King himself had stepped in and put a stop to it. Apparently, the French were emptying their cassettes into the sea. This staggered me. Could the French actually be this stupid and unthoughtful? The image of dozens of French walking down to the beach in the middle of the night emptying their crap into the sea was just too hard to imagine. We had heard or seen a few situations that either turned my stomach or made me wonder what some of these campers' mindset was. For Bet and me, it was quite simple. We would either use hotels or restaurants. If we used the cassette, we would simply go on site every few days to top our electricity up, empty our cassettes and fill up with water. It was a no brainer. The old saying applies; leave nothing but your footprints.

Some people, in their ignorance, spoilt it for everyone. I think the gipsies spoil it for all. Having said that, why can't the governments or local councils come up with a solution like the French or Spanish and make money from it? It would be relatively cheap to set up spaces around the country with a cassette emptying facility and taps for water. Most campers resent paying thirty quid a night for the same thing I would happily pay, three, even five quid. The council would be making money, the local businesses would benefit even by a few bob spent.

Slowly, we were making it along the coast uphill and back home. We were getting a feel for Spain, France, even Europe and enjoyed exploring it. On this trip, our main aim was to explore and visit Spain and Morocco. Initially, I had started to keep a diary of many of the places we visited and the parking places we were finding. But after a few excursions and forays, we started to feel there was no need. Almost everywhere in Spain was camper friendly, if not tolerant. In France, there were Aires every few miles, in the country, by rivers in villages, in towns. It was brilliant. There were plenty of places to park up and spend the night to enjoy the local amenities in between.

In Benalmadena, we found a very pleasant, quiet area, one road back from the seafront, in Torremolinos, a similar place. But because it was so commercialised, too far from the seafront. We started to find we preferred the smaller, less crowded resorts. We knew my sister Doris was on holiday in Benidorm with her partner and daughter Patty, so we decided to pop in along the way to see her. Focused on our touring as we were, we only spent a couple of hours with them around the pool before setting off on our journey. Not being able to find the hotel they were in, we headed down to the seafront, ringing her and asking to meet us and direct us back to the hotel.

We could see her coming towards us at a fast and steady stride—miniskirt on and a top. A fit, healthy woman with a great pair of legs, not a vein or lump in sight, yet she was seventy-three. Bet, nor I could believe it. Unbeknown to us, and just a few short months later, unexpectedly, and completely out of the blue, she was given just weeks to live. Within five months of that short meeting in Benidorm, she was gone. I had never even bought her or the kids a drink, a pint of lager. My lovely sister. Gone, in the blink of the eye. Leaving Benidorm behind, we carried on up the coast, through Gandia, up into Tarragona, stopping overnight or for a couple of days before heading inland and to Andorra up in the Alps.

CHAPTER 36.

Andorra is a landlocked country in the Pyrenees in the historical county of Urgell, between France in the north and Spain in the south. A microstate, that says it all, really. It is believed to have been created by Charlemagne, first ruled by the Count of Urgell. It is headed by two princes, the Bishop of Urgell in Catalonia, and the President of France. Its population is a mix of Spanish, French Portuguese and Catalans. To me, its only purpose seems to have been formed as a skiing resort before they invented the skis. That and its duty-free seem to be all it has to offer. Being between the two countries, I was intrigued to see it and its purpose. I wasn't all that impressed; maybe we were looking at the wrong things. People came to ski, shop for duty-free, then pass through. Some just used it to pass through from north to south or south to north.

The main city of Andorra la Vella is bustling. The shops are busy. There is a feeling of affluence. Those mountains that seemed to keep everyone in poverty and isolation is now their saviour. We spent a couple of nights in Andorra le Vella parking for free on an Aire, adjoining the main supermarket just inside France's border. Unfortunately, we felt the only two things worth being there for were the duty-free shops and skiing. We were into neither one of them.

Leaving Andorra and getting into the Pyrenees, the contrast was breath-taking. The Alps were staggering in their beauty. Majestic and frightening. If nothing else, Andorra is worth visiting just for the experience of taking a breather and visiting the Alps on both sides of the border. Passing through the Alps, we were so overawed by the beauty we seemed to be stopping every few miles just to take pictures, take in the views while having a coffee.

We took a circuitous route into France because we wanted to visit the natural park of Cadi-Moixero, still within the Alps on the French/Spanish border. We debated whether to spend a couple of nights, but we wanted to visit Alt Urgell and Cami de la Liudriga between Montella and Martinet. Two alpine towns. It was a typical little skiing village. Out of the kindness of their hearts, the local council had set aside a camping Aire, right in the middle of the town, next to a beautiful, fast-flowing mountain river. We had arrived on Saturday afternoon, but most of the town had closed down. It was out of season, and the campers around us were the only ones there.

The site itself was a delight. A sign at the entrance stated that we were permitted to stay for up to five days. Water was available free of charge on-site, together with cassette emptying facilities, toilet, and shower facilities and even electricity hook-up, for a small fee. Behind us was a mountain backdrop, with farmland nestled underneath and beside the Aire. In front was the mountain stream across which lay the town and the Alps in the distance. At any time of the year, the views would have been breath-taking. Just to sit in our motorhome, a glass of wine in hand, looking at the views was enough. The fact that it was free was a fantastic bonus.

Before coming abroad, we had started to become resigned to the fact that we were expected to pay for a site if we wanted to park up for the night. Either that or made to feel like pikey's if we free camped. Here, in Spain and France it was completely different. There were Aires and places to camp up everywhere- the whole attitude was different.

Walking out at night, we visited a small restaurant, in which there were many, ordered a bottle of wine, sat, and enjoyed a very nice simple meal. It was something to savour. The prices were very favourable. Walking back to our motorhome, we stopped at the river, sitting on a bench to take in the ambience. The air was crisp and fresh. Our only question was, why don't the English do this?

From Urgell, we set off north into France proper, continuing through the Alps and dog legging to the right and Perpignan. Our plan, evolving as we went along, was to see as much as we could, taking snapshots of all the places we visited. We were free spirits, going where we wanted when we wanted. Perpignan was something on the map that we had heard about and would never normally visit. It was certainly worth the visit, and Perpignan was a beautiful city. We called in whilst a crafts fair was on with market stalls and cafes set up and selling their wares. It was a very pleasant experience. We had done it. We had seen it. If we were in the area ever again, we would pop in, but other than that, we would be discovering other places. There were just so many places to see, so many things to do. We were finding Europe one big adventure playground.

From Perpignan, we headed up again to the coastal resort of Gruissan, where we stopped for a couple of days, enjoying the nearby amenities. The beach and seafront of Gruissan were superb, with plentiful and adequate restaurants in abundance, all at reasonable prices. Down by the harbour were more expensive restaurants but the difference in quality was quite clear, with fresh seafood taking pride of place on the menu. There was plenty of places for us to park up by the beach, but I felt that was only because it was low season. France, without a doubt, is more expensive than Spain but each has its own qualities. For beauty and culture, France beats Spain hands down. A bottle of wine in France can be bought for a couple of euros. It's the beer that hits you in the pocket—a pint of beer in Spain, one euro. A pint in any restaurant in France, ten euros. After a couple of smacks, we learned to stick to the wine.

From Gruissan, we headed across to the main city of Narbonne, calling onto a very nice campsite with its very own shower, water, and toilet block. Again, how different to England, where you have to trudge across the field to the nearest tap for thirty quid a night. Narbonne, to me, was just another busy town. Born in Birmingham's inner city, I just saw no pleasure in walking around concrete blocks and shopping centres. After a couple of pleasant days around Narbonne and the campsite, we headed off to the amazing and breath-taking medieval city of Carcassonne. Now that was something else.

CHAPTER 37.

CARCASSONNE AND OTHER MEDIEVAL TOWNS

Ignorant as I was, I was never impressed with France. I believed all those stories, how we rescued them from WWII, how ungrateful they were. As for the frogs, well, we all knew they ate frogs' legs, disgusting, and drank wine by the gallon, all the while hating the English for being 'le boeuf' eaters. Worse, the French cops hated the English and persecuted them at every turn and point on the motorways and roads.

We were wrong on every count. We were continually being surprised and impressed with what we were seeing and experiencing. The big difference lay in how we see things. In my eagerness to get to Spain, I just ignored France, utterly not interested. What a mistake. It took a few passes to realise how wrong I was. In all our travelling, we had never heard of Carcassonne, Paris, Saint Tropez, Cannes, Nice, the Loire valley, the Chateaus. France, like England, is bursting at the seams with character and history.

Carcassonne was founded 2500 years ago. Its long double-surrounding walls stretch for two miles. It has fifty-two towers and, over the years, has been occupied by Romans, Goths, and crusaders. It was magnificent. It was breath-taking, as we were about to find out. Carcassonne is a city within a city. Imagine if you will the 2500-year-old medieval city built on a hill overlooking the surrounding countryside for miles and the modern city of Carcassonne below. Pulling into the large car park in front of the city, we were confronted by the two awe-inspiring towers leading into the city itself. Outside the towers and to the side was the graveyard serving the citizens of the city. Walking through the towers and along the cobbled streets, passing one building after another, which had been turned into shops or restaurants. The atmosphere and history just seemed to ooze out of every brick and stone. In England, we have our castles built to protect our kings and leaders together with their minions. Here we have a whole city where its citizens were housed and protected.

The city's centre opened up into the main square and to the side the main church, the Basilique des Saints Nazaire et Celse. Walking inside to see the stained-glass windows, we sat in silence. Lighting a candle in memory to those who had passed. The city and the church were crammed with what seemed to be every nationality, Chinese, Japanese, black, white, and yellow. Finding a restaurant, we decided to sit and enjoy a light meal whilst soaking up the atmosphere around us.

After a lovely day touring and swallowing in the city, we again set off, heading slowly home. Our next stop off at a little campsite outside Limoges, but first, as it was late in the day, we spent the night parked next to the river in Carcassonne. The next day setting off for the 240-mile run to Limoges. Limoges is famous for its porcelain manufactured in and around the city. Established over a hundred years ago because of the clay in the area. Having Stoke on Trent on our doorstep famous for the potteries, neither one of us was too bothered about spending valuable time in the city. So we decided to give it a miss during this trip.

Our main plan was to visit the city of Oradour-Sur-Glane, about twenty miles north-west of Limoges, where in 1944, for some reason, a German platoon travelling from Limoges had called into the small village, gathered all the residents, consisting of women, children and mainly old men into small groups and herded them into separate buildings, as well as the church. They shot and killed the whole lot of them, then set the village on fire. The only reason the story got out was that one or two people, including children, escaped. Otherwise, the truth would never have got out at all. When president De Gaulle heard of the atrocity, he ordered that Oradour–Sur-Glane be left untouched as a living museum, a monument to man's inhumanity to man. Instead, another town also named Oradour–Sur-Glane was built a few hundred yards away.

To the present day, no one knows for sure why the town was destroyed or its occupants. It was to some good luck that much of the population were at work on the nearby farms and in Limoges itself. Some small consolation. The Germans that carried out the atrocity were never discovered. The only plausible theory put forward was a train destroyed by the French resistance a few days previous, so it may have been a revenge attack.

Walking through the town sent a chill down my spine. Everything was deadly silent. Still being out of season, it was relatively quiet in terms of people and sound. Very few people spoke out loud. As we passed people, we could hear them murmuring in French, Dutch or German. German? What must they have been thinking? Their own fathers or grandfathers had committed this atrocity. The small tracks still ran through the town. Every building, house bar or café still stood. We saw a burnt-out car in the local garage. In the church, the broken window was visible from where a young child managed to escape outside. Not even a bird sang. It seemed as though the whole town had died with its people, the birds showing their respects by keeping away. Just outside and in between the two Oradour-Sur-Glane's stood the cemetery for those murdered. We felt it only right that we went in to pay our respects. Leaving Oradour-Sur-Glane behind, we made our way to the campsite to rest for the night and reflect on what we had seen and experienced during the day. For sure, Oradour-Sur-Glane would never leave our memory.

By now, we had been travelling for almost three months, covering over 5,000 miles at the cost of £1,250, Our spending money for the period less than £2000. Approximately £250 per week, inclusive of fuel and the odd campsite. Based on what we were spending, we realised that the longer we spent somewhere, the cheaper per month it would have worked out, mainly saving on the fuel costs. Building the actual costs up, we never set out to cheapskate. In fact, we never cheapskates at all. If we wanted to eat out, we ate out. If we wanted to drink, we drank - probably too much. We could have travelled down to Spain, spending the winter in the sun on very little. Many people still do. After spending two days at the campsite owned by a London couple, we set off for the steady drive home. We kept a bit of a diary, more as a reminder of where we had visited, how many miles we had travelled and just roughly how much we had spent. Before leaving the campsite, I went online and booked a ferry from Caen.

Arriving at Caen itself, we booked in, parked up in line, put the kettle on and feet up. The weather was overcast, and a light rain was falling. Looking outside, we were grateful for the comfort of the motorhome. People were either crunched up in their cars or walking around in the rain to get a bit of fresh air. Well, we couldn't invite them all in, could we?

CHAPTER 38.

OUT AND ABOUT BACK HOME

The eight-hour ferry home to Portsmouth was steady and uneventful. The drive home a drudge that we just knew we had to get over. Our holiday tour break had now come to an end. All we wanted to do was get home. It was a steady three-hour trip. Getting home was a pleasant and welcome relief. Some people live full time in their motorhomes, travelling the globe as they see fit. Whilst I envy them, we both enjoy getting back to our own little nest. Much as we love travelling and seeing the world in our motorhome, it's great to be back home.

Before buying our motorhome, our plans were quite clear and specific even more after we had bought it. The summers would be spent enjoying the natural wonders and beauty of our own country. We had camped in Devon, Wales, the Derby Dales, now we were looking forward to seeing more of it in the luxury of our motorhome. We were to be disappointed. After we initially joined both the caravan and camping club and the caravanning club, we were constantly surprised and disappointed with what we were getting for our money. I certainly don't consider us skinflints, but we have spent all of our married life in business. You can't be in business without knowing how to be careful with money. Both these clubs boast they are non-profit making charity-run clubs. I went along with this for a bit before starting to question why these same sites were more than many private sites in many cases. Yes, some were in pleasant locations like Wolverley outside Kidderminster, a short walk to the canal side pub with canal walks, but many were not yet. They seemed to charge such a great deal for what they offered.

In our tent camping days, part of the pleasure was getting out into the wilds, the woods or some isolated bit of farmland, permission granted by some kindly farmer without thought of charge. Today, these campsites look at campers as a captive audience, charging as much or almost as much for a tent as a caravan. Yet, in many cases, they never even had electricity. It was a pitch, and a pitch is a pitch. So much for charity. The caravans and tents really had no choice, but we were totally self-contained. To be stuck on a site was, I found, a bit suffocating.

Another advantage of the sites was the small CL sites we could use at far more reduced prices. In theory, these sounded great, but many of them were well out of the way, in the sticks on small farm fields or next to pubs. We had purchased and owned a pub in Hereford with five acres of land that came with permission as a CL site. This was fine. We wanted to build on the caravan site, but the first caravans pulled up and bought their five-pound fee in. I had to do a double take. The caravan clubs were charging £25 per night. We were expected to charge £5. They didn't even eat in our restaurant. They were using £2 a night in electricity, banging the cookers, heaters, and fridges on. We were on site for the campers. The camping clubs advertised and got wardens to look after the sites for free, well, with the privilege of a free camping pitch during their post. Very clever.

Then there were the rallies. These were organised by the clubs and the members themselves. Usually, a field would be rented from some local farmer for a fee. The rally would be organised, a steward would be enrolled to look after the event in exchange for a free camping break himself. Ok, the pitch was cheap and fine if you wanted that kind of thing. This was convenient for the caravan owners because they could buzz off out in their cars. Fine for the campers, not of much use or joy to us in our motorhomes. It was even worse when we happened to call into the rally tent one day to ask the steward for advice. The rally tent had been set up with a long table at one end, chairs set down along the other three walls. The steward's job was to keep the campers entertained; it was ridiculous. We had already been invited to judge a potato man competition at one site. This was not our scene at all, I'm afraid. When the steward thanked us for helping him escape, we definitely knew it wasn't our scene, even for a short time.

Being friendly is one thing, saying hello, having a chat, making friends, great. But in reality, we were finding very few campers wanted to socialise with their next-door neighbour and fellow campers caravan owners associated with caravan owners yet expected to be entertained by a steward. The more we went about, the more we found doors closing on us. Maybe we were just too fussy. Maybe we were expecting too much.

We had to rethink the whole strategy of our thinking. Now it was starting to become a matter of principle. Especially having experienced the freedom of travelling abroad, we were getting a taste for freedom.

In France, there were Aires all over the place, free camping spaces for the traveller. Ok, I know France is double the size of England, but why can't we have that opportunity here in England? I don't mean everywhere Weston-Super-Mare is a bit pushed for space, especially in high season, but maybe they might be grateful for the campers one day. Barmouth, for most of the year, is empty along the whole seafront and parking spaces. Whilst I appreciate the priority for the regular holidaymakers who stop in the hotels, I would have thought that the council could install a cassette emptying facility with a water supply and charge a reasonable fee. I'm sure most would be happy to pay for it. This applies throughout the country, not in every resort but in many. It seems a win-win situation to me, especially if campers were encouraged to at least have one meal in one of the restaurants or pubs, at least we were then helping the local community.

However, we were also starting to see the other side of the coin. We were starting to hear horror stories which we didn't like to dwell on. But at Barmouth one year, we pulled up at a car park on the far side of the seafront, we paid the parking charges for the night and settled down. Shortly, a caravan pulled in towed by a car that took up three spaces. When the warden called round asking the guy to park up a bit better and taking up less space, the guy gave him a load of lip. Turning to us, the warden muttered that whilst the council were happy to turn a blind eye to us as long as we paid the parking charges. Some people took advantage. Although the car park was empty, I could appreciate his point. Sadly, for whatever reason. Those same far off car parks have since had height barriers installed. The same thing had happened in Bewdley, the warden blaming it on the gipsies. Whether there is any truth in that, I don't know. If there is, then I wonder why the hell they can't do anything about it. At any rate, it seemed our options for touring and stopping overnight in or around England were dwindling. In the country areas like the peak district or the dales, we were either welcome or ignored. What we were finding was that being polite and respectful paid dividends. Leaving Barmouth after one trip, we called into Dolgellau for all-day Welsh breakfast at a town centre café. I don't know why they called it a Welsh breakfast because it was just a typical breakfast with all the trimmings, not so well cooked as the English breakfast, I might add.

Pulling onto the car park on the edge of town, I walked over to the warden and asked where we could park up as we wanted to spend the day in Dolgellau. Without hesitation, he pointed to the local rugby club's car park and mentioned that we would have no problem there. He was right. We parked up to the far side of the car park, where we spent a quiet, pleasant night. It allowed us to spend a peaceful day in a small town with a few drinks in the pub at night.

In the country like the dales or the peak district with plenty of open spaces, we found no problem finding somewhere to camp up for a day or two enabling us to spend time doing a bit of hiking or trekking. I don't think many people will appreciate the feeling of freedom that comes with parking up in the country, away from any crowds under the stars with only the odd murmur from a nearby cow or sheep to disturb the night. If places seemed difficult to find, then we would head for some local pub. Calling into one such pub in Snake Pass in the peak district, we asked the owner if we could park up overnight as we wanted a meal and a drink. The kind lady owner made us welcome and pointed to the far side of the car park. After a nice meal and a few drinks, we headed back to the motorhome safe in the knowledge that we could have a good night's kip without any disturbances. This is fine if you wanted a meal and a few drinks to go with it. If you're not particularly hungry or don't fancy too much to drink, it can turn out to be a bit expensive. The privilege of stopping at the car park cost us around fifty quid for the night. Not something we would like to do every night. One day I can envisage more and more of these pubs just charging a straightforward fee for the night, far better, and we would all know where we stood.

We were also learning to be a bit discreet in where we camped up. The reason for this was twofold. Number one was we were starting to find that some motorhome owners, just a few, were giving the majority a bad name by dumping litter and other rubbish. There was no excuse for it nor any good reason. We were on a couple of camping sites, some set up encouraging you to pass on favourite little places you could share with others. This seemed a great idea to us initially and at the time. But some of the posts were absolutely ridiculous. You would get posts like. The layby on the A38, three hundred yards in from the island and two miles outside the resort. Quiet and away from heavy traffic. What? What are we? Gipsies? Who would want to park up like that? There were loads of posts like this. How desperate are we that we considered something like that as normal? So you have a nice day in the resort before heading to the layby for the night. No, thank you very much.

Another downside to this idea of sharing was that someone would recommend a very nice resort-like Barmouth only to find when you turned up for a couple of days. The place was crowded out with other camper vans who had had the same idea. This was not conducive to happy relations with the local council, seeing their car parks rammed with motorhomes. This, in itself, was not so bad. Barmouth was a fair-sized resort with plenty of parking spaces, but there were other smaller resorts that I'm sure would not be so welcoming. Matlock Bath is a very nice, pleasant spar town outside Darley Dale. It was an ideal base to use for exploring the local area, Ashbourne Bakewell. Matlock was a delight that we had visited many times with our kids. This time in our motorhome, we found a little car park on the edge of town, hidden away and out of sight. The sign gave no mention of no parking for motorhomes, just a list of fees from an hour to twenty-four hours. That suited us a treat. The first time we called in and parked up, there was only one other rickety old motorhome. The next time we went, there were about a dozen vans. The litter bins full to overflowing. It had been mentioned on one of the camping sites which didn't fill us with excitement.

Slowly, we realised that we would have to start being more discreet about visiting and seeing. If we didn't, we feared they would be destroyed for everyone. We had found a lovely little village just inside the welsh border. It was a delight with free parking, and pleasant, clean, well-maintained public toilets. Next to the car park was a nice stream near a friendly little café and a couple of atmospheric pubs serving decent food. There was also a couple of tourist attractions nearby, in the form of monuments. What was not to like about it, it was delightful, and we spent many a short break there. Yes, it was something we would love to have shared, but more than one motorhome at a time on the car park we knew would destroy it. We were finding a few little places like this dotted around the country, few and far between. So, rightly or wrongly, we felt we had to be selfish and keep these little gems to ourselves.

Initially and right from our first purchase of the motorhome, we had decided that we would spend our summers in England, touring and enjoying small breaks. Enjoying the sunshine and good weather. The winters, enjoying the mild weather abroad with like-minded English travellers. We were to be disappointed on both counts.

CHAPTER 39.

Much to our surprise, we found the English holiday period international. I thought the annual two-week holiday spread over the two months of July and August to be purely an English trait going right back to the early 19th century dictated by the various factories and mines dotted around the country. Not so. The French, Spanish and much of Europe shared the same periods.

Go abroad in July and August the whole place was rammed. Germans, English, French, all sorts. Come September, the places started dying off. By October, the sun shining nice and hot, the places were dead. We couldn't believe it. Surely the biggest percentage of people who owned motorhomes were retired. Surely the same number would have paid cash for their motorhomes. Yet so many seemed to be stuck on peoples drives for months at a time. If we did go on sites, we found fellow motorhomers and caravaners kept mainly to themselves. In England, I could understand that. The sites, if nothing else, offered security to the campers. But abroad I expected to see more campers, either on sites or wild camping. Where were they? In France, Spain, and Morocco, we saw plenty of French and Germans, but English? Very few and far between.

We did wonder if maybe it could be the limited pension that people or couples were on. The average pension per couple was in the region of some £300 plus. Ok, not a lot if you're going to be extravagant. But if your careful, plenty enough, if you want to eat out at fancy restaurants every night, drink fine wine, and have breakfast out every morning. Plus living on a secure site, you're going to need more than £300 per week, more like a grand per week. It's all according to what you consider adds to your quality of life. We found frittering money away didn't suit us at all or increase our quality.

One year we had decided that it might be a good idea to store our motorhome down on a campsite outside Los Gallardo's outside Mojacar, Spain. The idea was to use it as a base for touring and also looking for a suitable villa or apartment to purchase. I drove down, sorted the storage fees, then decided to spend a couple of days on the campsite before getting a flight home. After some initial reservations, the main one being I just didn't see sense in buying and spending thousands of pounds on a caravan for it to sit on a site that you don't own and have to pay rent for, my viewpoint changed a bit after the second day.

The campsite was made up a little bit like a housing estate. One far end was made up of people who had moved to Spain, bought a caravan, and earned a living in the local economy. These I learned were known as the Nesbit's. In the middle section, the site was made up of more upmarket caravans that people left on-site to enjoy short summer breaks. One row was known as millionaires' row due to the quality of the caravans. The rest of the site was made up of mobile statics, known as Casas. Home in Spanish. Some were very nice, indeed. I didn't give a thought to any of this at all. I had just decided to have a little mooch around and get a feel for the campsite and the people. In the middle of the site, which boasted of being one of the biggest English owned campsites in Spain, stood the hub of the site, a great sized swimming pool, adjoining a partly covered eating out area next to a stage and another larger indoor restaurant area. Getting a pint of lager and sitting myself down by the pool, I couldn't help but be impressed. The longer I sat there, the more I was impressed. It was the height of summer. The sun was burning down above the shaded restaurant. People were sitting around enjoying the day, chatting, and laughing. The pool was almost empty, with only one or two people in it. I was beginning to love this place.

My first warning came from an old lady who informed me that she was only there, stopping with a friend. She had sold her Casa the year before, at a greatly reduced price. She was very disappointed, but her children had urged her. They felt she had no choice but to get out as soon as possible. Course, I just assumed this was the odd tale, the lady being on her own with a limited pension. I was to find out this was only the tip of the iceberg.

CHAPTER 40.

Getting a flight back home, we got the estate car sorted and packed before driving down to Spain to spend the summer. All the while, I'm filling Bet with what a great place it was. Bet, typically, keeping her thoughts to herself. Once on the site, I waited for Bet to get into the atmosphere and agree with me what a great pitch it was. The following week our daughter Louise flew over to spend ten days with us. If I bought a Casa, it would be going in her name. We would just use it for the odd break and as a base for our motorhome tours.

A few years earlier, we heard people were queuing up to buy these Casas. There was a waiting list to pay sixty to sixty-five grand for them. This was when the euro was 160 to the pound. Now it was almost level pegging. When it was at its highest, people on three hundred pounds a week pension were getting the equivalent of four hundred pounds a week spending power. Now, they had to pull their belts in. Now, you could pick a Casa up for as little as fifteen grand. I only saw the bargain. When I pointed out to Louise what I had in mind, she said, "thank you, dad, but no, sorry. The people on this site are too old for me." I don't think Bet was too disappointed. Why I don't know, but that was that.

It was only from then on, without looking for it, that I started to see the pitfalls. Many of the people living here were not wealthy, just ordinary guys who had sold their homes or put all their savings together to buy these Casas. It was a bitter blow for them to see their investment drop from some sixty-odd grand to less than twenty. Some of them were not happy bunnies. This was not helped too much by the owner, who was known as Mr ten per cent. If you wanted some work done on your Casa, he took ten per cent. If you wanted to slab your patio area outside, he charged you ten per cent. If you called the local mechanic out to fix your car, he wanted ten per cent. F*****g hell, the guy was well into it.

It was summed up one afternoon outside the pool when I was talking to a Yorkshire man. This typical blunt straight forward type said it as it was without giving a s**t for your feelings. Most of the camp never spoke to him or avoided him. This was all down to how he treated his wife, a lovely woman, by all accounts, when she became ill and put into the main hospital in Almeria. In Spain, you have to look after your partner, feeding her etc. He didn't feel he had the time or the money to keep visiting her daily. The poor woman died knowing he didn't give a s**t about her. Worse, and within days, or weeks, he approached another woman on the site whose husband had also recently died and in his gruff, blunt Yorkshire accent put it to her straight, "ay you. You're not going to survive on this site on your own, neither am I. Why don't you move in with me?" Well, I don't know how long it took her to work it out, but obviously not too long. The rental for the site, together with the television licence, water gas etc., came to £100 per week. If your pension was not much more than £160 per week, it didn't leave too much change. Unpleasant and blunt as he was, he had a point. Shrewdly, he made her sell her Casa and move in with him. This undoubtedly gave him the upper hand leaving her to walk around like it was close to the end of the world. Poor f****r, she was trapped. It also left me with the thought of what happened to his wife. Where was she buried? Was she given a pauper's funeral? How many over there were just dumped and given a pauper's funeral?

Just the thought of it sent shivers down my spine. My mind was almost made up anyway, but it really hit me in the face when I was presented with a bill for £70 for having our daughter on-site for ten days; I don't know who squealed on me. But that was the final straw. I thought we were paying for the pitch, not per person. We had spent a fair amount of money on the site between the three of us, with meals, drinks etc., to hit us like that was taking the p**s. When I mentioned it to other Casa owners, they didn't seem to know. They didn't seem to want to know. At the first opportunity, I got our motorhome off the site.

We were finding and improving on what we wanted and what suited us. Slowly, we were breaking things up into maybe three categories. Long breaks abroad in the sun, anywhere around Europe. Short breaks enjoying the English countryside and what it had to offer. In between, if a different type of break came up, we would look at it. We had had a few cruises from the Mediterranean east and west to Egyptian cruises, all of which were very pleasant and enjoyable. The next two on our list were a Caribbean cruise and an Alaskan cruise. Going online, Bet found a month's Caribbean cruise on Oceania, setting off and returning to Southampton for a grand. A four-week cruise for a grand? With P&O ferries, for a grand, fully inclusive? She got it booked sharpish. The bigger bonus, we were given an upgrade to an outside cabin with a porthole. A porthole, for heaven's sake. People paid hundreds extra for the privilege of looking out at the sea and the waves, whoopie doo. Now we felt even more upper class.

The great thing about a cruise is that you were treated like royalty, no matter who you were. You could feed until it came out of your ears. Even better, it wasn't as stuffy as we had feared. Ok, I didn't mind dressing up now and again. Neither did Bet. It was nice to wear a dinner suit or evening dress for the captain's dinner, but it was also nice to put on casual shirt and slacks. Maybe some cruises were stuffy. Maybe we had been lucky. We mixed with millionaires and ordinary people like us, many small business people, the odd one or two were stuck up their own jacksie but in the main, great.

If we found or saw an interesting short break in between, we would go for it. One such was a four-day hotel break in either Llandudno or Scarborough in a four-star hotel. We had been to neither one of them, so on the throw of the dice, chose Scarborough the next time Llandudno. We drove up in our jaguar and, following a pleasant drive, spent an equally pleasant break in a resort we had never been to before. After a pleasant week of eating fresh fish-n-chips and seafood, we returned home to Sutton. After another week of chilling, we started planning for our next break. This time we had decided we wanted to visit and tour Italy, Tuscany, the Amalfi Coast, Sorrento, Rome, and Pompeii. Italy just offered so much.

CHAPTER 41.

FRANCE AND ITALY

In the south of France, I got talking to an interesting guy travelling alone except for his dog. We were both parked up in a car park next to the beach. The guy was from London and was one of the very few English guys I had bumped into. Taking a picture of him standing outside his van with his dog, I asked him what he was doing in this part of Europe. His reply? Very simply, he drove to the ferry port at Dover, and after arriving in Calais, he then decided to turn left or right. I couldn't help but feel dead impressed. What a brilliant outlook; that was complete freedom. I didn't think we were far from that mentality, but I did like to have a bit of an idea of where we were heading before we actually set off from home. We felt a bit comfortable knowing where we were going before we even set off. Maybe one day?

Our plan was simple and straight forward. We had spent many a happy year touring, camping, and exploring England. Now we wanted to explore the rest of Europe. We had been fed the line that there was no better or beautiful country than England, with its beautiful welsh mountains and valleys, the Peak District, and the dales in Scotland. We believed it and agreed with it. But once we started getting abroad touring, we started seeing that much of Europe was beautiful as well, some even more so. Each country had its own beauty, its own magic. Its own individuality, its own character.

We had lost touch with our friends Janet and Ken after moving to Devon and buying our first hotel. Now we had found out where they were. Well, we rediscovered Janet. Sadly, Ken had died some ten years earlier after suffering a stroke followed by a heart attack. It is one of the sad facts that we find in life. We lose contact with our friends for no particular reason, drift apart only to find years later that those friends are not only years older, but their children, who we knew and remembered as children, are now adults with children themselves, such it was with Janet and Ken.

Following our renewed friendship, we had decided to get the ferry to Caen and drive down to meet Janet, where she now lived with Keith on a farm. Keith had bought the farm with his wife in the Loire valley, about an hour's drive from Caen. Both Ken and Keith were engineers. Having worked together, they also became firm friends. When Keith retired, he and his wife had bought a lovely fifty-acre farm just on the outskirts of Chateau-Gontier in the Mayenne. The river Mayenne ran through the town, which was beautiful and easy to see why they had bought in the region. Keith's father had been a strong union member in the north of England and a close friend of Arthur Scargill. Keith's wife had been a teacher, and their dream was to buy this farm, settle in France and into the local community. Keith also hoped and planned to make a living from the farm. I felt he was overly optimistic.

After only a few short years, Keith's wife had died. Ken and Janet were spending a few weeks holiday with them at the time. Within a few days of Keith's wife dying, lo and behold, Ken had his heart attack and popped his clogs. From then on, everything fell apart for Janet. Sadly, they had both been living on the hog. While they had a beautiful house with a swimming pool in a lovely village outside Sutton Coldfield, they also had a massive mortgage. No sooner had Ken died, the mortgage payments stopped. Within weeks the mortgage company grabbed the house back and sold it. Janet was devastated and, with the double whammy, naturally fell apart. Equally grieving for his wife, Keith pushed out his hand and invited Janet to move in and live with him, his daughter and brother Mark on his farm. It was a lifeline Janet was glad to grab hold of. She just had enough time to get a large van up to the house before the locks were changed and get her furniture out. Such was the situation when we got to them. Whilst all this had happened some ten years earlier, it seemed Janet and Keith had now progressed a bit further and had become a couple.

The farm was beautiful and something that many people would dream of. Indeed it had been Keith's dream, now his reality. They supplemented their income from renting a gite adjoining the farm, the bookings being taken through Brittany ferries. Just as well because the farm, delightful as it was, was not making any money. Instead, it was soaking their pension up. Keith made us very welcome as he had done with all of Janet's kids, treating them all as friends and family. Together they were great hosts. Settling us into a little part of the garden, we parked up, connected to the electricity, and filled up with water. Without a doubt, we were in our oil tot.

As well as the surrounding area of the Mayenne and Chateau-Gontier itself, they showed us around the Loire valley and some of the Chateaus it contained. There were literally hundreds of them throughout France. I thought the Chateau de Versailles was the only one, ignorant as I was. Janet introduced us to the Chateau d' Usse, Chateau de Chambord. Which was breath-taking in its beauty. King Francis had commissioned the building in the sixteenth century as a hunting lodge. His private hunting lodge, for Christ's sake. It boasted 335 fireplaces and a double helix grand staircase, all to show off his wealth. All I can say is I can understand why the peasants revolted and chopped their heads off during the revolution, especially after Marie Antoinette told them to '... eat cake.' We could only see a small sample of the chateaus, but along with so many other places, we were determined to spend a lot of time in France. Along with the medieval villages, France certainly had a lot to offer.

Janet and Keith fell in love with our motorhome. Jan and Ken, in fact, had the same make as ours, but along with the house, they lost everything, including the motorhome. Now they wanted to spend a couple of weeks with us touring Italy. We were all up for it but with minor hesitancy. A motorhome is a confined space. Visiting their farm, we felt it better to keep that slight distance by keeping to our motorhome. The surest way to fall out with someone is to be confined to a small space for a short period. I thought our friendship could withstand it. After all, we would be out much of the time. Hadn't we known each other for many years? I became even more nervous as the countdown came to the last couple of weeks. Janet rang me up with a confession. She had been considering cancelling the holiday. Why? she suffered from IBS. Irritable bowel syndrome - what did that mean? Well, it meant Janet was prone to visiting the loo all times of the day and night. I could feel my face freezing in horror. The toilet was right next to our bed. All kinds of thoughts crept into my head. None of them very pleasant. Oh bugger it, they are friends after all.

We had decided for convenience to pick Keith and Jan up from their home in Chateau-Gontier. We got the ferry to Caen. From Caen, the drive down to the farm took us about three hours. Stopping overnight, we set off the next morning to Chamonix in the French Alps. At just over 450 miles, it took us most of the day to get there. Jan had a friend who had a campsite in Chamonix. But for the life of her, she couldn't remember where they were. No problem, it was quiet in the season, and Chamonix had a massive public car park in the centre below Mont Blanc. We weren't the only motorhomes to pitch there for the night.

Chamonix itself was very pretty, all the shops, restaurants and stores were open and plenty of people were walking about carrying skis. The atmosphere was friendly and lively. An air of quiet excitement pervaded the air. Walking up to the ski lift taking us up to Mont Blanc itself, we decided it was too late in the day to attempt it. At any rate, some of the lifts were closed for the day.

After a tour around the town, a coffee, and a few drinks, we settled down for the night. The next morning we set off for the chairlift to take us up to Mont Blanc. The day before on our arrival, it had been glorious with far-reaching views, now here we were, the sky was overcast and cloudy. The lifts to the top of Mont Blanc were cancelled, meaning we could only go up to about three-quarters of the way. Three-quarters of that little journey was blanketed by fog and mist, making it almost impossible to see further than a few feet in front of us. Maybe that was a good thing, when we did get a clear look below us, I almost got vertigo.

Reaching the furthest point, we got out along with the other skiers making our way to the start of the first piste, where we watched them setting off downhill. We had never been up in the Alps before, and I was quite surprised by how mild it was. We were high up in the Alps, thick snow on the ground, and people were walking around in light clothing. Heading to the nearby restaurant, we sat enjoying a pleasant meal, while enjoying the amazing views before making our way back down the mountain and into Chamonix, where we enjoyed yet another coffee whilst doing a bit of people watching.

It was by mutual consent that we had decided to set off over to Italy. None of us were into skiing. Whilst the experience of going up the mountain, having a nice meal and experiencing the town itself was very enjoyable, we felt that was enough. Setting off, we first hit the Mont Blanc tunnel. Almost ten miles long and connecting France into Italy, it was an experience I wasn't over the moon about, knowing we had millions of tons of rock above us. It cost over fifty quid to get through it. Getting to the other end was a relief, to say the least. I didn't fancy making that little trip again. I had no firm plan for Italy on what we wanted to see or do, my only criteria was I wanted to see the Colosseum in Rome, Pompeii and Herculean, both destroyed by the eruption of Mount Vesuvius. Other than that, I gave Jan and Keith free rein to go where they wanted.

Our first destination was Vinci, outside the metropolitan city of Florence. Vinci was the birthplace of Leonardo da Vinci in 1452. The famous artist and inventor, Da Vinci, was born the illegitimate son of the local notary, magistrate and a local peasant girl named Catarina. Set within the beautiful Tuscan valley, it was surrounded by what seemed like untouched countryside filled with vineyards.

Italy was a continuous revelation to us. Coming out of the Mont Blanc tunnel, we were met by a few very poor towns, run-down and slum looking. But the Tuscan countryside itself was stunning. From Chamonix to Vinci was some four hundred miles, giving us one overnight stop on a very nice free Aire next to a river. Walking up to the local village square, we called into a local restaurant. We ordered the inevitable pizza, which we ate on a bench overlooking the town.

Arriving in Vinci late afternoon the next day, we found a quiet spot in the local car park a short walk from Vinci itself. Walking up into Vinci, we were struck by the quietness and beauty. Apart from the telephone lines, you could easily imagine that you were in another time. There were not many people about. For those of us that were, we almost spoke in a whisper; such was the effect the town had on us. Sitting down at the local ice cream parlour, we all tucked into a big tub of ice cream. In England, we are known for our roast beef dinners. The French for their snails and frits. Here in Italy, it was the ice creams and pizzas. They had got both down to a fine art. The lady owner came out to say hello and enquired what we were doing. Telling her our plans, she suggested we visit the well-known restaurant further into the town and try the Florentine steak, famous throughout Europe. I think she was into the big sell, but when it came to food, Janet would start salivating. No doubt about it, Janet liked her scran, as Keith called it. The lady kindly offered to ring the restaurant to tell them we would be along later. I reckon it was her relative, but at any rate, we decided to call in later in the evening. We were the only ones there. Sitting down, Keith got in straight away and ordered the bottle of wine. Jan might like her scran, but Keith liked his wine. The staff were expecting us.

Having been told about this famous Florentine steak, we were all looking forward to tasting it. First, the waiter bought out a large lump of thick steak weighing about two pounds. This puzzled me as I wondered how it would be served up between the three of us. I didn't have long to wait. Whatever steak we have in England, in fact, anywhere, be it rib-eye, rump or sirloin, we expect it cooked to our preferred taste then plonked on the plate in front of us. This was not the case here; it had been cut up in the kitchen, then bought out in chunks and placed on our plates. I was not impressed at all, neither was I with the taste of it. It was neither here nor there. But Jan was guzzling it down, giving it the big, "mmm, delicious." I didn't want to spoil the ambience.

The next day we set off for the short walk to the Vinci museum. The main Leonardo museum was in Florence itself, but here we had the museum and Da Vinci's home. It was enough for me. We were all in awe of what someone from such a little village could go on to invent and create. I knew Da Vinci was a famous artist, but the man was a living genius, an engineer. The parachute, diving suit, a triple barrel cannon, then pulleys to pick up heavyweights. Where did he get that mindset from? He was born in a modest house in a little village where surely the majority of the population would have been illiterate. His mother was a peasant, though his father would have bought him up. He went to university in Florence, and he painted the Mona Lisa. So not only was he a famous artist, but he was also an inventor, years ahead of his time.

Walking out of his home and into the local church, I was still awestruck at the atmosphere, the ambience; it was like time had stood still. There was nothing to stop you from thinking you were in the fifteenth century. All of us were deep in our thoughts as we drove away from the town of Vinci and on to our next destination—Pisa. Some thirty-odd miles towards Florence.

Pisa was, I thought, a bit of a scruffy town. The leaning tower sticking out like a sore thumb in the middle. It was still low season, yet the town was rammed with tourists, a long queue leading up to the tower with people eager to pay to walk around it. We all decided to give it amiss. For myself, I just hated queues. Besides, I couldn't help but be surprised how much smaller the tower was than I had expected. In all the pictures I had seen, it appeared to be twice as big as it actually was. Keith and I decided to sit at one of the many restaurants overlooking the tower, enjoying a coffee, while Janet went for a walk and did a bit of shopping. What amazed and intrigued me was where all the money went. The town itself was heaving; the restaurants were making a roaring trade. We were all spending money, yet outside that small circle, there seemed to be a hardship. We were to find this time and again.

After a pleasant day, we again set off to our next destination, Rome, and the Colosseum, about 200 miles further south. I joined and became a member of ACSI, a discount members club. ACSI had fixed prices all over Europe with good campsites that they had vetted. It took a lot of uncertainty out of searching and finding sites with varying prices. We found a campsite just outside Rome with regular bus services into Rome itself and the Colosseum. After settling in, the first on our list was the Colosseum. We decided to have a coffee in the café directly opposite to just look at it and savour the view and atmosphere. Once satisfied, we headed across, joined the queue, and paid our entrance fee. We could have paid for a guided tour which in truth might have been better, but we all felt we knew enough about the history of the Colosseum to not need it.

Like our modern football and rugby pitches, the Colosseum was built to cater to the crowd's excitement. The only difference was back in those days, the public liked seeing lions eating the Christians and Gladiators killing each other. We had all watched Spartacus. What else was there to know? All I wanted to know, and feel was the atmosphere. This wasn't as easy as I thought it might be. No matter where I stood in the Colosseum, I just couldn't put myself back in the day. It wasn't helped by the constant flow of people walking backwards and forwards and the Colosseum's layout. It was messy. It was also difficult to envisage where the animals and slaves were kept. Everything seemed to be all over the place with no certainty or planning. Maybe this is where the tour guides would have come in useful. But it just appeared that whilst the Italian government were happy to grab the money, they didn't seem to want to put anything back.

In England, many of our stately homes are preserved and kept in good condition for the visitors, some still owned by the families that built them hundreds of years before. Aston Hall is a prime example of a property well maintained, despite the poor English weather. Here, in Italy, they had got the weather on their side, yet they seemed to do very little. The main overall structure of the Colosseum was solid and sound. Whilst there seemed to be some on-going maintenance, there didn't seem to be any major renovation work. There were dozens of films showing the Colosseum and how it might have looked back in the day two thousand years ago. There were canopies all around and on top of the building, no doubt supported by long tree trunks. Obviously, I wouldn't think that could be feasible to replace today, but the lower gallies doors, holding cells and galleries could surely be rebuilt and brought back to life? The government, or someone, made millions from the visitors to the Colosseum. The surrounding restaurants were raking in big money. People were being employed all on the back of the Colosseum, yet a lot more could be done with some forethought. We were to see this time and time again.

Our next foray was to see the Trevi Fountain in the centre of Rome. Who in the world has not seen or heard of the Trevi Fountain? Who can forget that image from three coins in a fountain? Getting the bus into the centre of town, we made our way steadily to find the fountain. The only problem was Rome was known for its fountains. There was a fountain in every square, in every centre. Keith was convinced each one was the Trevi Fountain. The first time I thought he was joking. "That's it," he shouted, "that's the Trevi fountain." Looking at his face, I was puzzled. Was it really the Trevi fountain? Maybe I was wrong. Nah, now I remembered the pictures. Surely, he couldn't be that wrong? Had he never seen the Trevi fountain? He said that twice more before we actually found the fountain. I think his first judgment was correct, then he tried to deflect it by pointing to every fountain.

The Trevi fountain was magnificent. The crowds were flocking around it, throwing coins in, and making wishes. If nothing else, coming to Rome just to see and visit the fountain was a treat in itself. Sitting down amongst the crowd, I couldn't help but be enchanted. We spent at least a couple of hours just soaking up the ambience and atmosphere before walking back through the town and getting the bus back to the campsite. The centre of Rome itself was enchanting and interesting, but we had a lot more to see and do.

From the Colosseum and Rome itself, Janet insisted on seeing the Vatican and the Sistine chapel. Entering the Vatican City, we then had to join a queue to enter and see the chapel. We had a choice of paying thirty quid to jump the queue and having a guide, or ten quid, sticking to the queue and seeing it for ourselves, we joined the queue. It was a chore. My obvious thought was someone, the Vatican, and the Pope must be raking in millions per year from the tourists. The queue was all along the block. Once inside, we were shuffling along ten abreast. Janet was enthralled, gushing non-stop.

In the chapel itself, I got my camera out to take pictures. Within seconds the security was over like a shot, "no, no, no pictures, please." It didn't stop most of the tourists from sneaking out their cameras and taking pictures of the ceilings and walls. Outside we strolled under the Vatican, hoping for a peep at the Pope who seemed well hidden. Neither Keith nor I were too overly impressed with what we had seen. Janet was over the moon and bubbling with excitement. To Keith and me, seen it, done it, got the T-shirt, never again.

Our next stop was the ancient city of Pompeii, buried for almost two thousand years beneath the ash from the volcanic eruption of Mount Vesuvius. It was utterly amazing how well preserved the city of Pompeii was. Even more impressive was the fact that the government were intent on not only preserving it but putting some of it back as it was before the eruption. The buildings and the streets were preserved as they once were. There were clear pictures still on the walls, some of naked women, one the home of a prostitute, another of a powerful leader in the town. It was very easy to sit and visualise how it must have been. The gardens preserved with fountains and statues as they once were. The roads laid out and preserved, wheel tracks worn into the stone from the countless carriages and carts that must have trundled along the steep-sided roads. Stepping-stones laid strategically for crossing. But for what I wondered? —not rain, surely? Maybe effluent. Where did they discharge their toilet waste? In the streets? Well, we were doing that in England over a hundred years later.

Really, we should have booked a tour guide, but we were anxious to get into and around the town. A good tour guide would have filled in all the gaps that I knew we were missing, some of which I picked up much later. At home, for instance, the people of Pompeii did not have such things as kitchens in their homes or did any cooking. Rather they ate out. Dotted along almost every street were cafes or eating places. Large clay containers set into equally large worktops and heated by clay ovens. The people would simply walk along, choosing something to eat from one of the ovens, maybe a soup or a meat stew. Perhaps a jug of wine to go with it.

It was only once we had got home that I watched a film appropriately called Pompeii, with Keifer Sutherland, about a nobleman's daughter falling in love with a gladiator slave. Whoever produced the film had certainly done their homework. The roads, the buildings, even the stepping-stones allowing the carts to pass over them were exactly as we had seen them. For anyone intending to visit Pompeii, I would strongly urge them to watch the film before going. It will fill in all the blanks once seeing the actual reality. For myself, next time we go, and there will be a next time, I will hire a tour guide.

Next off was the other town buried by Vesuvius, Herculaneum. This time on the coast and above Pompeii. Whilst Herculaneum was first discovered in circa 1700, it wasn't properly excavated till quite recently. For some reason, the difference between Pompeii and Herculaneum was the way each city was preserved. In Pompeii, as the ash and lava fell, the bodies were disintegrated by the vast heat, then preserved in the hot lava. This enabled the bodies, or forms of the bodies, to be preserved in the shapes they fell, usually curled up into lifelike balls. Even dogs formed and preserved as they died.

In Herculaneum, the bodies were first covered by ash, thus preserving the whole bodies, then by a lava covering them and protecting the people and the city. Many of the bodies, or rather skeletons, were found in the boatyards down by the sea edge. I didn't think Herculaneum was as well preserved as Pompeii. However, it was still awe-inspiring, tragic, and moving to see and experience. Even more so to realise that, unlike Pompeii, only a small portion of Herculaneum had been discovered. The city's biggest part was still buried under the more modern city built some twenty feet above. This seemed quite amazing to me as I couldn't help but shout up to a lady hanging her washing, going about her life completely unconcerned at us meandering about below. Herculaneum seemed the same yet quite different to Pompeii. To me, Pompeii seemed so much better preserved. There was so much more to it. Maybe this is waiting to be discovered with more excavations. At any rate, it certainly gave us food for thought. Standing there, trying to imagine what was going through the inhabitant's minds as they must have first heard the eruption.

Then starting to panic and rush towards the seafront to escape. Did any escape before the ash descended on them?

From here, we got the coach up into Mount Vesuvius to see the volcano itself and look down towards Pompeii and Herculaneum. The specially built coaches, adequate as they were, could only get up to one hundred yards from the summit. From there, we had to walk. Keith, pacing himself to keep pace with his pacemaker he'd had installed. It was quite awesome and thought-provoking to stand there, on the rim of the volcano. Looking down from where all that hot ash and lava erupted before flowing down in that relentless and deadly flow below. From the volcano, we descended to a campsite below and next to the city of Pompeii for a couple of nights relaxing and enjoying the immediate area.

Again I was surprised at the poor state of some of the areas within Pompeii and Herculaneum. The flats above Herculaneum seemed shabby and social housing. This was fair enough, I suppose, as the flats had been built before much of the city had been discovered. Pompeii had been discovered many hundreds of years before. Yet, the surrounding area was also a bit shabby. Apart from the restaurants in the immediate area, I guessed, were doing very well selling meals and the inevitable pizza.

Maybe I was wrong, but I felt that in much of Europe good quality tourist attractions attracted better quality houses within the area. Windsor being one example, the peak district. Pompeii was attracting hundreds of tourists a day, maybe thousands, like the Vatican, but where was all the money going? The improvements, renovations and rebuilding would obviously be costing a great deal of money, but not to the extent of what it was taking in each day. Maybe it was me; I was always questioning things.

From Pompeii, we headed down to Sorrento and the Amalfi coast. The Amalfi coastline was the be-all and end-all of coastal routes. Everyone and their uncle would say to you, you must

see and drive along the Amalfi coast. It is beautiful, it is stunning, it is nerve-wracking. They were right about the nerve-wracking bit. Driving my motorhome along the narrow, twisting, busy roads was nerve-wracking, to say the least. When we pulled into a viewing point overlooking the coastline dotted around, my only memorable moment was stalls selling different items, including strawberries and other fruits. Keith's eyes lit up, and like a shot, he was over and ordering a bag of strawberries and a bag of plums. I had offered to pay and got my money out, thinking about ten euros. The tout on the barrow raised his hand up as I proffered the ten euros. Puzzled, I offered fifteen. Looking at Keith, all I got was "luverly. Oohhh, luverly," as he was throwing strawberries down his neck. I ended up paying thirty euros for two bags of fruit I valued at no more than ten euros max. Without a doubt, I was going to have to keep my eye on both Janet and Keith. Neither one seeming to have any real value for money. All the way down into Sorrento, from behind, all I got was "oohhhh, luverly," as they filled their faces with plums and strawberries.

Sorrento was a beautiful and clearly affluent city. After a brief walk around the immediate area, we got onto one of the little trains that wound their way around the streets, giving us a tour. Sorrento was not only affluent; it was romantic and well worth a visit. The sun was shining and warm on our backs. Within a couple of hours of setting from Sorrento heading northwest and up into the mountains, we were into thick snow and throwing snowballs at each other. We were leaving it to Janet to go through the ACSI books and find us somewhere to camp up in the mountains on our way to Venice, our next major destination. The campsite was on the mountain's actual spine that spread from north to south in the centre of Italy. It was amazing not only for its level position but for the fact it was the only place that had no snow.

The site itself was beautiful, simple, rural, and rustic, truly back to nature. Pulling in, we were beckoned to a pitch by a guy in a wheelchair chatting to a young couple in front of a nice roaring campfire. The guy was named Alan. Chatting to him later and becoming friendly with him, we couldn't help but be impressed that he was not only in a wheelchair but was also towing a caravan. Hang about, here was a guy in a wheelchair, on the top of a mountain, towing a caravan. The roads just leading up to and around the mountain were a hazard. It was bad enough in my motorhome. After parking up, we went over to have a chat with him. We never know what goes on behind closed doors, especially in relationships, but when I mentioned my admiration for anyone to do what he was doing and, in a wheelchair, to boot, he told me his situation in a somewhat sad voice.

For whatever reason, his marriage had broken up. His children didn't speak to him. Looking at him, I couldn't help but sense he wasn't a violent man, neither did he seem a druggy. Was he a womaniser? Didn't sense that either. He was quick to point out that he wasn't fully disabled. He could walk a few paces, enough to back his caravan into a space, get out, manoeuvre it into its position and put the legs down, unhitch the car and move it away. He seemed totally unfazed as I looked at him with incredulity, my brain going through all kind of scenarios. We were in bear country. There were signs all over the place warning us about the bears. We had seen a couple come up to the van in the two nights we were there. What if he broke down on the mountain road? The possibilities were endless, yet he shrugged it off. I was thinking, 'but what if something happens? Like, say you kick the bucket.' He read my mind. "Oh, it's all sorted. My nephew has my instructions. I'm sure when I die, it won't take someone long to notice." Nodding towards the campsite office, his nephew's phone number would be visible. He was instructed to cremate his body, throw his ashes wherever he was, take the four-wheel-drive car, the caravan, do what he wanted, sell it, and cash in the money. Well, I was flabbergasted, sad, and full of sad admiration. Alan had got it sorted, and all figured out. I was f*****g gobsmacked. Janet and Keith gave him their number with an open invitation to their farm in Chateau-Gontier. Within a month of getting home, Alan had paid them a visit. He stopped on the farm for a week, at the end of which he sold Keith and Janet his four-wheel-drive car and caravan, the proviso being they had to meet him back in England pick up the car and drive it back.

For the bargain price of the car and caravan, they were more than happy to do that. The caravan was chock-a-block with all his worldly possessions. His plan from then on was to use the money to visit his friend in Australia. Dying there if need be. None of us ever heard from him again. How many other lost souls were out there like Alan. How close were any of us to being in that position? I had grown up in a strong, working-class family in the slums of Birmingham. I had a strong sense of knowing who I was, where I came from. Growing up and getting married, I then had a strong urge to make ourselves secure, build a nest, buy a nice house. People like Alan made me shudder. It also made me fully aware of what a major difference a solid and secure marriage made.

CHAPTER 42.

For getting away from it all, this mountain-based campsite was certainly that. To build a campfire, sit alongside the trees amongst the forest, watching the wild bears and even wolves hunting for food was an experience never to be forgotten. We were more or less dead centre in the middle of Italy, set into a levelled piece of land below the mountain. But now, we were setting off northwest and on to Venice. Janet and Keith's venue of choice. It was a nice leisurely drive through a beautiful country with two stop-offs before reaching Venice itself. Whilst we had the sat-nav, which I reckoned was one of man's best inventions since the wheel, it was Janet's job to find us the campsites next to the venue. She was doing a good job. The one site was just a short bus ride into Venice itself. It even supplied the bus and canal taxi tickets. But getting to it was a bit of a challenge.

The campsite was set near an island, close to a flyover at a very busy junction. It took me three passes to realise I was taking the wrong turnings. Keith shouting louder and louder, "you're taking the wrong turn! – YOU'RE TAKING THE WRONG BLOODY TURN, MAN." Keith is a big bloke over six foot tall; shouting down my lug holes in that situation was not good for my peace of mind. If I didn't have two hands on the wheel, I swear I would have put one on his chin, Janet not helping by repeating behind me, can I be of any help, boys? "NO."

The campsite was delightful, nicely laid out plots, a swimming pool as standard and toilet/shower facilities of a high standard, meticulously cleaned throughout the day. Throughout our travels in Europe, I was constantly surprised by the superior quality compared to English campsites. Pull onto a campsite in England your charged top bat, pointed to a piece of grass and the concrete shower and toilet block over there. Freezing cold floor. With dull cheap tiles. Sometimes you're even charged extra for the shower, and they think they are doing you a favour. Pulling onto one camping and caravanning site on Cannock chase, the warden said, "sorry, we've got no pitches available."

Puzzled, I said, "what about there?" pointing to an empty field.

"Oh no, you can't park there, it's on a slope, and you will sink into the ground." Well, why don't you put more gravel hard standing down then? And these are charity run?

Here, in Europe, it's a whole different ball game. With my ACSI discount card, we were paying less than half price. The more time I spend in Europe, the more time I want to spend in Europe. Yes, England was just for short breaks. Settling into the camp for the first day, we purchased tickets and set off the next day for Venice itself. The bus stop was across the road and directly opposite the campsite. The bus took us directly to within a short walking distance of the canals. Venice is small, compact, romantic, and historic. The canals, the gondolas, and colourful buildings. It was all an assault on our senses, the Doge's Palace, Rialto Bridge and The Bridge of Sighs. We had decided to just walk along at random first walking into the heart of the city, St Mark's square. From there, we set off at random, exploring the city. The bridge of sighs so-called because it was the city's last view as prisoners were sent away.

The Rialto Bridge was awe-inspiring and swarming with people, all posing and taking selfies. We were happy to join them. The views from the bridge were equally amazing. Young courting couples had put small padlocks along the length of the bridge with signatures swearing their undying love for each other. There were hundreds of them; they must have weighed tons. The council eventually had to remove them from the bridge due to the potential damage and maybe the bridge's collapse. All those lost lockets dumped or sold for scrap. The expressions of love lost to eternity. There are many must-sees and things to do in Venice, including a Gondola ride; we gave that a miss. Another was a canal-side meal, but when we just asked if we could enjoy a can of coke, the waiters started panicking, "no, no, no, sorry." Oh no, they wanted the eaters, the big spenders. Taking up a ringside seat for a can of coke was not on. I could understand.

At one Gondola park, I heard a local explaining to a couple of tourists how the Gondolas were made. I was mesmerised listening to him. I just thought a boat was a boat. Whether it be a rowing boat or a powered boat. But a Gondola is completely different and built differently. A Gondola is built at a curve, like a banana. This enables the gondolier to keep the boat going in a straight line whilst rowing the boat in the manner he did. Who thought of that, I wondered? How long ago? What kind of brain, and for how long did it take for the man, or men, to think of, then design it? A marvellous piece of engineering.

We were happy with a sandwich or a baguette as we went along, maybe a couple of ice creams. The only little disappointing experience was the knowledge that so many traders were on the rip-off: the restaurants, even the ice-cream sellers. More than once, a seller first mentioned four euros, even five, before dropping down to two-fifty. A joke. But it wasn't a joke. After a busy day, weary, we would set off back to the campsite, sated and satisfied. We would either have a meal in the very nice clean restaurant on the campsite or maybe even a barbeque. We would often eat out. Without a doubt, we found the campsite restaurants very clean and reasonably priced. The owners knew they had to compete with surrounding eateries. Again, a lesson the English campsites could take on board. If they even bothered. A decent meal on a campsite can be had for as little as six or seven euros, a pizza, two or three euros.

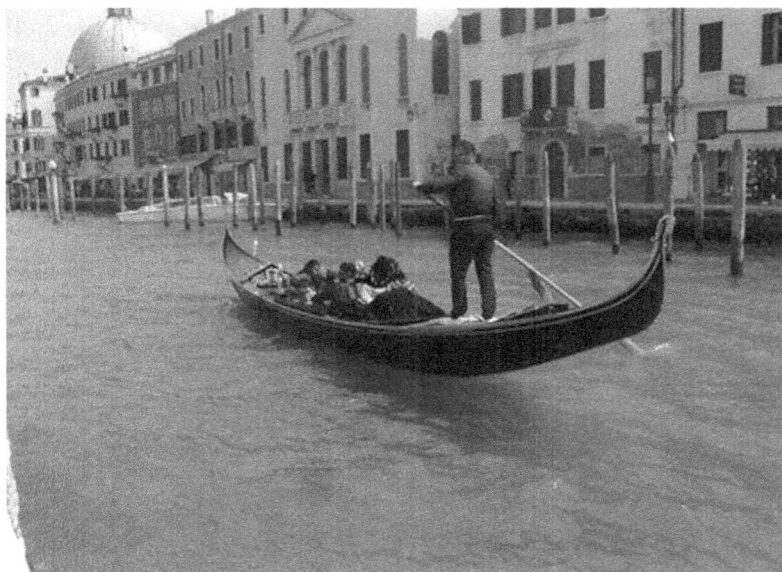

After four days on the campsite and touring Venice. It was time for Keith and Janet to head home. We had had a wonderful time and, surprisingly, retained our friendship after being in such close proximity for such a long period. Thoughtfully, they insisted on getting a taxi to Marco Polo airport rather than me having to go through the hassle. Spending the remainder of the day on the campsite, my plan was to set off the next day. East over to Slovenia, then Croatia turning south into Bosnia, Serbia, Montenegro to Albania before crossing over the mountain border and into Greece. My first stop was Trieste, the furthermost city in Italy. Trieste itself was a very strategic seaport during WWII. And the city was in itself beautiful with its majestic buildings, a big banner in the windows of one major building overlooking the square, begging the Americans to please come back and rescue them.

Trieste was just a short drive to the Slovenian and Croatian borders. I found a parking spot right on the harbour front right next to a couple of other camper vans to my deep pleasure and satisfaction. Obviously, a blind eye was deliberately turned to this habit, brilliant. After a very enjoyable walk around the town, I found a nice restaurant not far from the harbour. After a pleasant meal, I headed back to my van, enjoyed a nice bottle of wine whilst overlooking the sea and people watching. After a night's sleep, I set off for first Slovenia, then into Croatia.

CHAPTER 43.

SLOVENIA, CROATIA, DOWN TO GREECE

The first country I hit just a few miles from Trieste was Slovenia. Slovenia was famous for its lakes, and I was determined to visit the Plitvice lakes and their many waterfalls. Just inside the Slovenian border, I hit the small town of Zadar. Within minutes I found an Aire, with free camping spots just off the main road, within walking distance of shops and restaurants. Parking up amongst a dozen or so other motorhomes, I set off for the short stroll around the town to get my bearings. The town was pleasant and modern. Finding a small restaurant, I walked in, booked a table, and ordered a simple meal. I just wanted something hot and simple, too tired to cook.

The one great bonus that I thoroughly loved was the freedom of driving around Europe with its no borders. Although I voted for Brexit, I liked the principle of the open, European market. I just did not like the idea of a dictatorship, having our laws and our lives dictated to by faceless bureaucrats in Brussels. But to drive from one European country to another, brilliant. After a decent night's sleep on a full belly, I set off over to the lakes. It was quiet and uncrowded, with only a few people walking around. Paying my fee of a few euros, I was directed down to the lakes where we caught a small boat over to the island and the lakes proper. There were numerous walks from the steady amble consisting of about four miles along a level easy route, to the mountainous route taking you to the top of the falls across and down, maybe of some ten miles. Not wishing to bring on a heart attack, I went for the easy route.

The Plitvice lakes were beautiful and inspiring, waterfalls in abundance. The walks, all marked with coloured markers of different colours for different routes, each easy to follow. Often, I would just sit and soak up the atmosphere whilst watching and listening to the falls. After about four hours, I reached the pick-up terminus by a little café. From here, the small bus took us down to the entrance, from there a short walk back to the Aire, and another night of camping up. The next day I set off for Croatia and Zagreb. My plan was simple and two-fold. I wanted some dental treatment. In England, the prices were disgraceful for what is really an essential need. I had found a clinic over the Hilton hotel that sounded first class. I'd tried Bulgaria, but they didn't fill me with confidence; plus, like Morocco, they were starting to get greedy with the tourists.

I had made a tentative appointment, intending to confirm the exact date once I reached Croatia. Once over the border and approaching Zagreb, I text to say where I was, making an appointment for the next day. There was only one campsite in Zagreb, so I made my way to it. The surroundings of it were not that salubrious. The campsite was in my ACSI book, but parking up and calling into the office, they informed me, with a smirk, that yes, whilst they were in ACSI, they were not now. Hence, it was normal fees, only thirty euros for the night. "Thirty euros?"

"Yes, we are the only campsite in Zagreb."

Ahhh, so that's it, they think they had me over a barrel, well f**k you. Off out I drove. I did consider parking up outside, but it didn't look too healthy to me, so I set off towards the dental clinic.

Driving up and down the main route leading to and alongside the clinic, I eventually found a car park set back from the road and behind some offices. Pulling in, I found a nice little pitch next to a kiddie play park. From there, I walked around to the main road and caught one of the famous trams down to the dentist. Getting the lift up from the hotel, I went in and booked my appointment for two days' time. Arriving back at the car park, I was pleased to find that after six pm, the place was almost empty. Most of them had been there for the offices and workshops, very nice. Finding a local pub, I sat down for a drink, internet included, I was in my oil tot. The next day, with time to kill, I decided to visit the famous Lake Bled in Croatia.

The Lake Bled was famous and a designated world status UNESCO heritage site. Finding somewhere to park up, I walked down to the lakes, which were quite busy, unlike the Plitvice lakes. In the middle of the lakes was the famous church, and a steady stream of boats berthed up beside the lake, taking groups of us at a time over to the church. You could see by the eagerness on the rower's faces how keen they were to make money, counting our bodies as we got on board. Engines were not allowed because of its heritage site, so it was all rowing to get us over. The rowers all had muscles like Popeye.

I never gave any thought to the church or its position. Well, a church is a church. It was only once I got over to it, I saw the problem. It had a million steps leading up to it. Why so many steps? I had no choice. I was stuck on the island; I just had to bite the bullet. It wasn't as bad as I thought. I got to the top without suffering a heart attack; looking at some of the others, I doubted if they all were going to escape that fate.

The church itself was beautiful and well worth the visit. The outside views were also well worth the visit. Sitting down at one of the many tables outside the café sipping on a coffee, I had an hour or so to savour before getting the boat back to shore and back to my motorhome. The next day I got the tram down to the dentist, who, after inspecting my mouth, gave me a price for the work needed. I was pleased, a great difference to rip-off English prices. It was agreed that I would fix the next appointment on one of my numerous future trips. I set off the next morning from Croatia from my nice little pitch in the car park planting it in my memory for the next visit. From Croatia, I set off into Serbia, my plan being to drive into Serbia, then into Bosnia, Montenegro, then Albania and on into Greece across the mountains.

The countries of Croatia, Bosnia and Serbia had once been one country called Yugoslavia. After the Bosnian Croatian wars of the late 80s and 90s, characterised by bitter fighting, ethnic cleansing, and systematic rape, mainly perpetrated by the Serbs, the countries were split up. Ignorant as I was, whilst I had been aware of the fighting, it wasn't much of my concern. Worse, the map book I had was old, so I was still referring to it as Yugoslavia. My first impression of Serbia was it was a very third world. The contrast between Serbia and Croatia was stark. The people in Croatia were civilised, normal Europeans. We spoke on a level footing. You could feel an air of prosperity and growth. Serbia? People sat in groups, muttering, sour faces, shifty and sulky looking. You could sense an air of distrust wherever you went. Pulling up outside a café, I was met with sullen stares. I decided to drive on.

Pulling into a bigger, busier town, I was struck by how stuck in time it was. The lorries and tractors were from the fifties and belched smoke all over the shop. There was no such thing as zebra crossings. If you wanted to cross the road, you took your life into your hands, yet there was something almost nostalgic about it; it was like a town in the wild west. Maybe how England could have been in the forties. I don't think there was any road covering, tarmac, concrete, or cobbles. The road just seemed a dust track with lorries kicking it up as they drove through. Spotting a café, I parked my motorhome up and headed for it. I felt an air of utter disinterest. No one looked at me with curiosity. Reaching the café, I hit obstacle number one. No one spoke a word of English. Everyone could understand coffee, so ordering a coffee, I sat outside watching the life going by and going on. It was interesting.

But my next goal was to sample a bit of the Serbian cuisine, sit, eat a local meal, sip on my coffee, and soak up the atmosphere. Into the café I go, no one could understand me. I did the little fingers into my mouth bit, still no understanding. In the end, I saw a picture of something on a menu card, which I don't know, but it looked like local food. The girl took my order, and after a few minutes, she brought it out to me on the veranda with a few chunks of bread. What was it? It looked like a scrawny misshaped sausage stuck on top of something, but what? It wasn't potato because it had some colour to it. Maybe swede, I took a few tentative bites of god knows what. It was tasteless and disgusting. I looked at the sausage and conjured up all kinds of things. Even in England, there's the fear of getting your burger or sausage made up of a dog or cat. What would they serve in this country?

After a few attempts, I decided to give up. I was brought up on good healthy food. Eating crap was not in my mindset. I decided I had had enough of the town of Serbia and headed out and over to Bosnia. A few miles from the Bosnian border, I saw the sign for a campsite. Following the signs led me along a narrow winding lane to the top of a mountain and a farm. The lady came out telling me yes, they ran a campsite, had internet, and charged ten euros a night. Directing me in, I found a suitable spot, after a bit because the options were many. The pitch and the views were amazing, looking for miles in any direction. The owners had obviously got it well set up with a running mill wheel, waterfall, and barbeque, to the side, and an undercover eating area, with benches and tables, very rustic and welcoming.

This was low season, but the appeal of the place would be obvious. The female owner came over to me and asked if I was ok. Bringing my camera out, I asked to take her photo. This is where she got all coy, "no, no, I will come back," she said. And so she did, a few minutes later, obviously dolling herself up for the camera. She was a little darling and very attractive. Even better, she was flirting outrageously, telling me she was sixty and asking how old I was. Blind as a bat, I ignored the signals thinking, 'no, This ain't possible. I'm on a farm, and her family is just a bit further up the field.' It was a mistake I regretted for some time. After topping up, I sat back on top of that mountain, enjoying the views and the ambience using the internet. I was the only camper up there. It was fantastic. The next day I set off the few short miles to the Bosnian border.

CHAPTER 44.

BOSNIA.

On reaching the Bosnian border, I experienced yet another different attitude to Croatia, even Serbia. Christ, even the border guard couldn't hide his dislike, contempt even. Maybe it's me, maybe I'm a bit sensitive,

"Where are your documents?" he demanded. Passing him my documents straight away, he pointed out that I wasn't insured for Bosnia. Obviously, it is outside the European Union. Ok, no problem, I'll do a U-turn back into Serbia, then down into Montenegro. With a surly growl, he handed me my documents back, minus my passport. "I will hold this. You go over there," he said, pointing to another office fifteen yards away.

Reaching the office, an equally sullen attendant, this time a woman, demanded ten pounds and printed out and handed me ten days insurance cover. "But I am only driving through," I said, while thinking to myself, 'I don't want to see your f*****g country!'

"It is minimum," she said.

Grabbing the printout, I headed back to the passport office. The guard hadn't cheered up. Checking the insurance cover, he handed me my passport and waved me off. This seemed like a scam to me, but ok. Getting back into my motorhome, looking at the surrounding shops, houses and sullen people shuffling about, I decided to get through Bosnia as quickly as possible.

Being a layman, my ignorance of politics is right up there with the second coming of Christ. But many things in life puzzle me. Politicians, to me, mean well, I know and believe. The father of my good friend Colin Lawler was Wallace Lawler, the MP. He was a true gent and had integrity. Further, I knew first-hand that he fought for a better condition for his constituents living in Birmingham's deprived areas. But in the main, any, and all politicians looked after themselves, number one. You always hear of politicians of bent countries, backward countries lining their pockets, never the British. But how many politicians live in a council house.

Croatia looked and felt like a prosperous and ambitious country. Yet, right next door, Bosnia and Serbia looked like right s**tholes, its people walking about with sullen faces. Africa is far bigger than America. 100s of 1000s of Europeans struggled and fought to get there over the last three hundred years, then by wagon train or whatsoever, they headed out and spread across the country. Now it is the most powerful country in the world, well, it was before Trump got in, but Africa? It's split up into about fifty countries, each with its own king, its own president, each taking backhanders and living in palaces, whilst its people live in mud huts. Yet surely Africa is far richer than America in minerals and agriculture.

Driving through Bosnia, I wasn't passing through anywhere that made me feel that I wanted to stop. I passed through village after village, similar in many respects to what I had witnessed in Serbia. Each small village or town was surrounded by countryside, each house set in plots of some half to one acre. Obviously, I assumed this was by some government decree to enable each householder to grow his own crops. Sure enough, each householder had got pieces of their land set aside for various and different crops. Some were split into three or four different sections with different crops, quite a few with a cow or a goat, in a cut off section. I guessed the idea of much of this would be to run it as a cooperative and share it with a neighbour—socialism at its best. If I did stop, just to ask for directions, the small groups of people seemed friendly and amicable. Unable to speak Bosnian at all, and with them unable to speak English, I would shout the name of a major city, pointing ahead of me. They would smile and confirm by pointing ahead. Some even shouted out, "Brexit, Brexit." So from then on, in many countries, with many people, I would confirm where I was from by shouting Brexit.

Driving into the nearest big town, I found somewhere to park up for the night. Having a walk around, I found a café and walked over for a coffee. Sitting down, I steadily took in street life and scenery. I saw and felt something but couldn't quite put my finger on it. The streets were tidy and clean, a lot of the buildings fairly new and modern, but what was it? I was heading for a bank to get some euros out. Letting myself in, I waited in line till I could speak to someone who could speak English. Shortly, I was directed to a smart and pretty looking girl in a side office. Approaching her desk, I then commented on how pretty I found her town, then I put my foot in it, "I noticed there are no Asians or Muslims in your country?"

With what seemed like sadness in her voice but no irony, she murmured, "no." Maybe that was a mistake. Feeling I had touched on something sensitive; I kept my mouth shut. Taking my money, it only occurred to me when I had got out and back to my motorhome, the truth hit me. Just a few short years ago, the Bosnian wars were all about ethnic cleansing. They had wiped out 1,000s of Muslim minorities, and she would have it fresh in her memory. Whoops.

My next country to enter with a border was Montenegro. The very name Montenegro conjured up romantic images to me of some far-flung Caribbean hideaway. Yet, Montenegro was a small country only formed in about 2006 on the Adriatic Sea. It was famous for its beautiful beaches, pink flamingos, and salt mines, at one stage being the biggest salt producer in the Mediterranean. Pulling into customs, I was again reminded that I was not insured to drive in Montenegro. Oh, right. But for fifteen quid, they would supply me with a ten-day cover note. I paid up, this time thinking to spend a few days.

Within about ten minutes of leaving the border and five miles into the country, I was pulled in by a single cop on the side of the road.

"Hello, can I see your documents, please?" He asked.

Bringing out my new insurance, driving licence etc., I passed them to him. There was something funny here. He didn't seem right. He was looking at me with a smile. Looking back at my documents, he said, "it is ok, no problem. But did you know you were speeding?" Well, I didn't, and I hadn't seen any speed limit signs, and the only gun he had on him was in his holster. He had clocked something on one of my documents that clearly made him sit back.

I gave him a big smile, "but officer, I was not speeding."

He carried on, "but normally, this is a one hundred euro fine." With a quizzical look on his face, I sussed it. He was trying to figure me out. Now I gave him a bigger, knowing smile. He's looking for a bribe. "It is ok, there is no problem, will ten euros be acceptable?" I had to smile at his naivety. He was quite young and fairly new to it. I bunged him a ten euro note, he gave me my documents back and off I went, his thanks ringing in my lughole. Well, at least crooked as he was, you know where you stand. You can be doing five mph over the limit on a straight clear country road with no traffic in England, and you get walloped for sixty quid and an endorsement.

My next stop was Kotor, a very nice seaside resort and coastal town. Kotor was a beautiful town. Like many other seaside towns I visited along the coastline towards Albania, and worthy of another, longer visit in the future. Finding a quiet place, I parked up and had a meander around the town, stopping for a meal in one of its many restaurants. Having a coffee, then driving on the next day. No wonder Montenegro was such a favourite holiday destination. It was like a beautiful jewel locked in between a group of ugly rocks on all sides.

After a pleasant short stay in Montenegro, I then set off to Albania's border, again, another bit of a culture shock. Here the guards like the Serbs and Bosnians were surly, miserable, and resentful. Checking my documents, he snapped, "you are not insured for Albania."

"Ok, shall I go back?"

"No, you must pay. Go over there, and I will hold passport."

Going over to the office he directed me to, I was asked for fifty euros. "Fifty euros," I spit out, "I've paid ten euros in Bosnia. I'm only passing through your beautiful country. I will be out of it within one day."

It made no difference, "fifty euros, you pay." I paid.

The nearest city to the border was Tirana, so I decided to head for it. I was debating whether to spend a couple of days to try and get my fifty quid's worth. I was still debating as

I pulled into Tirana. It was a Saturday and market day. The place was buzzing, and I was determined to soak up some of the atmosphere. Doing a quick turnaround in the centre square, I spotted a space and pulled in quick. Seeing a local traffic cop, I gestured if I was ok parking there. He nodded back. Albania was interesting, to say the least, and Tirana was amazing. Finding a café, I sat back to savour and soak up the atmosphere, the ambience. For some reason, all I felt was corruption. It hung in the atmosphere, what the average wage was, I don't know, but I was watching new and flash Mercedes passing back and forth. Then I saw a motorbike pushing a two-wheel cart. The male driver on the bike, his son or wife on the back, clinging on for dear life. Four or five family members in the cart on the front, heads above the sides staring around as they drove. I was mesmerised. It was an even bigger contrast than Morocco.

I guessed, like Morocco, these were peasant farmers bringing their wares down to the market to sell. Just like Morocco, no airs, and graces. Walking around, I saw stalls laid out with fruit and veg. If not stalls, the market seller would throw a tarpaulin sheet on the ground and throw his wares on it. On one was a catch of massive tuna fish. The trader would cut off chunks as you wanted it. I was fascinated and lapping it up.

After a good few hours, I debated spending the night but wondered if I would be safe in the town centre. Heading out and over the mountains, I headed for Greece. Just outside the city of Tirana, I pulled into a roadside café with its large car park. Walking in and grabbing the menu, I ordered a Fanta orange and a spaghetti Bolognese. Well, you can't go wrong with that, can you? After he had taken my order, which cost about three euros, I then asked if I could park up for the night in his car park. He nodded, yes, but suggested I bring my motorhome up closer to the café building. I didn't have to query why. Bringing my Spaghetti Bolognese out, I stared, trying to figure it out. The spaghetti was easy to make out, but the rest I don't know. It was dotted with small pieces of pink meat, maybe ham, it tasted nothing like Spaghetti Bolognese. Oh well, it was a meal, and for three euros including a camping spot, I wasn't going to argue.

CHAPTER 45.

After a good night's sleep in a quiet car park, I set off the few short miles over the famous Pindus mountains between Albania and Greece. The drive was interesting, amazing, and breath-taking in equal measure. Within three miles of leaving the café, the road disappeared. One minute I was on a tarmac road; the next, it became a dirt track. It wasn't even level, potholes all over the shop. Old lorries or brand-new Mercedes cars trundling along without a care. It reminded me of our first taxi ride in Bulgaria.

Climbing steadily up into the mountains, the views were fantastic. The difficulty I was finding is where do I stop off? There were just so many beautiful, interesting places along my route. France? Italy? Each country was a revelation. Sometimes, I felt a minor twinge of anger that I had been conned for so many years by people who had said, "oh, England is beautiful, it's the best country in the world for architecture, villages, mountains, countryside." Yes, there are some beautiful places, but there are many places around Europe equally if not more beautiful and interesting.

I had not spent much time in any of the countries I was passing through after Italy. My main aim was to get a feel for the country. Have a brief look around and mentally note it, with the intention of having a more detailed visit at a later date. Bosnia and Herzegovina, I was not too impressed with at all. Nor Serbia, really. Montenegro was well worth another visit. As was Albania. France was growing on me all the time. But other countries are equally as fascinating or have something to offer, especially if you're in a motorhome.

Here up in the Pindus mountains, it was like being in a different world. I had been in a few forests, been up a few mountains, but nothing like this. I had visions of America, Canada, even Brazil with its rainforests, and it felt like that here. With the poor roads, it felt like I was the only one on earth. The views, the quietness, it went on for mile upon mile. Initially, I was very tempted to find somewhere to park up for the night. Fascinating and tempting as the thought was, to be tucked into a little forest clearing on the top of the mountains, eating a simple meal while sitting around a little log fire was the stuff of dreams and something, I dearly loved doing. But I felt I had to get on and over to Greece.

Where I was, I don't know. I had no sat-nav, my only knowledge of where I was transpired from my phone, which kept disappearing due to no signal. But eventually, still within the mountain range, I came to a crossroads—a narrow mountain road with a signpost pointing to Filiates to the left, Igoumenitsa to the right. I had no knowledge except that the sea must be to the right. Then it went dark very quickly. The sky became overcast and opened up very quickly. It was terrifying and fascinating both at the same time. I dived in for cover as quickly as I could. The sky opened up, and the thunder and lightning came out with a vengeance. So powerful my van shook. I wondered how high up in the sky I could be. It felt like I was in gods back garden, never had I heard thunder so powerful.

It must have been terrifying to any of the locals to hear such loud noises in years gone by. This went on for about an hour when, as quickly as it began, it stopped. The rain stopped, the clouds disappeared, and the miracle of miracles, the sun came out. The drive downhill along the winding, meandering road was steady, passing small hamlets and villages tucked away into the mountains and forests. I spotted a couple of elderly folks in traditional garb tending their garden after the storm. A little café was almost hidden away with a small group, sitting outside, chatting over cups of black coffee. I kept thinking to stop, slamming my brakes on before realising I was too far past. Ok, I'll stop at the next one, then I made the same mistake again.

I was desperate to stop off, say hello, have a coffee or a Fanta. Eventually, I came to a little village. Seeing a café and pulling in, I walked across and ordered a Fanta orange. It was a lovely feeling. I wondered what these people did all day. How did they survive out here in the mountains? You couldn't grow anything. But then I started coming to the conclusion that some of these people, like in Serbia, Bosnia, like in Morocco, lived on very little money. Finishing my Fanta, I got into my motorhome and carried on down the hill.

It was difficult to judge how high the actual mountain was that I was descending. Stand at the bottom of mount Snowdonia, and it's a straight-up view; here, it's gradual. From the top of the mountain where I had been, the road down to Igoumenitsa was some ten-fifteen miles. Personally, I felt I was climbing out of the clouds. Eventually, the road started to open up into industrial estates, factories, shops, even an Aldi store. Back among the civilised, I soon hit the town and seafront of Igoumenitsa. It took me quite some time to find somewhere to park before getting into a good-sized car park next to the seafront. Hearing that the Greeks were quite lenient with camper vans, I decided to see how I would get on. I was directly in the centre of the town. With a café across the road, I went and ordered a coffee while I got my bearings and a feel for the town. I was in a very visible position in the car park, so if I wasn't welcome, I was sure someone would soon tell me, no one did. I had a very pleasant three days there.

Igoumenitsa was a beautiful little town and a busy little resort, but in the main not for the tourists. This was a Greek town catering for the Greeks, with the odd group of tourists welcomed and tolerated. The Greek church was directly in the centre of the town on the seafront. At night and weekends, it was the social hub of the town, with young children and adults socialising within the grounds as well as going inside for prayers. Set back from the first line, the town was set out into little squares with romantic little cafes and bars. Venturing out at night, I enjoyed sitting back at a café table amongst the locals and having a black Greek coffee and or a meal. It was a delight to watch the locals enjoying their free time as families with their children. Like the Spanish, the Greeks were very family orientated. They were also very religious. Whilst I am not, I do respect other people's beliefs. I don't think anyone could speak English, even the shopkeepers. That in itself was unusual and an indication of how few English visited here.

After a few days, I decided to head off to the beach that I had passed on my way down the mountain. I had seen the sign for the campsite which was next to a beautiful long sandy beach. A couple of motorhomes were on the beach, but I needed to empty my cassettes and top-up with water. Calling into the site, the owner came across. Showing him my ACSI card, he said, "no, no. How long you going to stay? I will do you better price than that." That was music to my lugs. Inside he showed me to a pitch, right by the beachfront. It was magical.

My intention was to have maybe a month on the site, and the owner agreed that he would only charge me 100 euros a week. I was up for that. But the toilets and showers were dire. I had debated having a couple of days on the site then head over to the beach, but his fees were that reasonable, it didn't make sense. There were periods of thunderstorms and showers at regular intervals, each centred on and around the mountains. After a few days, I was determined to have some more of it, so leaving my passport with the owner, which cheered him up, I set off back up into the mountains. Reaching a small village, I saw a couple of shops, a store, and a restaurant. Pulling into a nearby layby, I called over to the restaurant that was just closing up.

Not speaking a word of Greek and them not speaking a word of English, I eventually got the message that they would be open that night. Sorted. Walking across the road to the local store, I ordered a couple of cans of lager, a bottle of vodka and a carton of orange. Heading back to the van, I settled down and waited for the restaurant to open.

After a respectable period, I headed off on my little walk into the restaurant. It was small and cosy. Heading for the counter, I looked across to see the owner working away. To the one side wall was a griddle with a spit spreading from one side to the other, about six-foot-long. On the spit and spread out were six whole chickens. Not able to understand a word of what either one was saying, I went for the easy option and pointed to the chicken. I don't know if he did anything else, there was only one other young couple in the bar, and they went for the chicken also, so I guessed that was it for the night at least. Ordering a beer, I went and sat down and waited. Before too long, his wife came across with half a cooked chicken and chips on a plate with a thick cut chunk of bread and placed it down on the table in front of me. It was a delightful experience, and even on my own, I enjoyed and savoured every minute. The meal was cheap, the atmosphere friendly and relaxed, and after a couple of hours, I set off, just as the sky opened up and the thunder and lightning started.

I hadn't locked the van up here in the mountains. Getting in, I left the door wide open, opened the side windows, poured myself a large vodka and orange and sat back to enjoy the fireworks. It was awe-inspiring and brilliant. Lightning bolts shot down all over the place, the rumble of the thunder rolling right on top of my head. Following a beautiful chicken dinner, I couldn't wish for a better end to the night. I was in my oil tot. The next day, sated, I headed back down the mountain to the campsite. Before reaching the campsite, I had a drive back into town and along to the major port. After inquiring about the price, I booked a return ticket to Corfu, a small island resort a couple of miles offshore.

Corfu is a small island off the west coast of Greece, about 39 miles long by 17 miles wide. Its coastline is 135 miles long. It took me just over an hour to reach it from Igoumenitsa. My first destination was Corfu itself. What a disappointment that was. It looked a right dive, broken down veranda's, shops and houses in dire need of repair. I know it is out of season, but everything looked abandoned and desolate. Where were all the locals? To my understanding, Corfu was notorious as a wild 18 to 30s holiday destination. Maybe this was its problem. With a reputation like that, no one would want to visit it at any other time.

I had a steady drive around the island, spending a night in one resort where I met a few English people. Driving along one beachfront road to the west, I saw an English flag outside a restaurant bar. Pulling alongside, I ordered a drink and asked if I would be alright parked up outside. On being told that there wouldn't be a problem, I ordered a meal and another lager, that was it. I was in for the night.

The owner was an English lady who had bought the place with her son, both of them running it together. The lady kept dropping hints that she was on the hunt for a nice man but was not having much success. For a quick few seconds, my ears pricked up. She was in my age bracket alright, but she was a ginger nut, there are redheads, and there are ginger nuts. Both can be beautiful, redheads can certainly be beautiful, but ginger nuts just don't do it for me in a lot of cases. After a nice few beers, I had a quiet night alone.

The next day, I drove further along the west coast when I spotted a lovely secluded little cove. Pulling in, I parked up on the beach next to a small rowing fishing boat. Next to that were a shower and a freshwater tap. What more could I ask for? Opposite and spaced apart were a few restaurants. Calling across, I asked if they would be open. The second one I called into asked what I might be requesting. When I said, "well, definitely mussels for starters," he replied, "oh, no problem, we always keep mussels in." that was it. I was over there for seven pm.

The dining area overlooked the cove and my motorhome, sitting next to the little rowing boat. I was in my oil tot. A more scenic picture I could never wish for. When my order of fresh mussels came along, with a few chunks of fresh bread, that was it—a lovely night. The next day after a peaceful night's sleep with my door wide open, listening to the waves gently lapping the shore, I set off for the steady drive back to the port and the ferry back to Igoumenitsa.

CHAPTER 46.

BACK TO ITALY AND VENICE.

Arriving back at the campsite, I spent the remainder of the month topping up my tan and lazing on the beach. A few pitches away from me was an English couple, enjoying a few weeks touring. They admitted that they spent a few days off and a couple of days on a site, which I thought was quite sensible. I had told them that I intended to spend a further few days outside of the port and on the quayside before moving and asked if they might wish to join me. The campsite was great for its position if nothing else. But I wanted to spend a night on the beach further up, which I did, then a few nights next to the port near the town centre.

Pulling up at the quayside, it was obviously a known spot for motorhomers passing through. It is either just to spend a few days enjoying the local amenities or before and after getting the local ferries. I was not bothered at all by the local police or locals.

It was a busy little waystation with all sorts pulling in for a day or two. One day a very colourful camper pulled up with a Chinese couple onboard. They were very friendly and open to telling me they were partway through their trip, travelling all the way from China. It sounded amazing, a bit daunting to me, I thought, but fair play to them. The German in front of me saw the opportunity to liven the atmosphere up, brought out his little Wurlitzer wind-up organ, and started playing tunes on it. The Chinese, delighted, started dancing. It turned into a right little party with a little crowd gathering around for a couple of hours. I suppose it was a reflection of life, really. You could go for days in pleasant quietness, then all of a sudden, a party atmosphere can spring up spontaneously. It was something I had grown up with, nothing planned just a spur of the moment thing.

I then got a phone call from my granddaughter Sammy. She had got a week's holiday coming up and thought she might join me. This was a regular thing and something I took great pleasure in. it might be just a few days in Barmouth where my daughter and grandkids might join me. My daughter Louise might fly over somewhere for a short break. It provided a great opportunity for them to have a short holiday for little or no money.

There was no airport near Igoumenitsa except for Corfu. As that was a no go, I told Sammy I would ring her back within the next twenty-four hours. Going up to the port, I was quoted 150 quid for a one-way ticket to Venice. This was a no brainer really, it cut out the long and arduous drive back on myself but also the cost of fuel driving there.

Booking my ticket for two days, I pulled up at the ferry port and waited to be called. Driving onto the ferry and showing my ticket, the ferry staff were busy mumbling to themselves, looking from the ticket to my motorhome. I knew what it was. The independent ticket seller had given a shorter length for my motorhome. I had queried the price difference he had quoted me, so he simply gave me a lower price for a shorter length. Out of sight, he wouldn't care if I got to the ferry and was then charged more. Thankfully, it was quiet, and the ferry staff were not too bothered. They waved me on board. Well, it wasn't my fault, was it.

I set off on the ferry, which sailed up the Adriatic Sea overnight. Passing Albania, Montenegro, Bosnia, and Croatia to the starboard side. Reaching Venice the next morning, I had a day to kill before meeting Sammy at Marco polo airport. It had cost Sammy sixty quid for a return ticket which we both felt was a bargain. She didn't drink, she didn't cost me a fortune in food, and she had a wonderful week. After a little tour of the local area, I had booked into the same campsite I had spent with Janet and Keith a few weeks earlier. Now being familiar with the area and the scene, made for a whole lot easier break. We spent a pleasant two-day touring Venice, which I think was a new delight for Sammy, for me a tad boring. I'd done it before.

On the third day, we were both ready for some sun. Walking down to the local beach, we came to a row of four-star hotels along the seafront. Walking in as bold as brass our towels under the arm, we walked into the hotel. We joined the others around the pool, quickly sinking into the local surroundings, making ourselves invisible. We were just two amongst dozens of people, and I knew our faces would just blur into the crowd. Many people enjoy swimming in the sea, lying on the beach, getting sand into every orifice. I didn't, and I don't think Sammy did either at least I never heard any dissent from her.

The site fees, with ACSI, were circa 14 euros a night, less than £100 for the week, we could have wild camped, but we would never have the convenience that we had on this very nice site and so near to Venice. Although Sammy had her own money, I gave her fifty pounds spending money for any treats she wanted for herself. If she spent any, I never saw it. When it came to food and eating, I've always eaten very simply. I believe in eating to live, not living to eat. Some people go on and on about food. "I must have a McDonald's burger," "I must have a pizza," crikey, has anyone ever tried eating a cold burger. Others see it as the must-have, the norm, to eat out in fancy restaurants, fine, I don't mind a nice meal, but I'm not paying through the nose for the privilege. Waking up, Sammy would maybe make herself a couple of slices of toast. If I were in the mood, I might have a couple of slices of marmalade on toast—plenty enough. I rarely ate during the day. Out on the touring trail, we might have a snack as we walked along. Most nights, we would eat out at some restaurant or even in the camp restaurant, which we found very reasonable. All in all, I don't think I spent more than 200 quid, including the site fees, and we had everything we wanted.

After an enjoyable week, I took Sammy back to Marco polo airport. I think she had had a good week. I certainly enjoyed her company, my only regret being that she came alone. I would not be the best of company for such a young girl. She could have done so much more; she could have enjoyed the nightlife in Venice instead of being stuck with me on a campsite. But ay, she had a nice week's holiday for very little money.

CHAPTER 47.

HEADING HOME

Having seen Sammy safely off at Venice airport, I decided to make my way back home. It was some 1000 miles to home in a fairly straight line to Calais. Across the ferry, then home. It would take me some four to five days of steady driving, stopping off as and when it suited to admire any particular town or village. I was becoming more aware of how many medieval towns or villages there were in France. My growing aim was to see more and more of them. On my travels, I had passed through, stopped at, or visited eight countries, from France, across to Italy, round into Slovenia, Croatia and down to Greece. Then back to Italy. The tour had been thoroughly enjoyable, informative, and exciting. It had also been, surprisingly, a lot cheaper than I had imagined or thought.

I didn't set out to travel and live cheaply, but as I undertook each journey, I couldn't help but notice how little I was spending. I am in a fortunate position. Many people who buy motorhomes are pensioners. The biggest expense is the motorhome itself, but once purchased, the only real cost is the fuel, day-to-day running costs, and maintenance. Most people own a car. To me, with a motorhome, you get out of the driver's seat and into your lounge or bed. To compromise, many people will buy a small transit type motorhome with a pop-up roof, using it as a means of ordinary transport and a travelling home on wheels.

Not for me, I'm afraid, at eighteen —twenty maybe, at my age, no, thank you. I like my comforts; I like to stand up or sit down as I please. I had seen fellow campers on sites, cramped up to a table playing cards waiting for sleepy time. Or having to sit outside, huddled under overcoats for a breath of fresh air. No, we chose sensibly in the size we chose. My only minor misgiving was that we could have more or less got what we wanted for less than half the price. Motorhomes are not like cars; they are looked after and with far fewer miles on the clock.

The drive home was steady and uneventful, I tried toll roads once or twice, but the problem with toll roads is you miss out on all the scenery. Worse, I find toll roads a pain in the backside. Those toll booths come along very quickly. Out you get, cash or card, the prices seem to vary all over the shop. My aim is to avoid them as much as possible.

It was a delight to get home, walk into my own lounge, see familiar things as I had left them. I lived in a pleasant part of the country, on a road, I feel comfortable locking up and forgetting. It was low maintenance and fairly easy to keep clean. It was now coming up to the full summer. Time to think about short breaks around England, but first to take stock.

I had covered in total some 2700 miles from start to finish. At some twenty mpg, it had cost me just short of seven hundred pounds in fuel. Two hundred and fifty pounds for the ferry. Over ten weeks, I reckon I had spent approximately one hundred pounds per week on average, plus an odd couple of weeks on sites. All in all, not much more than two thousand pounds, £2,000. Two of those weeks with company, including Janet and Keith plus my granddaughter Sammy. We'd all had a great time; I had seen and experienced a host of countries not many people would have the pleasure of seeing. For two grand? A bargain by any measure.

Some people sell up and live their lives in their motorhomes. Again we were fortunate enough that we didn't have to consider that. The time when I would have wanted to do that was in my twenties when I had no money. Now I was comfortable. I liked my creature comforts. The idea of touring fulfilled everything I wanted, seeing different countries, tasting different cultures, the freedom to come and go as I pleased. And even better, being able to park up virtually anywhere was a great bonus.

The more I had travelled abroad, the more I preferred to travel abroad. I had spent much of my life enjoying the British countryside, yes, it was beautiful, there is not much to beat the British countryside on a nice warm day with the sun out. The mountains of wales, the dales of Derbyshire, but most times when we had got there, it was peeing down with rain. Enough I say, here I had just been seeing some beautiful countryside in many countries, and with the sun shining even in low season. No, England and the countryside or seaside were for the odd few weekend breaks. Many times with the grandkids.

It would have given us a great sense of pleasure to have had our kids borrow the motorhome and enjoy many a break around the country. Following in the footsteps of my wife and me, having had many enjoyable memories. Sharing with their siblings a day on the beach at Weston-Super-Mare, a few days on the seafront at Barmouth, a hike in the derby dales, a couple of nights on Cannock chase, listening to the deer walking around within feet of you. So many beautiful places. Sadly, it was not going to be.

I suspect most people will not share their motorhomes for their own personal reasons. I had one friend and neighbour who was adamant that no one would ever use his toilet, even for a pee. No, no, no. Others maybe did not like the idea of someone else driving their motorhome. The fact is our motorhome is not just a shed on wheels. It's our home, our personal space. Our living room, our bedroom. Our personal toilet and kitchen.

Shortly after we had bought the motorhome, we decided to take her down to see our younger daughter Rachael who lived in Oxford with her husband. With our other daughter Louise sitting in the back, we set off for the short drive down to Oxford. Rachael was hosting a pig roast. They do that in Oxford, don't you know, very middle class. Pulling up outside, we sat, waiting till someone caught on that it was us and would tell Rachael. Eventually, they did. It was Rachael's mother-in-law that first saw us, one of the biggest snobs on the planet.

Joining them in the garden for the pig roast, Rachael asked if she and Justin, her husband, could go and have a look around the motorhome, "of course" I said. Justin was a barrister and just like his mother. I swear, if their noses went any further in the air, they would get frostbite. After a suitable period, we walked up to join them in the camper. Asking then what they thought, they admitted, with a studied quietness, that they quite liked the motorhome. "Do you think me, and Justin might borrow the motorhome, dad?"

"Well, I don't see why not. Of course, you can. You would have to spend some time getting used to it." This was not like a car where you just jump in and drive off. There were a whole host of gismos you had to get used to. Power converters, control panels, various switches. Most motorhome owners will tell you they are still learning; we were. Although Justin was a barrister, I still felt it wasn't as simple as he thought.

With his little nose in the air staring imperiously around saying nothing, I asked Rachael what she had in mind. I was hoping she would suggest that they would maybe go away for a few days with one of her siblings. Oh no. I was wrong there.

"Well, we would go away with our friends."

"Your friends? —and where would they sleep?"

"Oh, they could sleep anywhere, and don't worry, we would valet it so that it was cleaner than before we had it." Sadly, she just never got it.

"Rach, that's our bed, me and your mom's bed, our personal space."

"Oh, dad, don't be silly. It's only a bed. How many different people have slept on hotel beds?"

That was it. Without realising it, they lost the opportunity to have some nice quality time and have some nice breaks. Yes, she was right about the hotel, but we weren't in a hotel. We were in our own little home. I didn't want her mates, strangers, bonking on our bed, crapping in our toilet. I don't think Bet liked the idea either. Kids ay.

Another time, Rachael asked again if she might borrow the motorhome; I think she had forgotten the first time? This time she wanted to bring her two dogs. Now they ain't normal dogs. They are massive like a pair of Alsatians, worse, with long hair. "But where will the dogs go, Rach?" Now I thought she would be a bit respectful and say, "oh, don't worry, dad, they will stop outside and sleep in the garage?" But no.

"Oh, they will share with us, dad. But don't worry, it will be valeted afterwards."

Great ay. Wrong answer again. My kids make me laugh, all very well educated, the two youngest private school. But sometimes, I feel they don't see the bigger picture. By sharing, even if it's small amounts, a tent, a motorhome, a car, maybe even a second home in Spain, everyone gains by being that bit unselfish. By demanding, everyone loses. I suspect I'm not alone in my generation who thinks like this.

CHAPTER 48.

With time we were getting sorted with places to visit or even stay overnight, without objections. But I was also learning lessons as we went along. I had joined a few motorhome forums on Facebook. One devoted to sharing little places to park up. But honestly, some of the recommendations were pathetic, many on laybys, nice little lorry pull-in off the A38, six hundred yards from the island, two miles from the resort, for gawd's sake. How not to feel like a gipsy. There is a fine line, I find, between parking up somewhere with dignity or squeezing under cover of darkness like a gypo. I fully respect that there are a lot of people out there who cannot really afford expensive site fees. This is where the government should shake their heads up like the French and provide places around the country. But to consider parking up in a lay-by is beyond the pale. Ok, if you're travelling somewhere, it's late, and you're tired, fine. If a nice safe layby is handy, by all means, pull in, but for regular everyday use? No, thank you. The other problem I found is if you find somewhere nice, you risk losing it by sharing it. The next thing you know is hordes of motorhomers turn up, dropping rubbish, putting camping chairs outside, and generally abusing it. So no, one has to learn to be a bit selfish.

Barmouth gives me a great deal of pleasure to visit. I'm surprised the council doesn't install facilities for motorhomes for the amount of parking space along the front. Apart from the odd, rare weekend, the place is empty. The council would get back a great deal in revenue for the cost of installing waste emptying facilities or a simple tap, plus the local businesses would benefit. A win-win all around. Matlock Bath is the same. A massive car park is hidden away to the back of the town, twenty-four-hour parking, which is fine. We have many other hidden away little places, little treasures I consider them. A quiet little tucked away spot in a little village, a pleasant stream free public toilet, a couple of village pubs serving nice meals, a historic monument nearby. But if more than one motorhome pitched up on the site, it would be crowded, and the locals would scream. One local, a fellow motorhomer, had already approached me and politely suggested that more than two nights was too much.

Over the years, I had garnered enough places to satisfy my needs for the short breaks I required. In this country, the Derby or Dale, or Yorkshire Dales fine. In fact, many pubs are now taking up the baton, of offering or inviting you to park up in the pub car parks providing you have a meal or a few drinks. This is fine if you want a few drinks or a meal. Sometimes it's nice to do that. We pulled into a little country pub in the dales one afternoon. Now, as it happens, we wanted a meal and a few drinks. The landlady was very nice and friendly. But at the end of the night, we had spent in excess of forty quid, spending that every night for seven nights when you have your own drink and food on board is not the best way of conserving cash.

But you can't go away every weekend. That then takes the fun out of it. It's the spontaneity, the freedom of just deciding on a whim. Being able to say, "ay kids, wanna few days in Barmouth?" They were moments and periods to treasure. Before we know it, time whizzes past. I had also started to keep a diary of places of interest to view or visit all over Europe. Medieval towns and villages in France like Carcassonne, the Chateaus, hidden resorts, castles, and other places of interest in Italy. I was building up a whole portfolio. Now it was getting to the stage of sitting back, revisiting places that we had enjoyed seeing and savouring them all the more. Unlike the guy, I met in one beachside resort who told me that he simply waits till he gets to Calais before deciding whether to turn left or right, great, but I couldn't do that. I had to have some idea of where I was heading.

The following year soon came round. It was spent checking, rechecking the motorhome, stocking up with provisions, Fray Bentos pies, coffee, powdered milk. My clothes and cutlery never come out of the van except for cleaning or changing; underpants, socks, swimming trunks, sandals, and shoes. No matter how you plan, there is always something you've either packed in that you don't need, or you've forgotten. Motor homing is a continuous learning curve. One fellow camper posted how she never wasted water. She simply used a paper towel to wipe clean her non-stick saucepans. So simple, so petty, yet I never thought about that. I've heard of some money saving tricks that, frankly, I'd rather not know about or mention. If you have to resort to such levels, then go on sites. Let's face it, if five of you are sharing a motorhome, it's not going to take long to fill up a cassette. In our case, we had a rule that I would never use the toilet, or our grown-up kids, my wife and grandkids had priority. We would always find a hotel or café, if not we went on sites. We used water sparingly, never, ever drinking water from the tank. We always carried a small one-gallon container or even a five-gallon container. If we were abroad, we bought bottled water.

CHAPTER 49.

EUROPE AND A BIT FURTHER.

My next foray, tentatively, was to get the ferry over to Calais. Then head east to Bulgaria, getting my implants done in Croatia on the way, hitting about twelve countries. As the time arrived, I booked the late ferry. No matter how or where I book it from, I make sure I always book in advance. Why, because the ferry companies like the tunnel, take the p**s. Book tickets at the terminals, and they charge you double according to the mood they are in. The tunnel is a definite no-no to me. I've tried it a couple of times. Yes, it's convenient, and it's fast. But you would expect it to be cheaper. But no, it's double the price. What do you expect, it's a train company, as far as they are concerned it's a licence to print money? So no, I prefer the one hour twenty minutes on the ferry, and I always book in advance.

I also make sure I get to Dover late for the ferry crossing at midnight or thereabouts. I had heard enough horror stories from lorry drivers and campers about the brutal behaviour and little scams carried out by desperate immigrants at the border—cars pulling in front, pointing to your rear wheel in order to make you stop. Giving you a slow puncture at some garage, enough to force you to stop two miles further on, so no. When I get off that ferry, I put my sat nav on, head for the gates and don't stop for at least a hundred and fifty miles. The roads are nice and quiet, with very little traffic and a dream to drive along, even the toll roads.

This time around I didn't feel much inclined to stop or enjoy anything available along my route or northern France. Paris is beautiful. The Palace of Versailles, breath-taking and out of this world. But we had been to Paris twice, both times on short four-day breaks, which we found ideal for us. Seeing the roads around Paris, there was no way I wanted to risk driving anywhere near there. There was plenty to see in front of me, so the first port of call was Switzerland. Simply, I thought it was a must-do, one of those places that you must see just to say you've seen it, not on the actual bucket list but ok, you're passing near, go and visit. That was a big mistake.

It was a comparatively short drive to the Swiss border involving one overnight stop at an Aire service station, one of many along the route and dotted around France. Some experts and experienced drivers will advise you against parking up and sleeping overnight in garages. I'm not going to dispute and/or argue with them, but my motto has always been one of using common sense at all times. I have seen Aires signposted along main roads or motorways and pulled in only to realise that they are totally isolated, miles from anywhere and with no one around. Vehicles will pull in and use the toilets, then drive off. I avoid such places like the plague.

Garages I find very different. They are open twenty-four hours. They all normally have a café meaning people are pulling in for fuel and refreshments all night. They have vast swathes of parking areas with designated places for caravans, cars or lorries, and an even better bonus, most have a free internet connection. I never park in the far distant caravan/motorhome section unless it's daytime. Instead, I park up as close to and within shouting distance of the café or garage itself. Failing that, I park up amongst the lorries, snacking in between. It can sometimes be a bit of a pain with the stopping and starting and running engines, but at least I've always felt safe.

Switzerland was covered in a blanket of twenty-foot snow. What was so appealing about the place except for skiers or St Bernard's dogs? The only problem was I saw no snow. My initial reaction on entering the country was one of growing amazement and awe. I was impressed. Everything felt so clean, so fresh, no litter anywhere, just green valleys and snow-capped mountains. Then the inevitable beautiful Swiss chalets. Considering Switzerland was so small, I was surprised how much space there seemed to be. Swiss chalets were dotted around in fields with space around them, outside everyone a ton of logs or more piled up in readiness for winter. Even in the small villages, there seemed to be plenty of space with no overcrowding. Maybe it was that German thing. Germans were notorious for their need for their own space, we've all seen them nick the sunbeds at holiday resorts, even digging little isolated plots on the beach. There are a lot of Germans in Switzerland.

Slowing down my speed by a few miles, I was determined to soak up every moment. My first destination being Chur, in central Switzerland. I had heard of the Bernina train and wanted to experience it. On reaching Chur, I drove around the town centre until I found a car park to spend the night. Parking up, I then headed to the train station some miles away. At the ticket office, I was given a return ticket for the princely sum of £110. This might seem like a lot, but if my expectations were right, this was indeed going to be the trip of a lifetime. It was.

After a decent and uninterrupted night's sleep, I set off to reach the Bernina station for ten am the next morning. The bright red train stood at the platform, with plenty of people shuffling forward to get on it. The narrow-gauge train was not packed, with just enough people to make it comfortable. The train would set off across the Alps into Tirano, northern Italy, zig sagging all along in order to cross. Setting off from Chur, we were soon climbing the Alps, the snow getting deeper and thicker. It was truly amazing, breath-taking, and I was not alone in thinking the same. People were getting up and crossing side to side to get the best views, clicking away non-stop with our cameras before sitting back down to discuss it. We made a short stop at the very top of the Alps, at a ski resort to take stock, take in the views and take more pictures. After fifteen minutes, we were off again and down into Tirano, the journey taking four hours.

In Tirano itself, we had approximately an hour to experience the town, have a meander around and maybe have a meal or a snack. Wanting to try the local cuisine, I walked into a local restaurant, sat at an outside table waiting for service. I was last in the queue. The sun was out, it was quite warm, so I decided to move on and instead have one of the ice creams that Italy was famous for. After an hour, we got back on the train heading back over the Alps and onto Chur. This time the journey wasn't so eventful. We had seen it, done it. Apart from the odd newbie on board making the journey for the first time, most of us just sat back and enjoyed the ride. As my motorhome was back in Chur, I had no alternative but to head back. But in reality, it would have been nicer to have had a night in Tirano. It had been a long but pleasant day. I decided to spend the second night in the car park, before heading off to Bern the next day.

CHAPTER 50.

Bern was one hundred and forty miles to the east of Chur. Being a medieval city, it was a designated world heritage site with its cobbled streets and beautiful buildings. The city was beautiful and a delight to walk around. I sat and had the obligatory coffee whilst taking in the scenery. Nothing about Switzerland disappointed me, except the prices. The views, the cleanliness, the fresh, invigorating air was enchanting. But the prices. Walking around the shops, I would like to have bought a cuckoo clock. I had always wanted a cuckoo clock. Just the thought of that cuckoo clock on my wall, popping in and out giving its little cuckoo, made me want to own one. Until I saw the prices. £500 for a clock? A cuckoo clock? How do they get away with such prices? Who could afford to pay them? This, to me, was a mick take, especially after I had seen them in Belgium a couple of years earlier for less than £100. No, sorry, I wasn't going to have that little cuckoo on my house wall, neither was I going to have much else by the looks of the prices. Looking for something, a memento for the kids, I decided to give it a miss.

Bern was beautiful without a doubt but having had a good walk around enjoying the sights, I felt it was time to move on. Next stop, Lake Lucerne, 50 odd miles to the west. The town and Lake of Lucerne were again beautiful, both equally tranquil. The lake nestled between the mountains with houses and villas dotted around. I soon found somewhere to park up for the night alongside the lake. The next morning I explored the town and took a boat trip across the lake. Both were a wonderful experience, the town was peaceful and pleasant, and the prices were reasonable.

Unlike Bern, I decided to spend the next night on a campsite before heading off to my next destination. Finding a site in my ACSI book, I pulled in, flashing my little magic card. The site was very nice, clean, with stunning views across to the lake. I was constantly being surprised and impressed with the quality, cleanliness and tidiness of the sites compared to what we had had to put up with in England. This site in the ACSI book was £12 for the night, including hook up. It was worth that just for the views.

My next destination was Zagreb in Croatia to get my teeth sorted. But first, I wanted to cross the Saint Gotthard Pass. Famous for its stunning views. After checking on his computer, the campsite owner kindly let me know that the pass was indeed open. Setting off, its reputation was justified. The views were stunning. Apparently, there were some twelve or fifteen famous passes across or out of Switzerland. I made a mental note that Switzerland was a must-see country to come back to.

I had whizzed through many countries, as was my intention. I had got a bit more to do, but eventually, my aim, goal, and plan would be to spend more quality time enjoying the countries I had shortlisted. Getting through and over the Gotthard pass, I decided to pay a visit to the little country of Liechtenstein. Nestled next to Switzerland and Austria, Liechtenstein is the only country in the world with 100% of its country in the Alps with 38000 people. It was one of the smallest and least visited countries in Europe, I was to find out why.

Once in the city, I parked up next to a garage and had a walk around to get a feel of the town. Calling into a local restaurant in the high street, I went in to enjoy a bowl of traditional homemade soup. Walking back out and looking around, I could see the main street seemed to be the only level bit about it. To left and right, one end to the other was the Alps and steep hilly walks. Not for me, thanks. I headed back to the motorhome.

It was then I noticed the sign above the garage. CO-OP, CO-OP? That's a British company, surely? I decided to have a bit of banter. Opening up my internet, I went onto one of my motorhomes camping sites. I had kept a bit of a blog of my travels, with more than a few people telling me they enjoyed my stories and the countries I visited. So I put the following:

'Well, well, well. Some of these foreigners astound me—the complete ignorance of them and their inability to speak even a smidgeon of English, never fails to amaze me. I've just called into this local garage in Liechtenstein, a CO-OP. If you don't mind, an English company. I asked for my favourite paper, the Sun, and no-one can understand a word I'm saying. Looking at me blank like a docile cow. How pig-ignorant can these people be?'

I added a picture of the CO-OP garage and made a point of exaggerating it a bit for people to get the joke, then sat back for the response while I drank my coffee. Well, I nearly choked when the posts started coming in thick and fast. I expected the odd one to really believe me. But I also expected the majority to get the joke and enter into the banter. How wrong can I be?

'What an ignorant bloke this Thomas Lewin is. How can he be so ignorant to go into a foreign country and demand that they speak English? You should be ashamed of yourself for expecting people to speak your language.'

Another, 'what do you expect? He's a Sun reader.' I could feel the air of superiority in his tone. This went on, line after line. I couldn't believe it. No one saw the joke. Then eventually, someone did get it.

'Hang on, this has to be a wind-up. No one can be that serious.'

Then I replied, 'well done, take a blue peter badge.' This inflamed the others even more—especially the guy who insulted me because I mentioned the Sun newspaper. No one likes being made a fool of, and this lot were certainly being foolish. 'Guys, guys, calm down. I'm having a joke. I thought it was clear I am an experienced traveller. I'm keeping a blog. How can you take it so seriously?'

It was no good. This lot were really p****d off. I tried apologising; it was no good. Eventually, I was blocked. Admin had blocked me from the site. In truth, he should have blocked them for having no sense of humour, but I suppose there were that many he felt he would have lost all his members, simpler to sack me. I was sacked.

CHAPTER 51.

Dejected, well, not really, I set off for Croatia and Zagreb. Some 450 miles east. After nearly a year, it took me a few turns up the main road before I spotted my little car park, a camping spot behind the mix of offices and private flats. Driving in, I went to the far end by a kiddie's park, thinking I would be out of the way. I was, until I realised my own position; single, elderly male, in a camper van, next to a kiddie's playground. I moved sharpish the next morning, down to the other end.

The clinic, set above the Holiday Inn, seemed to cater for everything. Tummy tucks, facials, etc., including dental work. From my experience, I would recommend them highly to anyone. However, from my first visit the year before, there had been a small but potentially very expensive misunderstanding. My boxing period had left me having to have a couple of teeth removed from my upper jaw. Having had the implants inserted and paying a deposit, I was then seen by the main technician dentist who was going to do the works. Only this time, after a lot of faffing about, he made it clear he would not do the top set unless I had an equal amount done to the bottom set. His argument was that having the top done without the bottom would cause them to break. This p****d me off no end, and I genuinely thought I was being ripped off. How do I get out of this? I had half a mouth with screws in. The fact is, he should have done the first part of the job as well. He was now saying my jaw was too strong. Well, I knew that. They should have known also.

The legal eagles spout their worldly advice and tell you how to handle it at a cost more than you have paid in the first place. All the way to Serbia, I was trying to plot my way out of it. I know, I'll insist on paying by cheque then blank the cheque. No, that won't work. By the time I had got to the beautiful mountain top campsite in Serbia, I had come up with a plan. I composed a detailed letter of complaint by email. Expressing my anger and that once I got back to England, I would be getting my solicitor to write to the highest authority both in England and Zagreb. I didn't expect to get anywhere, but at least I had vented my spleen.

Low and behold and knock me down with a feather. Two days later, I had got an email back from the clinic apologising profusely and offering to do the rest of the work for free. That took me completely by surprise. I could never see an English dentist doing that. Further to detailed confirmation, I had graciously accepted. Now, here I was, in Zagreb, to get all the rest of the work done. The work was booked over ten days, which might not seem a lot, but ten days can be a bit of a jaunt. Sometimes there was a two-day break. Sometimes I would have to go back the next day at a difficult time, which made it awkward to plan anywhere. On those days, I'd spend the night in the local bar, free internet, having a few beers topped off with a few vodkas to knock me out.

On a free day, I would get the tram into Zagreb itself. The tram ride was very nice. I'm not going to knock Zagreb, but I just wasn't overly impressed with the city. It was just another city. Some of it was impressive, others not. In actual fact, I was more impressed with the people themselves, both young and old, modern, self-assured, confident. Happy, a major contrast to neighbouring Bosnia and Serbia and it's very sullen people and backward countries.

One day I decided to visit its main museum, two kilometres from the dentist office in a straight line and setting off,

I reached it about lunchtime. To me, a museum is what I'm used to seeing in Birmingham, we have some very impressive museums. In Egypt, I had seen some impressive museums. Here in Zagreb, I was not impressed at all. Looking around. I came away with the impression that the western world had felt sorry for them and bunged them a few throw-outs that they had stuck in their cellars. I walked out a tad disappointed. Walking back to my motorhome, the heavens opened up, adding to my woes. I was soaked, weary and knackered—another drunken night.

I decided to have another day in Bosnia. I intended to spend the night and a couple of days. Calling into a café and ordering a Fanta, I asked the young guy behind the counter if there was any nightlife? Anywhere to visit? He looked blank. I decided to just have a drive around getting to know the area, the town. Again I wasn't impressed. People shuffled around, not looking very happy at all. The most interesting thing I noticed was a funeral.

Maybe I aroused suspicion by driving back out of Bosnia within the day because, within two miles, I was pulled over by a cop or a gendarme who wanted to search my van. He was sullen and very diligent. I tried taking a picture of him for my records, but he clocked me and insisted on checking my camera. By luck, maybe, I hadn't taken it. Like British cops, even a couple of cops in Switzerland pulled me over for no good reason. They didn't like having their picture taken. Why not? These are public servants. What he was looking for, I don't know, and by the sour look on his face, I thought it prudent not to ask. Three miles further on, another car started to wave me down. There were two people in it. We were on an isolated stretch of road, I thought I ain't having this, but they were persistent. Overtaking them, I pulled up alongside them as they were stern-faced and waving me down, pull in, pull in. I guessed by then they were coppers.

Pulling in, I said, you do realise we are on a lonely stretch of road, and you're in an unmarked car? No response except, "we want to search your van." This time they went even more thoroughly than the first one a few miles back, pulling back bedding, mattresses, even looking underneath cupboards. What on earth are they looking for? Tobacco? Booze? —no. Eventually, they told me. Bosnia is well known apparently for smuggling immigrants into the west. Oh, right, and you're going to find them in my cupboards then? They were polite, serious, and efficient. Fair play, I understood. They had a difficult job to do.

Eventually, my treatment with the dentist had come to an end. He had matched my teeth up exactly and did a brilliant job. I had to go back in the morning for one final check-up-instructions not to eat anything solid ringing in my ears. Getting back to my motorhome, I did a thorough examination in the mirror. I was over the moon. I did no more than call into the modern local shopping centre, spent £100 in Krona on flowers, chocolates, and other treats. Well, I looked at it this way, the clinic had carried out an extra £5000 worth of treatment that I felt I didn't need or want. My ten-day stay in the centre of town had cost me zilch. Just the odd meal. And a few drinks. It was a good result for me, a terrific result. The least I felt I could do was repay the dentists kindness with kindness.

I returned all the gifts to the clinic, plonking them on the counter in front of all the smiling staff and customers. I was feeling very benevolent. Going back the next morning for my final check-up. The dentist and his staff were all smiles. Pointing to the flowers in the corner, he beamed and went all over my teeth again, double-checking, filling down a bit more before expressing his satisfaction. We left on very nice friendly terms.

CHAPTER 52.

ONWARDS AND EAST TO BULGARIA.

Leaving the dentist, making sure I had spent all my krona, I put Sunny beach into my sat-nav and set off. Sunny beach was 800 miles from Zagreb. Having been in and around Serbia, I didn't feel too inclined to spend more time there. I stuck to the motorway taking me directly into Bosnia, sleeping overnight at one of the many free, open garages and Aires along the route.

It took me three days of steady driving, stopping off for a few hours in Sofia on the way. Wanting to get into Sunny beach fresh, I started to look for somewhere to park up for the night. Some cafes or bars were too isolated to risk spending the night, but eventually, I came to a lorry/car park, a few yards down from what looked like a police station. Can't have anything safer than that, surely? Pulling in behind a couple of lorries, I tucked in out of sight. Waking up, I had a better look around, hang about, what's going on down there? Outside what I thought was the police station, I could see traffic cops pulling people in left, right and centre. This wasn't a police station. This was a custom vehicle pull-in point. Cars and lorries were being pulled in left, right and centre. This was a faulty vehicles graveyard, full of abandoned cars and lorries. I was glad to getaway.

Getting into Sunny beach, I saw the sign for a campsite. Calling in, the owner came out telling me it was five euros per night inclusive of electricity. Very nice. I decided to have a look around. What a disappointment. What a dump. This wasn't a campsite; it was a bomb peck. I noticed a couple of campers dotted about. One with the owner sitting outside, he didn't look very happy at all. He wore a pair of shorts and a grubby T-shirt. I wondered if he was on the run. Just looking across, it was clear this wasn't just a five-minute scenario; he was just existing. As I drove out, I told the owner who was waiting to trap me, "I'm just off to get some supplies. I'll be back in an hour." With that, he stood back and let me pass, relief. I was out and never looked back.

I spent at least an hour driving up and down three rows back from the main front before finding a suitable looking hotel with parking outside. Well, I thought it was suitable for parking, it was dark. Calling into the hotel like a native, I saw the sign saying two euros for twenty-four hours of internet. I was wary, but I didn't question it. I bought a ticket and walked back out to the camper. The hotel was a very nice four-star, with an excellent swimming pool and a couple of bars. Any thoughts I had were dashed within minutes when security pulled over.

"You cannot park here." He stated.

"What do you mean I cannot park here?" I replied.

"It is forbidden to park here."

Irritated, I said, "but I have just come out of the hotel. I have paid for the internet."

"Oh, are you in the hotel?"

I grimaced my face up, not wishing to tell a blatant lie.

"You have friends in the hotel?"

"huh, yes." I stuttered.

"Oh, that is no problem, follow me."

He led me around the corner to the main entrance of the hotel. To the side was a large piece of land for future development.

"You can park there and stay for as long as you want, ok?" He said.

"Yes, ok, thank you very much." I replied, relieved.

The hotel was fantastic, with a nice atmosphere and a nice mix of people. I was half a mile from the main Sunny beach and shops, within a hundred yards of bars and restaurants where I could buy good quality English food for less than five euros. Like the Spanish, these Bulgarians certainly caught onto what pleased the English, good English food and cheap lager, I was in my oil tot.

The weather was gorgeous, not too hot, just nice tanning weather. There were three ways into the hotel, the main entrance to the front leading into reception, then out into the gardens. A rear entrance on the opposite side of the hotel, then the side entrance directly opposite my motorhome. This led directly to the pool gardens and pool. That was my entrance. The hotel was packed. Those who weren't out and around the town were around the pool. With my little carrier bag, towel, and magazines inside, finding an empty lounger, I set the towel out nestled down and started reading my magazine. Along the way, weighing up the local hotel life. Occasionally having the odd little swim.

Between the reception and restaurant were the main entrance and toilets to the side. Checking out the toilets, I was pleased to find they were up to my usual standards. Cleaned every couple of hours, you could eat off the floor. So, in one fell swoop, I had gotten my toilet and shower facilities and swimming. If the weather turned cold, I had some nice sofas with an internet connection. What more could I ask for? Now I know some people might consider me a bit cheeky. And that is fair enough. The more people who feel I'm cheeky, the fewer people out there will scupper my future chances. Don't do it.

In fairness, many hotels will allow people from outside to use their pools daily for a small fee. One or more people are not going to make much of a difference to a 500-room hotel. I had been in one or two hotels speaking to someone living in an apartment nearby, I saw no problem with that. But I had also seen someone spoil it for many others, on a campsite, by asking the owners if their family could use the pool. Even offering to pay for the privilege. The stupid idiots weren't even at the campsite we were on. Not only did the owners say a firm "no," but they also locked all the doors meaning everyone had to go to reception when they wanted to use the pool, which would be many times a day, a real nuisance. So no. My motto is not to rock the boat. If you want to be all pious, right on, and considerate, you have my full respect. I shall say hello as I pass you on the beach or outside your motorhome. For myself, I'm discreet, respectful and I spend money in the hotel.

I was on no strict schedule, having travelled from France onto Croatia, my loosely held plan was to have a few weeks in Bulgaria, then head on round to Greece. Once in Greece, I intended to coast-hop down to Athens, then round to Igoumenitsa. My days varied as to how I felt. Most days, I would spend the day around the pool, soaking up the rays. At night, I would pop down to the beach and maybe into one of the many bars that had entertainment on, in the main, good entertainment and decent food. Although, I couldn't help but be a bit cynical towards the Bulgarian attitude to the holidaymakers.

In fairness, the Bulgarians were doing a fantastic job in catering to the tourists. Bulgaria had emerged from a satellite communist country of Russia and had jumped on the holiday boom. Sunny beach was very Europeanised, but behind the shutters, you could catch glimpses of a different culture. Five miles outside Sunny beach, the country was as bad as Serbia and Bosnia.

We had visited Bulgaria in 2007 just before it part joined the euro. In the hotel we stayed in, the owners would regularly do a pig roast for their family, sitting around the table with a pig as the centrepiece on the table. We, the customers, were irrelevant to them, fine by me. But it gave me an insight into their character. There was also the mafia element with lots of rumours that they were into the hotels, restaurants and even growing property market. I had looked at the idea of buying something, feeling properties would be cheap, only to find that was far from the case. On the contrary, much was overpriced and jerry-built. Gossip or not, when I heard of one family who had bought an apartment only to realise, she had made a mistake and wanted to sell it, she was told she could own, live in, and use the apartment for life, but she would never be able to sell it.

Either way, I wasn't too impressed. Besides, on the build-up of joining the euro, the properties were being hiked up higher than in Spain. No, thank you. Now here I was in 2019, and everything had grown and come on a bundle. Almost every hotel had become a central park. Swings, slides, plumes, and bouncy castles were everywhere. The whole idea was not only to get you in but also to keep you in.

I was beginning to see why Bulgaria was surrounded by mountains, the Balkans, many snow-capped. I think whoever came up with the name Sunny beach deserves a medal for ingenuity. Yes, the sun did come out in high summer. But the weather was inclement, often raining. The Bulgarians had a very short season in which to make their money. If they didn't get the balance right, they could fold. Some resorted to ripping the customers off, which struck me as really stupid and short-sighted. I think many got carried away thinking they were going to make a killing only to find that wasn't the case.

I found Bulgaria nice, for a one-off break, and interesting. But the only other place of real interest is Nesebar, a few miles away. Unless you're into touring the local villages and towns or the non-stop noise of all the various funfairs etc. In fairness, it's great for families with kids, cheap with plenty of entertainment.

My newfound friend in the hotel was Daniel. Or Danny, as we all called him, the barman in the outside bar. Most nights, we would sit having a chat if it were quiet. Not many people used the hotel bars preferring the entertainment of the local bars down by the beach, plus the drinks were half the price. Personally, I felt it only fair to repay my use of the hotel by spending a bit. Maybe this wasn't such a good idea as one night Danny observed that he never saw me going into evening dinner. Oh dear, then he added, "but you must be here just for breakfast, no?"

"Yes, yes," I replied. Flip, that was a close one!

"But, you are here for a long time, yes?"

"yes," I said, "I'm here for a month."

"Ah, you are very lucky."

It's just as well I wasn't stopping any longer, really. But a month was plenty enough for me. I reminded myself that if I stopped any longer, I needed to be even more discreet. Danny was fine, but the restaurant's manageress was a right tiger with eyes like a hawk. How she hadn't caught on to me yet, I don't know, but anyone trying to get into the restaurant she was onto like a shot. Any staff not pulling their weight or making a mistake, she would be over shouting and bawling. I made a big point to be very, very nice to her.

CHAPTER 53.

GREECE

I was starting to get restless, so after a very pleasant month, I hit the road. Heading to Thessaloniki, Greece, 370 miles south. I had finally had a solar panel fitted to my roof. I had chosen a 100-watt thinking this was adequate for me. Some people ran computers, televisions and more. Apart from the odd video, 100 watts was enough for me. It guaranteed my batteries were charged up at all times, which is a great blessing for long-term wild camping.

The drive to Thessaloniki was steady, with one overnight stop in a small village. My only consideration being whether to turn left for Turkey or right for Greece. No, maybe Turkey another time. Thessaloniki was beautiful. A city renowned for its culture, food, and vibrant nightlife. It was romantic, with million-pound yachts along the harbour, posh restaurants in abundance serving quality food and, even better, seafood. I just love seafood when I'm by the sea. Finding somewhere to park up was a different matter. Thessaloniki was the second biggest city in Greece. It was a million miles away from sunny beach, very refined, no funfairs here. I wanted to spend a couple of days at least, even sampling the local gastronomy.

I had spent barely £200 in the month I spent in Bulgaria. Cheap as it was, most of that was on drink more than food. Here in Thessaloniki, I intended to push the boat out and enjoy a couple of nice meals. Maybe it was our work ethic during our business life, but for years we had learned not to waste money. I think most people in business are exactly the same. Work for someone else; you get a regular wage. You can plan accordingly until the proverbial crap hits the fan. In business, you allow for that every week, every month. You learn to live on the minimum. The advantage is knowing if you want it, you have got it there. I finally managed to snuggle my way into a little spot to the harbourside before heading off to wander around the town.

The atmosphere around the harbour was truly vibrant. It was tangible. Finding a table right by the harbour, I sat down, soaking up the atmosphere as I waited for my order of freshly cooked mussels to arrive. When it did, together with the obligatory chunks of bread I got stuck in with relish, savouring every morsel, there is nothing quite like fresh seafood. It was even better knowing it was only a fraction of the cost of Puerto Banus in Spain. Looking around, I felt very middle class. A million miles away from the ragged arsed, snot-nosed kid from the slums of Birmingham. Thessaloniki was definitely on my must-see again list. Definitely, I would have stopped longer if I had had better parking. Whilst the wealthy yacht owners with their big-spending power were welcome, I don't think us motorhome owners were.

My next destination was Athens, 300 miles further south. I coast hopped as I went along, calling into little seaside resorts or coves. It took me just under a week to get to Athens, stopping off for a day here, a day further on. I had always been led to believe, from other campers, that Greece was a great country for welcoming motorhomes. They were right. I encountered no ill will at all. In fact, many of the beaches I had to myself, a choice of restaurants aplenty.

Athens was a different kettle of fish altogether. Dusty, dirty, manic. The roads were wild, like one big banger car racetrack. Driving around in circles, my nerves were shredded, trying to find somewhere to park up near or in the vicinity of the Acropolis. Even the Greeks here were different. Bullish, unfriendly, and aggressive. I finally found somewhere in a car park. A guy who saw me waved me in as he was getting rid of a coach driver. "Five euros," he offered.

I was glad to pay it. I was glad to just get a break from the lunatic Greek drivers. Amazing how a city can have such an effect or alter the personality of someone so drastically. I knew quite a few Greek Cypriots from working for them back home. They were, in the main, laid back, easy-going. Even in Thessaloniki, along the route and the many resorts I had stopped at, it was so much different to here.

The Acropolis was impressive. Packed with tourists but well worth the visit. We had viewed it a few years before, during a Mediterranean cruise, but from a distance. Now, here I was, close up and in it.

I was glad to get out of Athens. Major cities are just not my cup of tea. Because of Greece's shape, I set a destination in stages. First to Corinth, then up to Antikyra. Then slowly back up to Igoumenitsa, in northern Greece. Corinth is famous for its two ports based on the Saronic Gulf coast and its canal. The Corinth canal effectively splits Greece in two. The canal leads from the Ionian Sea to the Saronic Gulf in the Aegean. It effectively made the peninsula of Greece an island.

The canal is awe-inspiring indeed. To stand on top of the cliffs looking down was breath-taking. It was built in 1881 and is four miles long, but who built it? Navvies? We have canals in Birmingham. In fact, we have more canals in Birmingham than in Venice. We are famous for our canals. We know all about the navvies; in the main, Irish labourers brought over to dig them out. But this. This is a vast difference. The sides of the Corinth canal are 100ft high. Who dug that out? No locks, so who did the final dig? The mind boggles, was the canal always there? It refers to it in 600AD. I can't imagine a couple of thousand navvies being brought over to dig that little lot out. And where would they dump the excavations?

I spent hours just sitting there taking in the views, watching the ships passing through before heading to the port of Corinth and spending the night by the sea. The next day I set off for Antikyra further up along the coast.

CHAPTER 54.

Antikythera is a port on the northern coast of Corinth, a pretty town, the most important part, as far as I was concerned, was its vast car parks along the front. According to what time of the day you called in, the car park varied in its occupancy. As per is normal for me, I headed off somewhere out of the way in the car park but was never isolated. Settling in, I locked up and went for a walk around the town and its bars and restaurants. Just one of the many things I love about Europe is its casual attitude to dining out. Whether it be France, Spain, or here in Greece, the air of relaxation is tangible. Sitting myself down at one of the many cafes, I ordered a drink so I could sit and take in the atmosphere. Listening to the Greeks around me chatting and laughing. Most of them seemed office or shop workers in casual clothes. The waitress was very friendly and, as soon as she heard my accent, asked me what I was doing here. Explaining what I had done, where I had been and where I was, she seemed quite fascinated in my travels. Antikyra struck me as a place not many brits visited. This, to me, was one of the bonuses of motorhome life. By its very nature, we got to a place many English never visited. This was great for me.

The only downside, especially in Greece, was the coffee. Maybe to the connoisseur, Greek coffee was maybe something else, something to be savoured and drooled over. Leave it out. It's that thick you can stick a shovel up in it. The Greeks sip it like nectar. Ok, I don't mind the odd one, maybe that's all you are expected to have, but I'm a cheap Nescafe man. Just give me the instant with a tot of milk and a spoonful of sugar. Coffee snobs astound me. Over the years, our attitude to food and drink has shifted, altered. As kids, a treat or a takeaway was fish and chips, particularly cod and chips, once a week. Then McDonald's tried to break onto the scene. Apart from the odd café like our el Greco that did a proper homemade burger, no one touched or thought of a burger. If we wanted meat, we cooked the Sunday joint. People took one look at McDonald's and walked away.

Not many people realised that McDonald's were losing money hand over fist. After six years, they were just about to pack up and go back home to America when someone came up with the brilliant idea of the Ronald McDonald clown and the free toys. The rest is history, of course. Parents would take their child to a McDonald's for a free toy, and that was it. Now whole families go en-masse to a McDonald's every day. It's called brainwashing. Now it's coffee and pizzas. People have their favourites like Costa coffee or 'Costa lotto,' as I call it. I tell you; it tickles my brain. We pay three quid for a coffee costing a few coppers.

I was on my second day in Antikyra when I got a text from a friend who was on the island of Zakynthos, Zante, as it's widely known, with her family and relatives, in all, about twenty of them. I weighed up the odds and thought, why not. The ferry for Zante left the port of Kyllini, just a few miles further up the coast. I had never been to Zante, just as I had never been to Corfu. The big difference is that now I knew someone on Zante; there would be company. The ferry cost me £150 for an open ticket. Maybe a tad expensive for a week or so, but we never know what doors open for us. Besides, this is the very advantage of wild camping. It's like that extra spurt you need when you're in the boxing ring or on the racetrack; when you want or need that little extra, it's there. I booked the ticket online, and on the third day, set off on the short drive to the port of Kyllini. From there, it was just a short haul over to Zante. The ferry was due the next morning, so parking up on the ferry docks, I took advantage of the time by having a pleasant walk around the port town of Kyllini itself.

The next morning, up bright and early, I was ready for the ferry in front of me. I had had a good sleep on the port quay, no hindrance, no security. The ferry over was relaxed and steady, taking a couple of hours. From the main town of Zakynthos, I headed south-west to a little town called Kyllini, halfway along the island where the group were in a little hotel called Dannie's. The hotel was in a nice little out of the way resort with plenty of bars, restaurants, and shops. It was a short walk to the seafront and beach.

Dannie's itself was tucked away in a little corner. Great, but not for me, there was nowhere to park safely, moving away a bit I found somewhere to park up whilst I nipped into the hotel and found my friend. Coming out, she pointed me to the rear car park of the hotel. Following her directions, I headed on a bit further and turned into a dirt track which took me to the car park directly at the back of the hotel and within sight and a short walk of the swimming pool. This looked very promising indeed.

The hotel was very impressive, and on a large plot of land, it was very popular with the English, and I could see why. It seemed to be more geared up to the self-catering with a very impressive restaurant set to the side of a good-sized swimming pool—the whole pool surrounded on three sides by the hotel with the car park at the end. The hotel was very busy and seemed to be full. My friend and her family came here every year. As such, she was known by the owner. It's always a great advantage if you've got an intro into any place. Travelling abroad, I found this even more so. Here, it seemed within hours, everyone had heard who I was and what I was doing there.

Before the day was out, the owner's son came over and introduced himself as Dannie. Impressed at the fact I had arrived here all the way from England. I had to remind him that I hadn't actually come straight from England but a bit of a circuitous route from France over to Bulgaria. He was even more impressed.

"Do you mind my parking here?" I asked him.

Expansively he said, "did I say no? —you can stay as long as you want. How long do you want to stay?" Before I could open my trap, he said, "do not worry, you can stop all summer if you wish." Well, this was an invitation indeed. All summer? I looked around at the pool and at the restaurant. That 150 quid open ticket seemed like a great investment. I was going to be spoilt. The food was simple and of good quality. The cooks had got the English breakfast off to a 'T'. Just like the Spanish, and the Bulgarians. If there's one way to an Englishman's heart, it's through his belly. I looked around at the pool. Next to the restaurant were the toilets. I was in my oil tot. Toilet's, showers, swimming pool, restaurant, and parking. What more could one ask for?

Zante is a beautiful island known for its sandy beaches and turquoise sea, also its Caretta turtles. I couldn't help but compare it to Corfu and found it a lot superior in many ways. From the lovely harbour, port, to Zante town itself. Clean and welcoming. Compared to Corfu town, which was tacky, cheap, and down market. Within reason and without spoiling it, both islands appeared ideal and receptive to the motorhome. In fact, I think I was the only motorhome on Zante. At least three people approached me asking about my travels and how I got here. It seemed all of them had got motorhomes but were hesitant about travelling so far, the simple logistics of it. To me, I just go for it, bite the bullet, and get on. If I couldn't get a ferry, so what? Maybe it might be a two day wait. Then I'll wait. I'm in my own home, it's no problem.

I was starting to feel that motorhomers were split into three main groups. The security conscious, these will only ever go on secure sites with electric hook-ups and facilities. From there, they will venture out on foot or by bike to explore the surrounding area. Then there is the wild camper, like me, who will just venture out to where their curiosity will take them. The only thing holding them back is the natural instinct for self-preservation and caution. Then you have the cost-conscious, the budget aware. Many of these were single travellers, usually guys on their own travelling around like the guy we met in Morocco in his little van. To be fair, these guys were normally on the state pension, which is circa £170 per week. On an average £25 a night camping charge that wipes the guy's pension right into a cocked hat. How can they go to a campsite? The only feeling I have on either one is some of the risky places they might choose to park up just to save a night's site fees. Around England and in Europe, you will see them snuck into little out of the way places, inside roads pretending to be inconspicuous. They are not sleeping in them, you understand, no, just merely parking up for the night. That's fine if it suits you. Personally, I find the mere thought of it very uncomfortable.

I had picked unsuitable places a couple of times over the years. Once in a car park near the beach in Benalmadena, Spain, I thought it was an ideal spot. It was, but what I never allowed for were the punters coming out of the nearby hotel, gathering right outside our motorhome. Some of the worst places were on the main roads like I've seen in Benidorm. I gather one guy, in bed asleep, got rammed right up his backside one night. A tipsy driver swerved into the parking lanes that he was parked in. So no, I like my freedom. I love the freedom of parking up in nice places wherever I might be.

But cheap skating is not my thing. Here in Zante, I felt completely relaxed. Even other bars and cafes inviting me to park outside their properties. From the hotel, we could venture out on little ventures around the island. In Zante town itself, we might spend a few hours around the town. Another day we drove up to the high vantage point above the town, giving us magnificent views across the bay and beyond.

Certainly, Zakynthos was and is a beautiful island, the people very easy-going and friendly. The week flew past very quickly before my friend and her family had to fly home. A coach came and picked them up on the departure day, and with goodbyes all around, they were off, down into Zante airport and the flight home. It was then, slowly, it started to hit me. I was on my own. Worse, I felt vulnerable. Don't get me wrong. I have no worries about stopping in any nice four-star hotel, especially a comfortable one. But here? – everyone now knew who I was. I was an outsider. My motorhome was right in front of us all, on show for all to see by people who had paid good money to use the very facilities I was using for free.

As the days edged on, I was starting to feel a tad more uncomfortable. No one said anything. Danny was his usual friendly self, "how are you, my friend? You can stop as long as you wish." But underneath was he saying, but now your friends have gone? Actually, it was very silly of me. Over the week, I had seen plenty of places equally as nice where I could have parked up, many places right on the beach next to beautiful, inviting water. I had been invited to park up in other places. But the uneasy feeling had crept in. I felt like I was imposing. After another week, I mentioned to one of the waitresses as I ordered my breakfast that I might be leaving. "Oh no, why?" She questioned. When I explained, she protested, "but you mustn't. You are spending money here and using the bar." True. She was right, but I was starting to get itchy feet.

CHAPTER 55.

ONWARDS TO ITALY.

I had spent and had a very enjoyable two weeks and more on Zante. Saying goodbye, I set off down into Zante town to get the ferry back to the mainland. I hadn't booked the ferry, I had got an open ticket, but reaching the port, I was told that I would have to wait until the morning for the ferry over to the mainland.

Parking up on the quayside, I decided to spend the rest of the evening walking up to and around Zante itself before making my way back to the port with a bottle of wine. Enjoying the views across the bay on a balmy night. The next morning I was woken by the ferry noisily banging its ramps down—stewards shouting and bawling all over the place. The ferry back to the mainland was uneventful. Pulling into the quayside, I sat and considered my options. I had covered a great many miles, seen some beautiful, staggering sights. I had driven through some beautiful countries, from France, Luxembourg through to Switzerland, Italy onto Slovenia, Bosnia, Croatia, Serbia, into Bulgaria. From Bulgaria round into Greece. Now, here I was on the north-west coast of Greece.

Looking at my sat-nav, I was 250 miles from Igoumenitsa. I decided to head there, stopping off at any coastal resort or place of interest as I saw fit along the way. It took me two days of steady driving to reach Igoumenitsa, by now a familiar place to me, with one overnight stop. Pulling onto the quayside, I noticed another couple of motorhomes also parked up. With the regular ferry services, Igoumenitsa was a popular destination point.

From my parking plot right on the seafront, I was in an ideal position for easy access into and around the town. Across the main sea road and just beyond the first line was a popular boulevard of restaurants and bars that attracted the Greeks at night and weekends. After a bit, I had managed to single out a couple of favourites. One such restaurant was run by a young couple and specialised in cooking chicken, fresh on a spit in the front of the shop behind the glass window. Effectively you could watch your meal being cooked in front of you. To me, a great confidence giver. The first time I had sat down there the year before, I had ordered a chicken dinner and a glass of lager. Within a few minutes, the girl had come out with a small plate with a few pieces of chicken, chips, and a bit of salad, and a glass of lager. This was my meal? I pulled the owner/waitress over, who couldn't speak a word of English. Eventually, she referred me to the guy on the adjoining table who kindly informed me that what I had in front of me was not my main meal. This was a free appetiser, provided before my main meal. I felt like a dickhead. Thankfully, I hadn't made an obvious big fuss.

There was only one problem, the appetiser was very nice, very fresh, and plenty enough. When my main meal came, I couldn't eat it all. The next time I sat there, I just ordered a small appetiser. Sure enough, they brought out a sample appetiser of chicken and salad, plenty enough for me. But it was hit and miss. Sometimes they brought out an appetiser; when they did, I would always leave a good-sized tip; other times nothing, it felt like we were playing cat and mouse. A little game between us. Now I had given up playing the games with them, ordering a meal I asked them please, no appetiser. If I had the appetiser, I couldn't eat the main meal. Worse, I was starting to feel a cheapskate. By bringing the main meal, honour was restored all around.

After another couple of pleasant days around Igoumenitsa, I decided to book a ferry over to Italy, this time a short hop across the Adriatic Sea to Brindisi in the heel of the boot. The one-way ticket cost me one hundred euros. From my position on the quay, it was only a short drive to the ferry terminal. Pulling in, I waited in line to be called onto the ferry for the short trip across the water. It was all very relaxed and casual, a great joy in itself. Soon, being called up to the loading slip, I handed my ticket over. Three of the crew huddled together, mulling over my ticket, mumbling, and pointing at my motorhome. I sat stiff, trying to act nonchalant. There always seemed to be some misunderstanding with my motorhome. Was it the height or the length? A couple of extra foot on a motorhome can make quite a bit of difference to the ticket price. No, here we go. They haven't got a tape measure. They waved me on board.

Disembarking the ferry at Brindisi, I had no hard and fast plans. Initially, I had thought to drive up along the coast to say, Bari, again, coast-hopping as I drove along north and up into France, having a few days here or there as I felt. Unfortunately, it didn't pan out so well. For some reason, the east coast of Italy, right up to and past Bari, held no attraction to me at all. The land was flat, uninteresting, unattractive. Bari itself was different. Being a port city, it is the capital of the Puglia region. The harbour and old town were very attractive but getting somewhere to park up to explore the town was a different kettle of fish.

I eventually managed to find somewhere out of the main harbour area between rows of shops. Having a short walk around to explore the area, I decided that I needed to travel on. This part of the coastline didn't appeal to me at all. Getting my map out, I studied it trying to figure out where to head off next. Then I spotted it, Gallipoli, yes, that's where I would head to, Gallipoli. Famous as a strategic seafront city during WWI, Gallipoli was on the eastern side of the heel, opposite Bari and 115 miles south. It was a steady drive through the countryside and on reaching Gallipoli, I drove around a bit trying to find somewhere to park up and explore the town. Initially, I found a car park not far from the historic centre and fortress dating back to the 13th century. The only problem was, I had got the wrong Gallipoli. The Gallipoli I was thinking of was in Turkey in the Dardanelles, idiot. Putting a picture up on Facebook with my typical little boast, I was put in my place sharpish by my friend David Bishop who knew his history better than me. Oh well. Let's get on with it; at least I was in Gallipoli.

Walking into the main port town, I couldn't help but be impressed. It was beautiful, full of character, and atmospheric. Following the walkway around the old fortress town, I could look across and down into the harbour and the mix of boats therein. I hit the first restaurant overlooking the harbour, first asking the waiter if they had fresh mussels. With the affirmative, I sat down. To me, no matter where I was, which coastal resort, my first routine was to find a nice restaurant near or close to the seafront and enjoy a bowl of mussels. Without a doubt, to me, there is nothing better than enjoying a seafood meal whilst looking across at the local scenery; a bowl of mussels with a few chunks of bread hits the spot.

My only little concern was my parking spot. The car park was a car park, and it was almost full. While no one commented, I felt it better to move on and find somewhere more suitable. Driving around the harbour port, and seafront I saw many suitable places where I thought it ok to park up.

My first spot on the seafront car park a few hundred yards from the old fortress and harbour. My only thought, why was I the only one parking up? Cars did pull up and park up but not for long periods. I kept looking around for ticket machines or parking bans but saw none. My only thought was maybe it was a little too far from the harbour?

After one night, I decided to park a bit further along from the harbour area. I found a car park next to a restaurant and snack bar kiosk, in front of the beach and seafront, sorted. Going into the restaurant during the evening, I asked the proprietor if my motorhome was ok where it was? Yes, no problem. After a nice meal, I looked forward to getting down on the beach the next day for some nice sea and sun. I woke up to find myself locked in, barricaded. The whole car park surrounded by barricades. What the flipping hell is going on? What kind of trouble am I in? I started to mildly panic. Seeing a cop, I asked what the problem is. "Do I have to move?" —he was quick to reassure me that I was fine to stop where I was, but he couldn't explain why the barriers had been erected. Was there going to be some kind of market stall set up? Maybe a small funfair of some kind, what about if it went on all day? Into the night? I would be locked in, feeling like a right dickhead, surrounded by crowds. No, no, I'd got to get off. Before anything at all started, I moved one of the barricades aside and got out sharpish. Now, where do I go?

I had moved twice already. If, at first, you don't succeed, take a fresh look at things. I got my ACSI camp book out and started to find any nearby campsites. Finding one two miles from the old fortress and seafront, I set off. Reaching the campsite, I walked into reception, confidently flashing my little ACSI card. The receptionist looked at me blank, "no, no, no, sorry, we are not ACCSI." I was stunned. But this is an ACCSI site? Walking out of reception, I had to take stock of where I was, what to do, my sat-nav had brought me to this campsite where had I gone wrong? After some thought, I walked back into the reception and asked how much their nightly fees were. Blow me down with a feather; they were cheaper than the ACCSI site. If I stopped longer than two weeks, the fees would drop again. I said I was thinking of stopping a month, the fees dropped yet again.

The site was called Miramar and was a four-star campsite. It was brilliant, with three swimming pools, a bar, a restaurant, and a bigger quality restaurant a short walk away. On being shown to my pitch, I noted I was just a short walk under a bridge leading to the beach. I couldn't believe it. Not for the first time had I found a better site in a better position with better rates.

The ACCSI site I had been looking for was on the opposite side of the Miramar campsite. When I found it, I called in to investigate what I was missing. Not a lot, as it turned out. It was overgrown and untidy, and no swimming pool. Talking to the first couple I came across sitting outside their motorhome, I asked how they found the site? Through the grunting in their reply, I guessed they weren't all that happy. I trotted back to the Miramar with a little hop and a skip. Yes, I was a lot better off. If I hadn't walked into this site, I would have been on the grotty one. It certainly pays to shop around.

I was the only Englishman on the site. The only other English couple I had met were the two grunters at the site next door. Otherwise, I had wondered if I was the only English man in the whole of Italy, maybe Europe, where were they all? For all the places I had visited, I saw very few English campers. Bosnia, I can understand. Serbia was another no go too. But I saw, touring through some beautiful places, some wonderful countries, yet hardly any English folk about.

The site I was on was less than 100 euros a week, 14 euros a day. This was a four-star site. Gardens and grounds immaculate, restaurants and bars reasonably priced and friendly; this wasn't a one-off. I found this throughout Europe, superior campsites at half the price of England. I was at the furthest tip in Italy, 1700 miles from home. If I were coming in a straight line, it would have cost me £1,000. Here a family of four could have a very nice months break for £2,000—a no brainer to me. The other bonus is the siesta. I thought it was just the Spanish who had the siesta. No, the Italians insist on their siesta also. I had turned up at the site at 2pm in the afternoon. Walking into reception, I was informed that I couldn't enter the site until 5pm, why not? I was baffled. The site entrance had barriers across. Walking around the site passed a bit of time, then I went and had a read and a nap in the motorhome until 5pm when the barriers were lifted, very strange indeed.

Siesta is so ingrained in the Italians' psyche, like the Spanish, that you feel if there were a gale-force ten or snow on the ground, they would insist on their siesta. It took me two days to fully realise the benefits of that. At 12pm, the pool area emptied, literally emptied. At 9am, the pool is busy. At 11am, the pool is chock-a-block, the grounds full, body to body everywhere, then almost on cue, everyone starts wandering off. I had the whole of the pool to myself. The campsite goes deadly quiet, even the grounds. It's like some sci-fi film when a silent whistle goes off, and everyone disappears.

Then at five pm, everyone re-emerges from their chalets, tents, caravans or whatever, and the whole site sparks up and comes to life, kids shouting, bawling, and laughing. Amazing, it suited me down to the ground. I didn't wake till late; I would take my time getting round to the pool, and when I did, it was at its hottest, exactly as I liked it.

The only thing I was finding, the downside, was the lack of English-speaking people. I was becoming starved of having a chat. I've never been a great socialiser. In fact, the conversation usually goes stone dead as soon as someone asks, are you a villa fan? Brummies' will ask, are you a villain or a blue nose? What's a bloody blue nose, for Christ's sake. I was born less than half a mile from villa park. I've even made money by buying tickets and reselling them. But watching twenty-two men kicking a ball about, what's that? But over the years, I've found out that it cuts off about 80% of the male population. If you can't talk football, that's it. Everyone goes brain dead. I prefer to talk to women.

An elderly lady I would see sitting outside the bar every night, most times sipping a coffee. Pulling up on my little electric scooter, she would give me a nice smile as she pointed to the scooter. I stopped offering her a go on it after the second time. She was obviously with her family, who would leave her on her own now and again. It was clear she couldn't speak a word of English. But that didn't matter. I was that desperate just for a chat I would have talked the hind legs off a dog. She was about twenty years older than me and using a disability aid, but I was just friendly. On the fourth time I saw her, I could see she hadn't got a drink. After half an hour and still not seeing her with a drink, I gestured to her, asking if she would like a drink? Blank. In the end, I walked into the bar and mentioned to one of the bar staff that perhaps I might buy the old lady a drink. No, no. It was made quite clear to me that the old lady didn't want a drink. It took me two days and two deliberate blanks by the old lady before I realised my mistake. I was mortified; the old bat had thought I was trying to chat her up.

This had happened to me a couple of times in different places and with different people. Once, at a campsite in Los Gallardo's, Spain, I had bought a wooden snake for a bit of fun, throwing it in the swimming pool to frighten the kids. The kids thought it was hilarious after getting over the initial shock, with one young girl pleading with me to get in the pool and play with her and her friends. It was only when I got out that my wife turned to me, warning me that the girl's grandfather was watching me like a hawk. For Christ's sake, he thought I was a potential pervert. I avoided those kids like the plague from then on. Now it was being thought that I was trying to chat up such an old lady. Blimey.

I would intersperse my days around the camp and pool with a few hours down in the old town of Gallipoli and its beautiful harbour and fishing port. A few places along the way were little beaches dotted about with the rare sandy beaches and a chance to swim in the sea. Most times, the sea along this coastline was very rocky and stony. I just saw no fun swimming in it at all. To the opposite side of the campsite and in the opposite direction to Gallipoli along the coast road were campsites and leisure parks galore. Still being low season, many were a bit jaded or neglected. Driving into a few, I was just glad I had hit on the Miramar, which I felt was one of the best sites in the area.

After a wonderful, relaxed month, I felt it was time I moved on, further north and towards home. My stay in Gallipoli had been relaxing and informative. I might have got the wrong Gallipoli, but the Gallipoli I was in was lovely and interesting, with something to do every day. With the entertainment all around me, I could see why it would be a popular place for Italian families.

Settling my bill on the final day, I was pleasantly grateful to find no nasty little surprise's. Not the case all the time. Once, calling into one campsite in Benidorm, I had settled into the pitch when one of the staff came over and informed me that I had left two years before, without settling the electricity bill. How could I remember? It was two years ago. Calling into the office, the receptionist asked if I would settle the plus 200 euros bill that I owed. She also told me that the male staff member who had first approached me had had to pay for the electricity out of his own pocket. I mentioned this to another couple of campers nearby, wondering what I should do. What would they do? Unanimously, it was agreed that no one could be expected to pay a bill presented after two years. On leaving the site, they had presented me with the bill, which came to over a thousand pounds. I paid it on the spot. No one mentioned extras like the electric bill. I had settled my electric bill for the recent two days I had stopped there, but this 200-euro bill from two years ago? No, sorry, I refused. That was it, the receptionist did her nut, threatening to report me to the police. Not wishing to fear being arrested at the border or when I re-entered the country, I decided to go into the local cop shop down in the town. They assured me that they would not get involved in such a matter. I don't think I would be welcome at that campsite in the future.

CHAPTER 56.

ONWARDS TO VIAREGGIO.

From Gallipoli, I headed off north, putting Viareggio into my sat-nav. Viareggio was a major and popular seaside resort and just a couple of miles from Lucca, the birthplace of Giacomo Puccini, who wrote the aria Nessun Dorma amongst other famous works. It was a must-see on my list. Setting off on my journey, I headed first to Foggia, on the east coast, then across the west coast to Pescara. Just outside Rome, although each place was only a short distance from each other, I would park up, stay overnight, and do a little tour of the town. Pescara was again another attractive little tourist resort clearly geared up to and for the Italians. Very nice, but the rocky volcanic beaches didn't make me feel inclined to want to stop there. It was bad enough trying to find a scrap of sand to sunbathe on. It was even worse trying to get into the water. You needed to be as nimble as a gazelle to avoid getting your feet torn and ripped to pieces. I was no gazelle.

Finding somewhere to park was the easy bit. But after a couple of days, I headed up and off to Civitavecchia, northeast of Rome. Civitavecchia was something else again, a bustling port city and obviously popular tourist spot with cruise ships calling in from around the world. I had found somewhere to park up for a couple of days but a fair walk from the town and port.

Next to the port was Forte Michelangelo. A beautiful historic building from the fifteenth century, the fortress symbol of the port, situated close to the Varco Fortezza passage inside the port. I spent almost the whole of the first day exploring the port and the fort. All the while listening to a cacophony of voices and languages from around the world. One minute I was having a friendly chat with some yanks, another a group of swedes.

A short walk away from the port was a large pedestrian walkway with restaurants and bars on all sides. Finding one outdoor restaurant, I sat and ordered a Fanta orange and a salad snack. Around me, I could hear different voices from different parts of the world. The atmosphere friendly and relaxed. The food and drinks not expensive. It was a delight just to sit there soaking it all up. Yet again, I heard no English accents. Had any English heard of this place? Civitavecchia, like Carcassonne in the south of France, was all new to me. I'd never heard of any of the places. It sometimes seemed to me that the whole world was visiting these places except the Brits. Santorini, an absolutely stunning, romantic Greek island, I'd never heard of until we visited it on a cruise ship. What a gem, as is Civitavecchia. Carcassonne. Certainly well worth another visit, and another.

The next day was market day. To some, just another market, yes it was, but it's the people who make the market, and this was no different. Listening to the different accents and the bustle with the sun shining down was a delight. My dad was a barrow boy in the old Bullring of Birmingham. I grew up on the banter and friendly atmosphere of the Brummie people doing their shopping. I headed to the Terme Taurine from the market, another historical site just a short distance away. Without a doubt, Civitavecchia had plenty to offer. I could have spent a fortnight here alone, but I had to head-on.

The next morning I set off this time to Viareggio. Just a few miles up the coast. The huge flat sandy beach at Viareggio stretched for miles in either direction. Following my usual habit of modus operandi, I drove up and down the seafront road looking for somewhere comfortable and accessible to park up. There were plenty of car parks on the seafront's southern side, the furthest two seemed the most popular, for cars. I drove onto the other larger neglected-looking car park, backing onto woods behind.

Parking up, I decided on refreshments from the pizza bar directly opposite me were in order. Sitting down, I ordered a Fanta Limon whilst I surveyed the local environment. The restaurant only seemed to sell canned drinks, coffee, or pizza. If you didn't want pizza, that was it. You were crackered. I didn't mind a pizza once in a while, not every day. That was it. I was crackered. Every country has their own traditional dish. Ours used to be fish n chips. Now it's the curry. Here, wherever you went in Italy, you were expected to eat pizza. Whole families would sit around the table in a restaurant and order a pizza. Picking a slice up, they would spend most of the night jabbering away while eating a slice of pizza.

After my Fanta, I decided to walk down to and around the beach, but I was puzzled. I couldn't figure out how to get out on the beach. Everywhere seemed to be blocked off. Hotels, boarding houses guest houses were all along the seafront. Seeing one pathway, I set off walking down it towards the beach. I hadn't got twenty yards when a young guy came out of nowhere bawling at me to go back, showing my ignorance. I threw my hands up in wonder; his English wasn't too good, my Italian was even worse, but I got the message. I was entering onto private land. How the hell do I get onto the beach then? This went on block after block. One section was cut off with eight-foot-high net fencing. It was guarded by a youngish man who had eyes like a hawk. As soon as I made my way to the entrance, he was over like a shot, demanding ten euros to use his section of beach. I couldn't believe it. I had never seen anything like this in my life. Yes, I knew about private beaches; there were enough in England along all coastline stretches, but nothing like this.

Throwing my hands into the air in exasperation, I asked, "well, how do I get onto the beach?" He then pointed to a section, also cut off with net fencing some six-foot apart, a channel. This was the entrance down to the beachfront, free. It looked about the only free section. By the time I had walked down to the seafront, I was exhausted. I needed an hour just to recuperate. It was the same down on the beachfront. The passage leads along to the one free section of the public beach. Great, the only thing was, for some reason, it made me feel like a second-class citizen. The private sections cordoned off with private bathers settled into their deck chairs, all fiercely guarded by attendants. Talk about the mafia.

So I'm sitting there, in my motorhome, chilling and enjoying the night, door wide open, feet up on the sofa, when I felt more than heard a small dog walk past the door giving a little grunt. A few minutes later, the dog returned, only this time he wanted to have a little nose into my door. It took me all of three seconds gawping at him to realise it wasn't a dog at all, but what was it? Having had a good little nose in the door, it then trotted off. Getting up, I went over to the door and stuck my head out. There in front of me, I could see the little blighter trotting away. Then another one came into view, then another. They were wild boar appearing from out of the forest. First, I saw the babies trotting around. Then their mother, then another, then another. In all, about ten of them appeared. In the meantime, I looked to the car park low wall edging the border. There were groups of locals sitting on the wall, with their children, feeding the wild boar.

It was a truly beautiful sight to see. This was clearly a regular event with the locals. Families coming out to feed and watch the wild boar. They were there for over an hour. The locals feeding them then running off. Both groups, humans, and boar were totally oblivious to me. In that one short period alone, it encapsulated everything that made wild camping worthwhile. Except for the isolated mountain campsite, we stopped at the mountains where we saw wild bear and boar. Nowhere else would you see such a sight as I was witnessing, and it was free, what more could you ask for?

Campsites are fine. I have no problem with campsites, except I find them quite restrictive. Sometimes, and very rarely, I have come across someone on a site who can play an instrument, maybe a guitar. As soon as they start playing, other campers start meandering around, even another musician. A lively atmosphere and a little party are going on before you know it, but this is very rare.

Normally, I find most campsites very quiet, very orderly. Most campers, both motorhomes and caravans, keep very much to themselves, heads down, sombre faces, mostly in twos. But even with children, the kids are under strict instructions to keep quiet, behave. Sometimes you could walk out thinking you were in an empty campsite when it was almost full. So no, unless it was for a good reason, I preferred the freedom of wild camping. That reason was to come about within a few days. I was on a very nice pitch, very convenient to the local shops and restaurants. In an ideal world, I would be getting up in the morning, having a snack, no chance of an English breakfast here, then down to the beach, toasting nicely, in between little dips in the sea.

The problem was the beach was just such a long walk. It was a bit of a chore having to find the little public passageways down to the beach and the long walk down to it. Another long walk to the public part of the beach and paying for the privilege went against my thinking. I found it a bit unsettling. Also, I found walking up and down the shops and restaurants more than three times enough. After a few days and nights of enjoying the wild boar, I decided to call and book into the local campsite. The nearest ACCSI campsite was less than a mile down the road. It backed onto the very woods that the wild boar came out of. With the heat, I needed a close and handy swimming pool. Trudging down to the beach every day spoilt it for me.

The campsite was very big and very nice and the price reasonable. It had a very handy shop/supermarket, a bar and a nice restaurant serving good quality food at reasonable prices. The swimming pool was just a short walk from my pitch. I hooked up to the electricity, and I was in my oil tot. I did need a site as well, for the facilities. My bedding definitely needed washing, and the site had a very good laundry room. Amazing. Like many others I found in Europe, this site was just the norm, vastly superior to most English sites at half the price. It's just the Italians; they are, like the Spanish, very strange in their ways. It was still midday, so I got up to the pool as soon as I could. It was empty. Well, there were about three people dotted around the pool. Finding a sunbed, I settled down to get some rays. After an hour and feeling like toast, I had a little dip in the pool, swimming a couple of lengths on my own, bliss. At five pm, bedlam hit the pool, all the Italians came out in force, kids, parents, the whole lot.

Strangely, very few of the adults used the pool, the kids were in and out, probably pissing all over the water, but the adults just seemed to want to sit under their umbrellas sheltering from the sun. Even the kids only spent so long in the water before coming out and sitting with their parents, I couldn't weigh them up at all.

This suited me down to the ground. I just slotted into the routine. Getting up in the morning, I would saunter up to the restaurant, have a leisurely breakfast, then a slow leisurely walk to the almost empty pool where I would enjoy the best part of the day. The Italians were hibernating in their chalets or caravans—what a treat. I was here for at least a week.

After a few days, I had built up the enthusiasm and interest to visit the birthplace of Giacomo Puccini, who wrote the aria Nessun Dorma amongst other opera compositions. Puccini was considered the greatest opera composer in Italy and was born and lived in the province of Lucca, just a few miles inland from Viareggio. He also wrote Madam Butterfly Tosca, Turandot and La Boheme. His home has been turned into a museum called Villa Puccini. In the beautiful tranquil setting of Torre Del Lago, beside his home was nestled a tranquil lake with a covered man-made bandstand. The lake was where Puccini composed much of his work. The whole area emanated peace and tranquillity. I could only sit and wonder in amazement how someone could sit there and come out with arias such as Nessun Dorma. Sitting at a small café that overlooked the lake, I could only sit in awe of the man and his home. As a memento, I bought two Puccini decorated mugs from the gift shop.

Lucca was in the heart of Tuscany. To my mind, some of the most beautiful country anyone could wish for just a short twelve-mile drive to Pisa. Driving back the short distance to the campsite, I felt satisfied and elated with how the day had gone. My list of beautiful places to visit was growing by the month—Switzerland, France, now Italy, which pressed all the right buttons. Any future travelling would be to visit maybe one country at a time, enjoying all it had to offer over a few months. Italy had so much to offer, from its beautiful beaches to its wild inland mountainous countryside, Pisa, Rome, Florence, Tuscany, so many beautiful places, and of course, you've got the weather.

Over the years, I have seen much of England, and, as everyone points out, England is great when you've got the weather. It is. But a more telling point to me, since buying our motorhome, is the restrictions we keep hitting as we travel around. Yes, maybe some people have buggered it up for the rest of us, but I find the reality is that England is money-obsessed, thirty quid to pay for a patch of grass and damp tatty grass at that. Most times, more for an awning, then more for a dog, doesn't make me feel very welcome. Here, in Italy, as in Spain and France, the attitude is more welcoming. I feel the freedom of being able to visit where I wanted when I wanted.

CHAPTER 57.

HOMEWARD BOUND, SLOWLY,

My days at Viareggio had been positive and rewarding, except for the unusual quirk of all the beaches being private and the problems it created. But just the experience of seeing the wild boar wiped that out. With the facilities it offered, the campsite left me pleased and happy to pay the fees asked. The pool emptying most times to suit me was another bonus. The home and lake of Giacomo Puccini was a memory that will remain with me forever.

Now I think it was time for me to set off again. Setting my sat-nav, I checked the map and where I was, was 200 miles from Monaco, France. I set my sat-nav for Monaco, keeping to the coast roads and stopping off as I felt, no pressure. Whilst I wasn't desperate to get home, I could feel myself coming to the end of my tour, mentally. I had seen and experienced such a great deal, as was my plan. I just had a few goals left, and then I would be homeward bound. There were literally hundreds of little resorts along the way, Chavan Recco, then Genoa. Pulling into one resort village town, I couldn't figure out what it was. There didn't seem to be any houses to speak of, just hotels, tourist shops, cafes, bars, and campsites. It seemed the whole area was purposely built or set aside for camping or tourists.

Driving up and down a few times, it took me a bit to figure it out and get my head around it. Yes, it was a purpose-built tourist village. At one end of the road was a large car park, opposite a large campsite. Finding a nice out of the way corner of the car park, I parked and had a walk around. To the back of me were woods and a pathway leading to the beach, a very long pathway. Many of the campers were crossing over from the campsite and following the path. Instinctively I decided to follow them, well, if they are leaving a campsite to go to the beach it must be worthwhile, right? Wrong, the path never seemed to end, I thought maybe a few hundred yards. No, it was nearer a mile. Ok, fair enough, the beach was superb. A nice little restaurant set back to the side. I needed refreshments after that jaunt. My legs were aching. Sitting down at the café, I ordered a cold drink and a snack, spending a couple of hours on the beach before heading back to the camper. I considered my options. I just didn't fancy getting up in the morning, taking that long walk to the beach, then back again after an exhausting day on the beach, and let's be blunt, lying on a beach all day is enervating. Especially doing a bit of swimming. That long walk back was daunting.

Looking across at the campsite from my motorhome as I drank a cup of tea, I wondered! Hmmm. The campsite had the usual barrier across the entrance road. The main reception was right next to the barrier. It was early evening, too late for a swim. But plenty enough time to take a look and have a walk around. Walking across, I joined the dozens of other campers coming in and out. No one gave me a second look.

Looking around the site, I can see it was split up into different sections, chalets on one side, caravans, motorhomes in another plot. Obviously, no one came into the site without being in one or another. I was just another camper, so long as I kept my mouth shut. Because there were no English here. Just

Italians. In the middle of the camp was a very nice large swimming pool, that was it, sorted.

Many Italians preferred going over to the beach. No, no, I didn't like all that sand. The next morning I was up, swimming trunks on, towel over my shoulder, and sauntered across to and into the camp. I passed reception, not giving a sideways glance either way. Making sure I've got my cap on, the Italians were sticklers for bathing caps. I got myself a nice little sunbed, tucked away in the far corner.

My days were spent browning nicely in between having a dip in the pool to keep cool. Occasionally I'd get up, leave my hat, and towel on the bed and make my way to one of the cafes for refreshments. It was a very nice interlude indeed. There was only one downfall. I could see why so many of the campers took that long hike over to the beach. The pool was full of Italian brats screaming, bawling, and laughing. Hardly any adults went into the pool. As normal, most sat outside and around, chatting, and relaxing. Only the odd adult joining in with their kids. I had started to try and second guess when the kids would leave the pool. For lunch or tea, then I'd get in and get some exercise. I could hardly complain; they were paying for the pool. Maybe I was becoming a bit jaded. I had been having too much of a good thing for weeks. At any rate, after the second day, I decided to move on, this time the short drive to Monaco.

.

CHAPTER 58.

I had heard much about the French Riviera over the years. Saint Tropez, Cannes, Monaco, just the names alone were so evocative. Bridget Bardot, Sophia Loren, Sean Connery, so many major film stars had villas there. Yet it had never appealed to me to visit it, certainly not before we bought the motorhome. After we did, we just wanted to get down to Spain, the sun, besides, just the names alone screamed money. France was bad enough. A coffee cost double that of England. We had been to Paris a couple of times. Whilst I never had a fit paying for a meal, the thought of eating out in Monaco gave me palpitations. I needn't have worried.

Monaco is as big as a postage stamp. What do people see in it? It is a sovereign city-state bordered by France on three sides, with the Mediterranean to the front, glamorous Monte Carlo casino and Grand Prix car race. It's one of the wealthiest countries in the world. It has a land border of three and a half miles, 33,000 people are crammed into it, yet it has one of the world's wealthiest populations. It has an area of less than one square mile. It was that small I almost missed it. Pulling in quick, I did a sharp left turn onto the road down to it. Within yards, the road started narrowing, winding, steep, narrow, bustling. The only thing that kept me going was the buses coming up the hill. It was nerve-racking and a potential nightmare. What do the people see in this place? Eventually, I reached the main seafront road leading up to the harbour. None of it appealed to me at all. My initial feeling was to drive straight out, so restrictive was its feeling. But no, no, I was here, let's have a look around. But where? If cars were not parked in every space, there were double yellow lines. It was ridiculous. Eventually, I found a small space by some yachts with only one yellow line. Parking up, I was determined to at least have a walk around to see what all the fuss was about.

The businessman Philip Green, billionaire, and tax exile has a yacht in the harbour. I have the impression he lives on his yacht with his wife, staff, and family. Floating over to Monaco when it suits him. I watched a documentary one time on billionaires and their yachts, competing with each other in Marbella or Puerto Banus. "Oh, that's Abramovich, the billionaire. He has the biggest yacht in the bay," I mean, think about it. Reading an article on Onassis the billionaire, I read that he used to boast and outdo his cousin on his superyachts' size. With that kind of money, why on earth would you want to resort to petty bragging? My tool is bigger than your tool. It's pathetic.

Walking around the harbour, shops, and restaurants, I just never felt, wow, I wish I had the money to live here, I wish I owned one of these superyachts. Ok, if I were that rich, maybe it would be nice to own a yacht just to visit for the Grand Prix or to lose a million in the casino. No, I don't think so. Getting back to my motorhome, I turned around and sought a way out; for god's sake, don't let it be the way I came in. Cautiously, I made my way along the seafront road past the yachts and superyachts to my left. Thankfully, and quickly I was out. I think Monaco traumatised me, short as my visit was. I just could not get my head around how anyone would want to live crammed in like rats in a box just to save tax and what? Impress each other? No, what is the next resort going to be like?

Cannes, now this was different. Cannes was massive in comparison, with plenty of room to move around and breathe.

Just outside of Cannes itself, I found plenty of parking, right alongside the beachfront. Pulling into a space close to the seafront, I got out to have a walk around, stretch my legs and breathe in the fresh air. This was more like it. Walking along, I came to several small restaurants and cafes with elegant elderly French ladies having a glass of wine or a meal. I decided to join them. With the sun shining down, it made for a pleasant, enjoyable experience. Stopping up overnight on the beachfront, I enjoyed a quiet, peaceful night. Being Cannes or close to Cannes, I did think the cops would pop along and tell me to move on, but no, I was fine. But again, I never felt a problem in France, or Spain for that matter.

The next morning, I set off to have a look and drive around Saint Tropez. Very nice, but it was difficult to find somewhere to park up, plus Saint Tropez was a bigger place still. I decided to drive on to somewhere more comfortable and welcoming. Eventually, after a few stops, I called into a beautiful, sophisticated little resort called Cavalaire-Sur-Mer. Literally means on the sea, and it was. It took me a few passes along the front before I came across a small side road, away and a short walk from the harbour. There were the odd few cars and scooters, so guessing I would be ok, I pulled in. To my rear was a closed restaurant, and another restaurant to my front that seemed closed, which only opened at night and had its own car park. The road was only an access road for a few restaurants, so it was nice and quiet for most of the time. This would do me for a few days.

Cavalaire–Sur–Mer was beautiful. The beach was glorious, long, and sandy and led down to the harbour and port. An extra bonus was a set of steps leading down to the beach just a few yards away from me. Getting my deck chair out, I carried it down to the beach, set it out and got down to some serious tanning. The sea was lovely, clean, and warm, providing no one came and told me I couldn't park where I was. No one did. I was sorted for a good few days of bliss.

After a pleasant day on the beach, I decided to enjoy some leisurely walking along the seafront towards the main town centre and harbour. Not as famous as Cannes or Saint Tropez, Cavalaire-Sur-Mer seemed more relaxed, upmarket but without that air of superiority or snobbishness, not that I saw any of that anyway. It was almost famous for its annual world jet ski races that were on the next day. The harbour area was jam-packed with motorhomes of all shapes and sizes, jet skis galore. This would be interesting. The harbour area was bustling with anticipation and excitement. The event was on for two days. The town was relaxed, pleasant and enjoyable to walk around, and surprisingly, not expensive.

Along and opposite, the seafront was lined with restaurants and hotels. I had had a snack of chips and salad at one café directly opposite my motorhome that I was not too impressed with. Further along was a more upmarket restaurant, based on a marine theme, with a sailor statue greeting us outside. Reading the menu, I didn't think it was very expensive and there staring me in the face was my must-have, Moules Mariner, eleven euros. For eleven euros, nice surroundings, and the pleasant view, seemed quite reasonable to me. I decided to book in after the racing the next day early evening.

Getting up the next morning, I got my deckchair out and made my way down to the beach, sunglasses stuck on my head—magazines in my little bag. Peaceful, then the whining started. Whining and roaring all day long, in between the commentator screaming out over the loudspeakers, all in French, foreign to me. Jet skis, whizzing in and out like wasps, loud wasps, it was non-stop, oh well, I'd picked the wrong time. The sea wall and beaches were packed with families watching the jet skis. Eventually, by six o'clock, it all died down. I put my deck chair away to enjoy my evening stroll up towards the harbour front and my meal of Moules Mariniere.

After a few hours strolling around the town and harbour, watching the jet skiers clearing their kit and talking about the day, all in French, all unintelligible to me, then an ice cream overlooking the harbour, a coffee overlooking the boats, I made my way to the little marine-themed restaurant and my mussels. It was still early. The place wasn't packed—only one family in front of me overlooking the seafront. As the proprietor came over, I gave her my order of Moules Mariniere and a large beer. I thought maybe she gave me a funny look, as she raised her eyebrows. I know what it is, she thinks I'm common, I'm in a genteel resort, I should be drinking wine. The Moules were going down a treat with a couple of cobs, followed by a lovely cold beer. The air was warm, the night clear. "I'll have another large beer please; it's going down like nectar." Another funny little look.

Eventually, sated and satisfied, I asked for the bill. I knew I'd have to pay eleven euros for the mussels. They won't sting me on the cobs, will they, no, or the beer. I thought maybe a couple of quid a glass, so maybe, twenty euros, maybe twenty-five if they're a bit greedy. They were greedy all right, ten euros a glass, plus a service charge, my bill came to over forty euros. I had to stiffen up to avoid falling off my chair. No wonder she was giving me the funny looks, a bottle of wine was only seven euros. Jeez. I should have known better. I'd been stung before on the beer, not by that much, of course, but enough to make me realise. If nothing else, the beer in France is about the highest in Europe. There were no two ways about it; the French were paying through the nose for the privilege of being in the euro.

A few years ago, we went to visit a friend in Puerto Banus. We had booked a fortnight in a hotel a couple of miles outside. On the day, he drove up to pick us up from his hotel and take us to visit his flat overlooking the harbour. The flat was very expensive and in a prime position. The overall thought we came away with after looking at the sparsely furnished expensive flat was that our friend was into something very dodgy. At any rate, after he had impressed us with his flat, he then took us down to Puerto Banus itself and showed us around. Our friend knew a few people, including a millionaire nightclub owner who was buying a one-million-pound apartment in the town. Interestingly my pal wouldn't eat around the harbour, choosing to eat a baguette instead, whilst Bet and I went over to a harbourside restaurant—too bloody expensive.

Sitting outside, we were in a prime position overlooking the harbour. The restaurant was packed. Taking our order of mussels and king prawns, off he trotted, coming back a few minutes later with some bread and olives. People can even like olives, never mind eating them, I don't know, even the table next door didn't want them. No, no, thank you.

The waiter brought out the mussels, eight on a dish between us. Very nice. We guessed we might be paying a bit more. After the mussels, he bought the prawns out, raw, six and massive. Impressed, he gave us a big smile. Off he trotted again, coming back about fifteen minutes later with the cooked prawns, three on each plate. To be fair, they were delicious, and we both felt like royalty, sitting there munching away, watching the Maserati's and Rolls Royce's passing within a few feet. Occasionally I gave the thumbs up to the odd driver. Well, no one was to know, would they? Informing the waiter that the meal was very nice, we asked for the bill. With a smile, he was off, returning a few minutes later with the bill on a silver platter, discreetly placed in between us both. Being the banker, Bet picked up the bill. All I saw was her face go stiff and f**k f**k, slip from her mouth in silent whispers. Well, we couldn't say anything, we had to keep composed, the place was chocka, the bill was 88 euros. I nearly fell off the chair, 88 f*****g euros. That's about all she had on her. No wonder our pal went for a baguette.

Getting back to our hotel, our pal agreed to pick me up later on in the night to bring me back down to the port. Bet didn't want to go, understandably, I thought. Still getting over the shock of the meal, we started hitting the bars, each time buying glasses that held just over a half-point. I quickly saw why, each glass was five euros, that was ten euros a pint, even the millionaire nightclub owner, seemed happy with the small drinks. Anywhere else, a pint was about one fifty euros. In Sinatra's, it was all about celebrity watching.

Over there, a famous boxer, here for a weekend of golf. Over there, a famous footballer, married with his little arm candy, having a few days nooky behind the wife's back. My friend and his millionaire friend were all casual about being on such an esteemed company's outer edges. Quite pathetic really, the celebrities didn't know them. But I could feel they would be living off these little occasions until the next celebrity turned up. It was almost embarrassing. After four drinks, I was glad to leave. That was the end of Puerto Banus for us.

Cavalaire-Sur-Mer was a delightful place to stay. After a full week, I felt it was time to head off, making my way steadily back towards home. Another beauty spot added to my growing list, so much, so many. It was some 800 miles to Calais, some 200 euros in diesel, along non-toll roads. With three stop-offs at Aires along the way, the drive was steady and uneventful. From Calais, I got the ferry over to Dover. After travelling 800 miles through France, the last leg from Dover to home was the worst. 200 miles of numb crunching boring driving, I was glad to get home.

Getting into my house, it was satisfying to feel the familiarity of my home and the comfort of seeing my pictures around the walls, with the luxury of sitting in my chair, turning the telly on, and winding down. It would take me a week of chilling to get back to normal. A lot of people have and continue to sell their homes to become full-time motorhomers. Maybe a different time, a different age, I might have considered it, not now. I love the lifestyle I have; I love the opportunities presented to me. The travelling, the touring, visiting different places, but I also love my home and the comfort of getting back to it. Then, of course, there is the planning for the next trip, the next tour, so many places, so many beautiful destinations.

I think I am now in favour of visiting Poland, seeing the concentration camps like Bergen Belsen and Auschwitz. Then from there, to visit friends I had made in Greece one year who gave me an open invitation to visit them, as they lived thirty-five miles from Auschwitz. From there, again down to the south of France, many more medieval villages, so many places, so much beauty. Yes, but first, we have to fight through Covid-19.

THE END.

Thomas Lewin is a semi-retired property developer and landlord with various businesses under his belt. He worked along with his wife, Betty. From shops to hotels to country pubs and a caravan site. Some good. Some not so good. Born in the so-called slums of Birmingham, he and his wife adopted the attitude that the glass was better half-full than half-empty.

Thank you for purchasing this book. This is Thomas' third book. *Against the Odds: From the Slums of Summer Lane*, his first book, about growing up in the slums witnessing corruption from an early age as an innocent child, is still not on the best-sellers list. Please help it along and purchase his first book, maybe even his second.